IMMORTAL HOUNDS

6

Ryo Yasohachi

VERTICAL COMICS

Table of Contents

Previous Volume Summary

In another world, "death" does not exist. However, Marie, the daughter of an officer with the Tousai Precinct, is murdered, and no one can figure out how it happened. Kenzaki has decided to pull Kazama out of the cryo-prison in order to delve into the truth of their world, even though Kazama is currently imprisoned in the deepest part of an UNDO-administrated facility. Members of the Tousai Precinct's Anti-Vector Unit and the Escape Artists have declared a temporary truce in order to cooperate on a mission to break Kazama out of the cryo-prison.

Characters

Escape Artists
A dark organization that hides Vectors from the law.

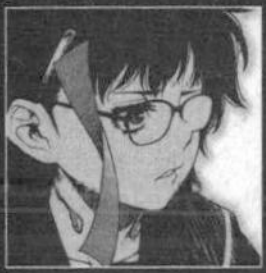

Fuurin
A beautiful girl who has infiltrated the MPD as a spy. Uses the false name "Rin Kazama" within the MPD.

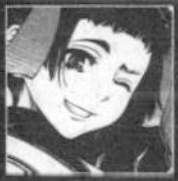

Kiriko
Helps Vectors escape alongside Rin. Competent but treated like a novice.

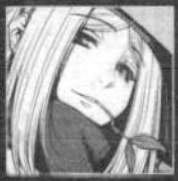

Karigane
Formerly an instructor. Very strong in combat.

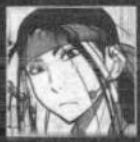

Sayori
Part of Kiriko's graduating class. Nicknamed "Miss Chin."

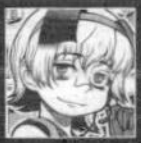

Misago
Another of Kiriko's graduating class. In charge of obtaining weapons.

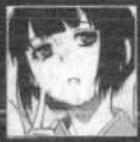

Karatachi
Mama's handmaiden.

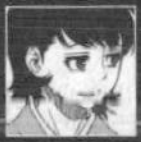

Hiiragi
Serves Mama along with Karatachi.

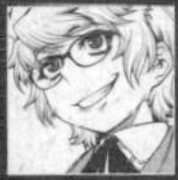

Mama
A mysterious woman who manages the Escape Artists. She looks similar to Fuurin.

Rescue

Tousai Precinct
A group of three led by Kenzaki comprises the Anti-Vector Unit.

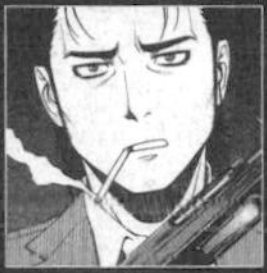

Shin'ichi Kenzaki
Chief. His sister, Ikumi, was killed by a Vector. A central figure in solving the mysteries of this world.

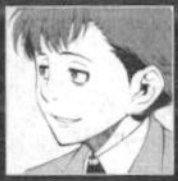

Masaki Wakabayashi
Kenzaki's subordinate. Has started dating Ikegami. Has a younger brother, Yuuki, a high schooler.

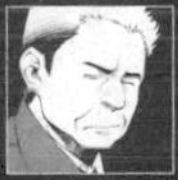

Kouzou Shigematsu
Kenzaki's subordinate despite being his elder. His daughter Marie died under mysterious circumstances.

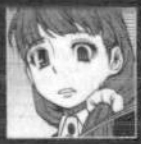

Kyoko Ikegami
Administrative officer. Wakabayashi's lover.

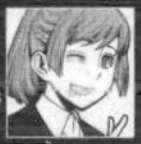

Naomi Tamaru
Married mother of one. Her husband works in a different precinct.

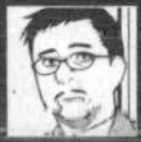

Takurou Kusunoki
Chief of the detective division. Classmate of Shigematsu.

UNDO
Short for the United Nations Disease-control Office

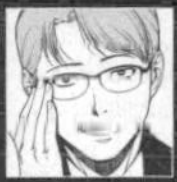

Kanai
Director of the Tokyo Branch. The UNDO has no right to carry out investigations or make arrests. Executes Vectors captured by the police.

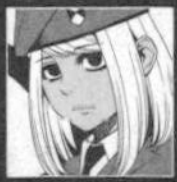

Camellia Kuribayashi
Kanai's aide-de-camp. A UN Military First Lieutenant. Her real name is Tsubaki.

Remove

Vectors
A group of murderers who spread Resurrection Deficiency Syndrome (RDS). Those who have loved them become incapable of revival.

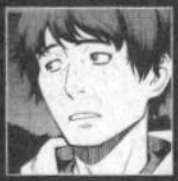

Teruyoshi Kouda
The Vector who killed Ikumi, Kenzaki's sister. Currently active as an Escape Artist.

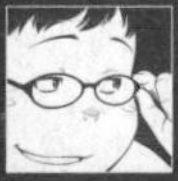

Tsutomu Takamiya
A Vector who has killed three women working night jobs. Called "Fatass" by Kenzaki.

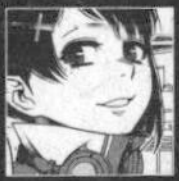

"Snow White"
A Vector who has killed 39 men. Is constantly on the move, quickly changing location.

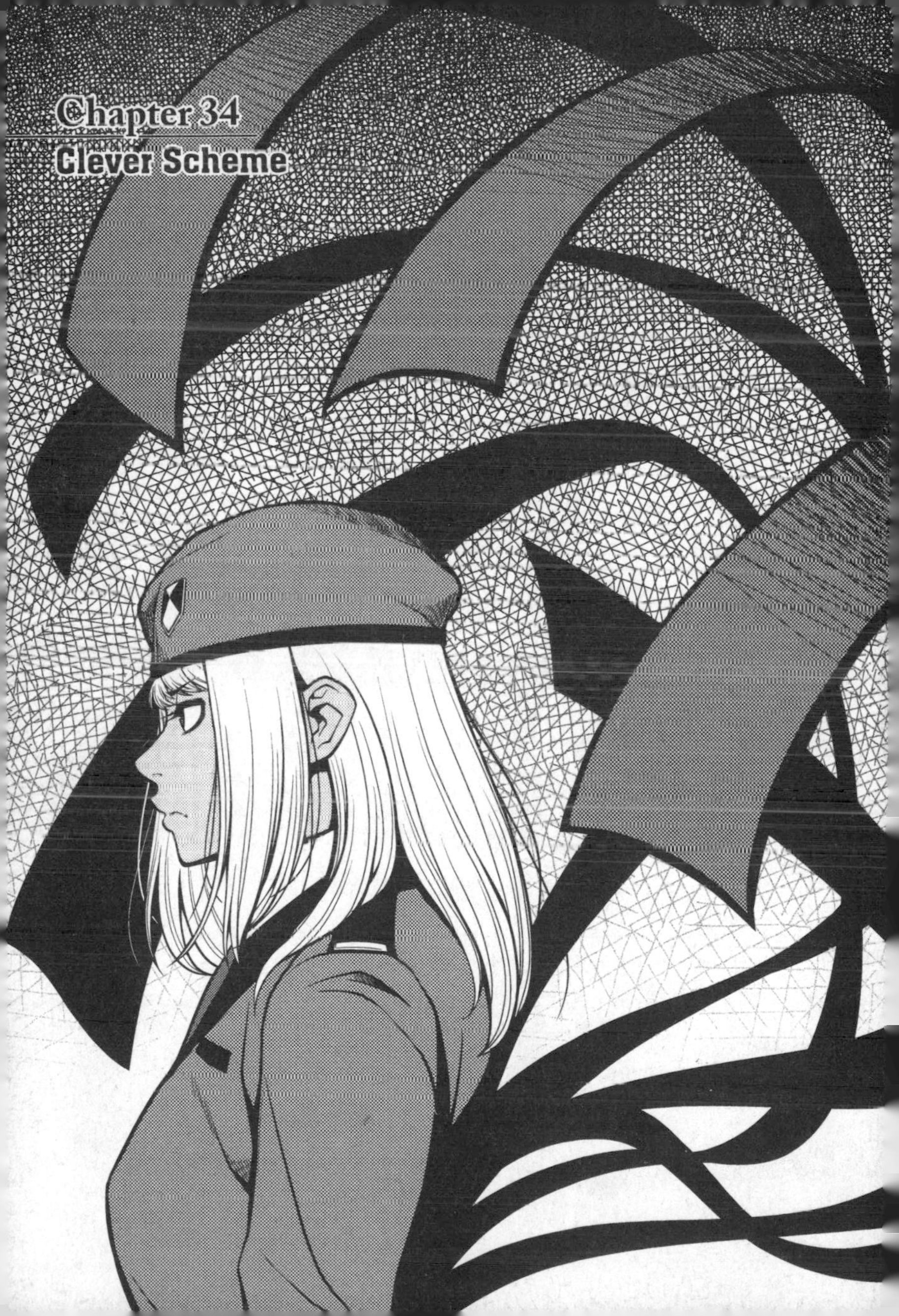
Chapter 34
Clever Scheme

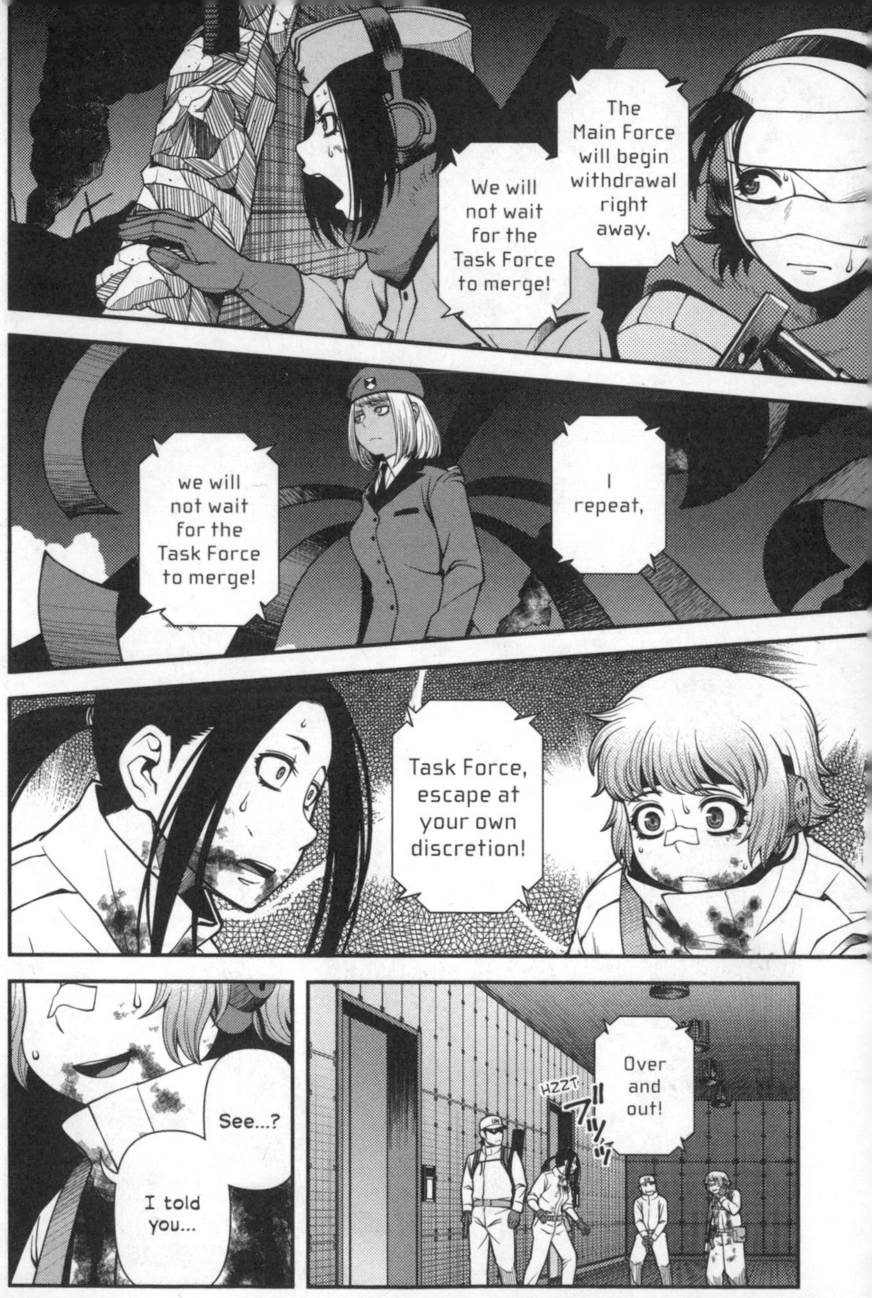
The Main Force will begin withdrawal right away.
We will not wait for the Task Force to merge!
I repeat,
we will not wait for the Task Force to merge!
Task Force, escape at your own discretion!
Over and out!
HZZT
See...?
I told you...

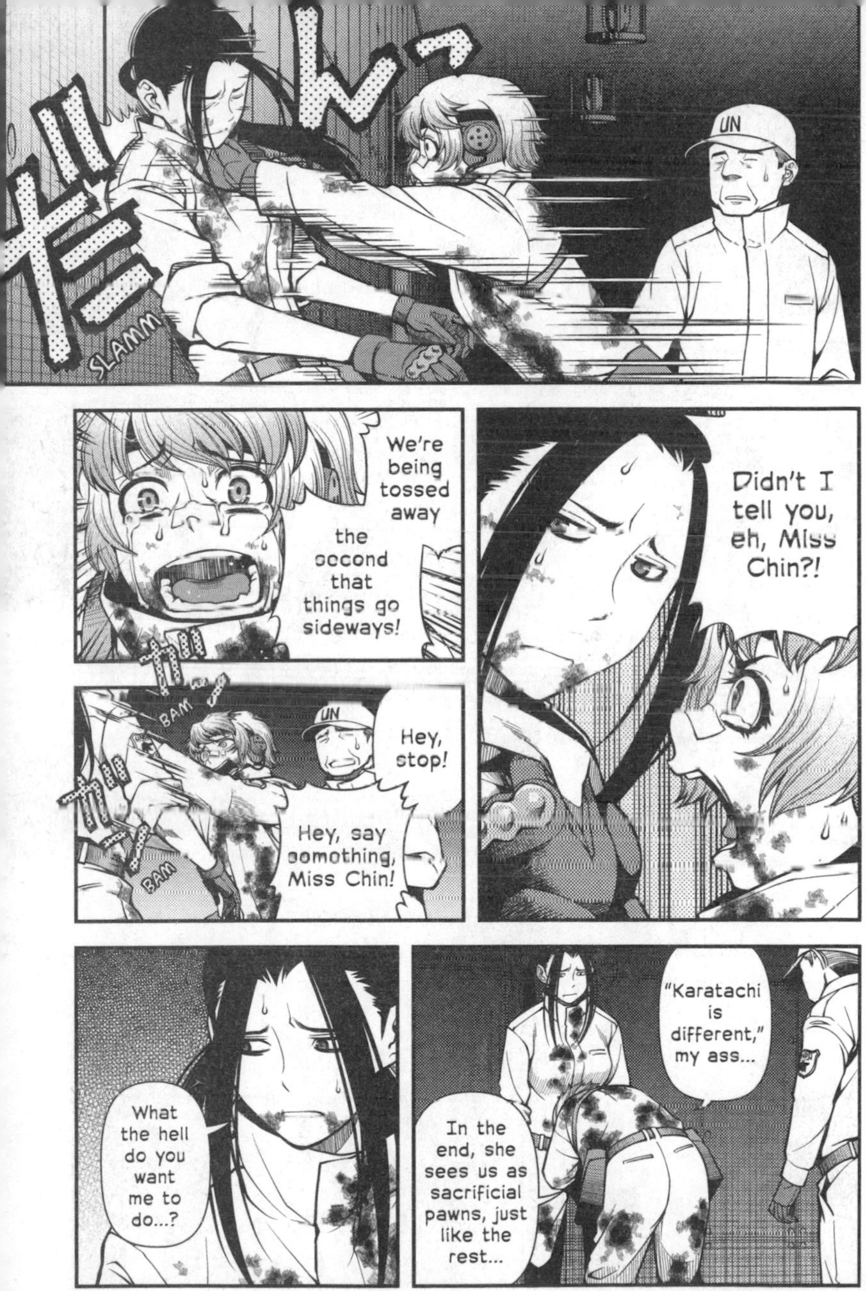
SLAMM
Didn't I tell you, eh, Miss Chin?!
We're being tossed away the second that things go sideways!
BAM
Hey, stop!
Hey, say something, Miss Chin!
BAM
"Karatachi is different," my ass...
In the end, she sees us as sacrificial pawns, just like the rest...
What the hell do you want me to do...?

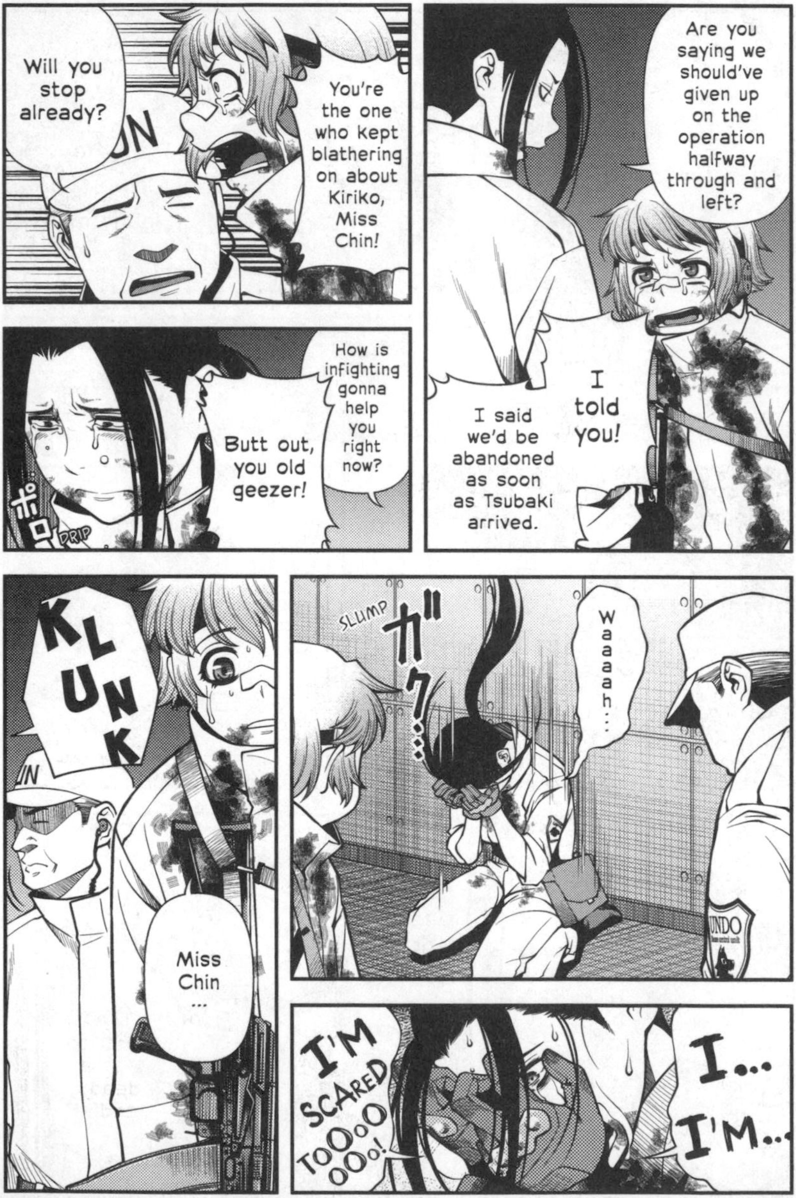
Are you saying we should've given up on the operation halfway through and left?
I told you!
I said we'd be abandoned as soon as Tsubaki arrived.
You're the one who kept blathering on about Kiriko, Miss Chin!
Will you stop already?
How is infighting gonna help you right now?
Butt out, you old geezer!
ポロ
DRIP
SLUMP
ガク…
Waaaah…
I… I'M…
I'M SCARED TOOOOOOOO!
KLUNK
Miss Chin…

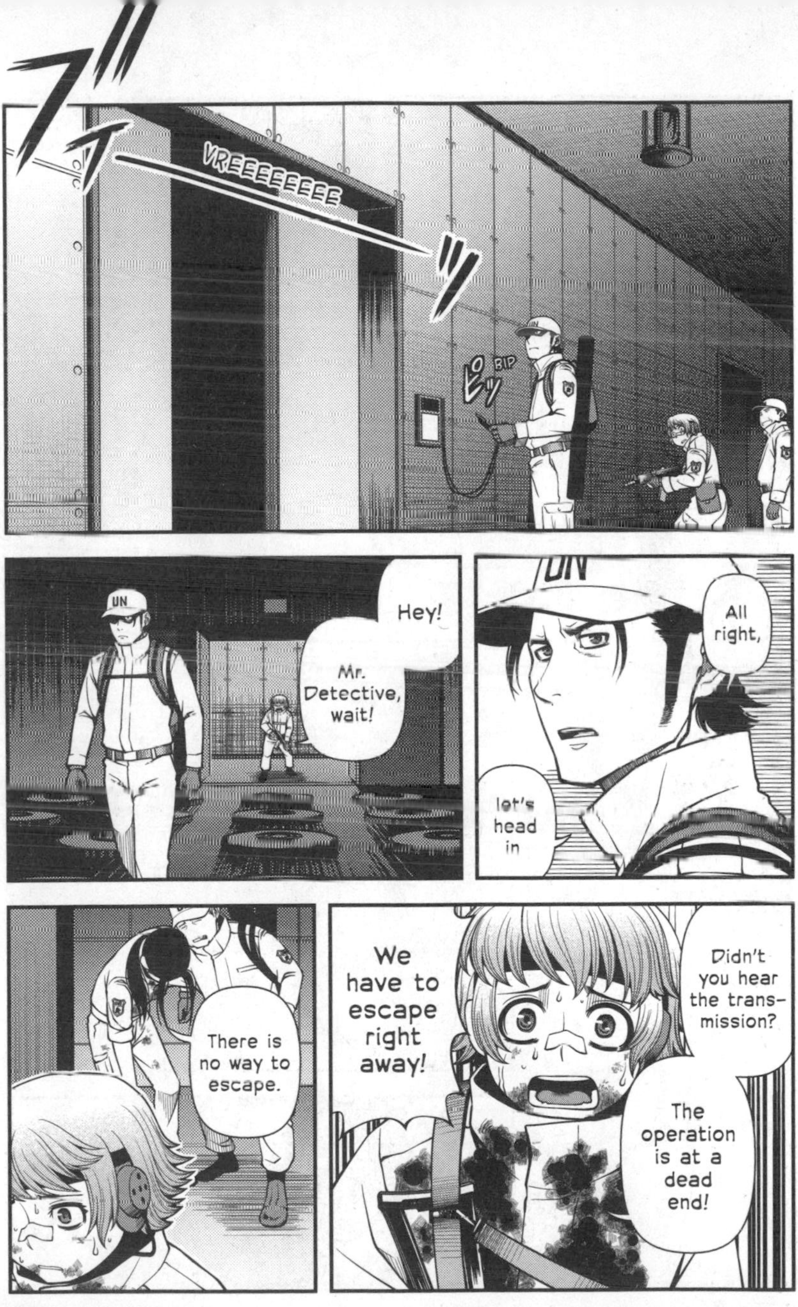
VREEEEEEEEEE
BIP
All right,
let's head in
Hey!
Mr. Detective, wait!
Didn't you hear the trans-mission?
We have to escape right away!
The operation is at a dead end!
There is no way to escape.

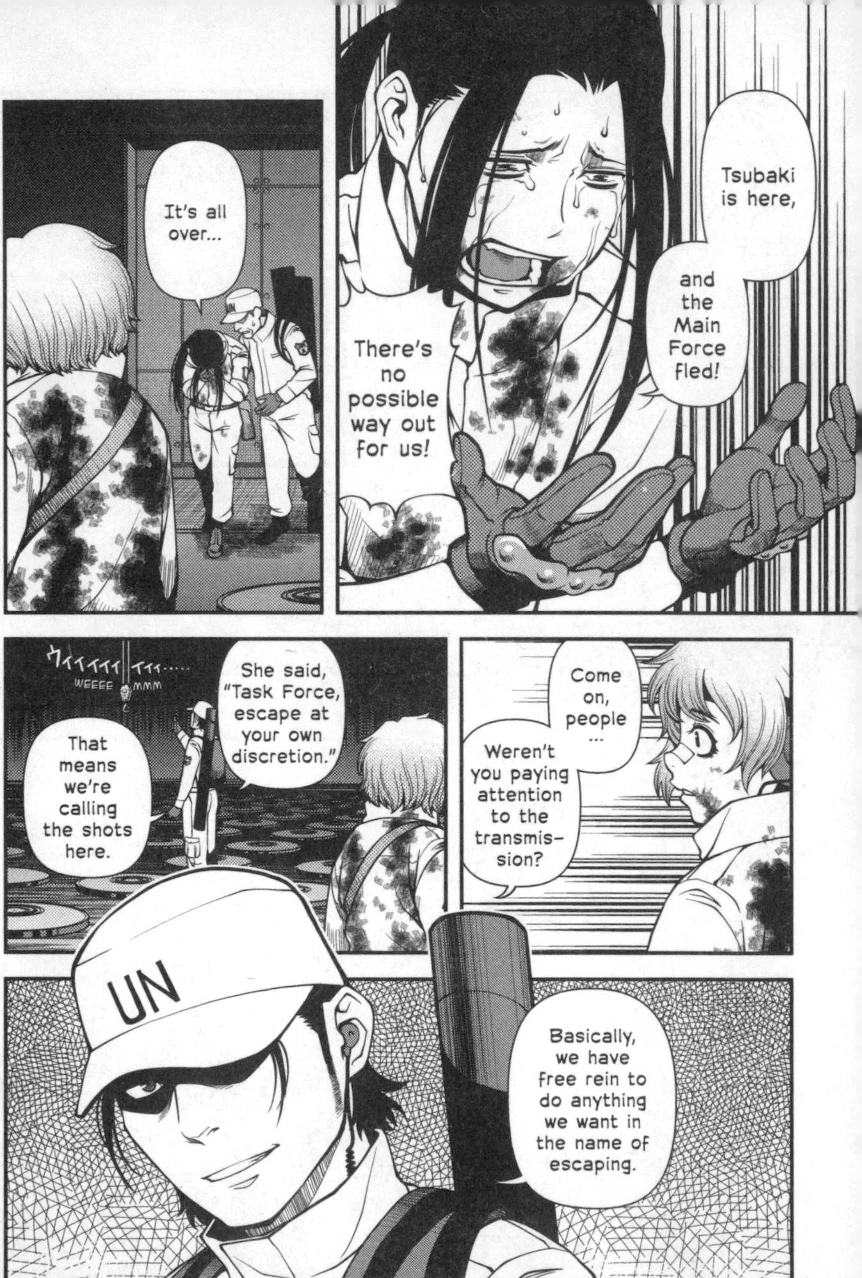
Tsubaki is here,
and the Main Force fled!
There's no possible way out for us!
It's all over...
Come on, people ...
Weren't you paying attention to the transmission?
ウィィィィィ ィィィ.....
WEEEE MMM
She said, "Task Force, escape at your own discretion."
That means we're calling the shots here.
Basically, we have free rein to do anything we want in the name of escaping.

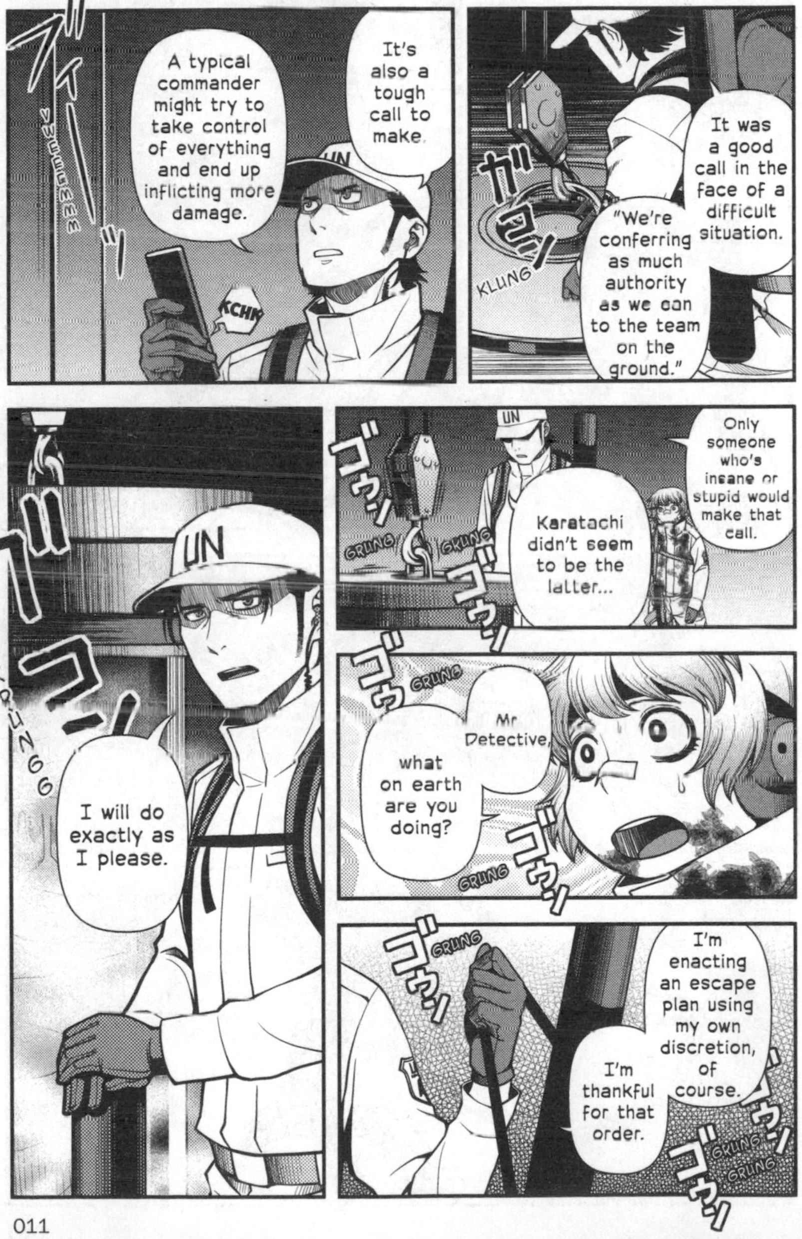

It was a good call in the face of a difficult situation.
"We're conferring as much authority as we can to the team on the ground."
KLUNG
It's also a tough call to make.
A typical commander might try to take control of everything and end up inflicting more damage.
VWEEEMMM
KCHK
Only someone who's insane or stupid would make that call.
Karatachi didn't seem to be the latter...
GRUNG
GKUNG
Mr Detective,
what on earth are you doing?
GRUNG
GRUNG
I'm enacting an escape plan using my own discretion, of course.
I'm thankful for that order.
GRUNG
GRUNG
GRUNG
I will do exactly as I please.
KRUNGG

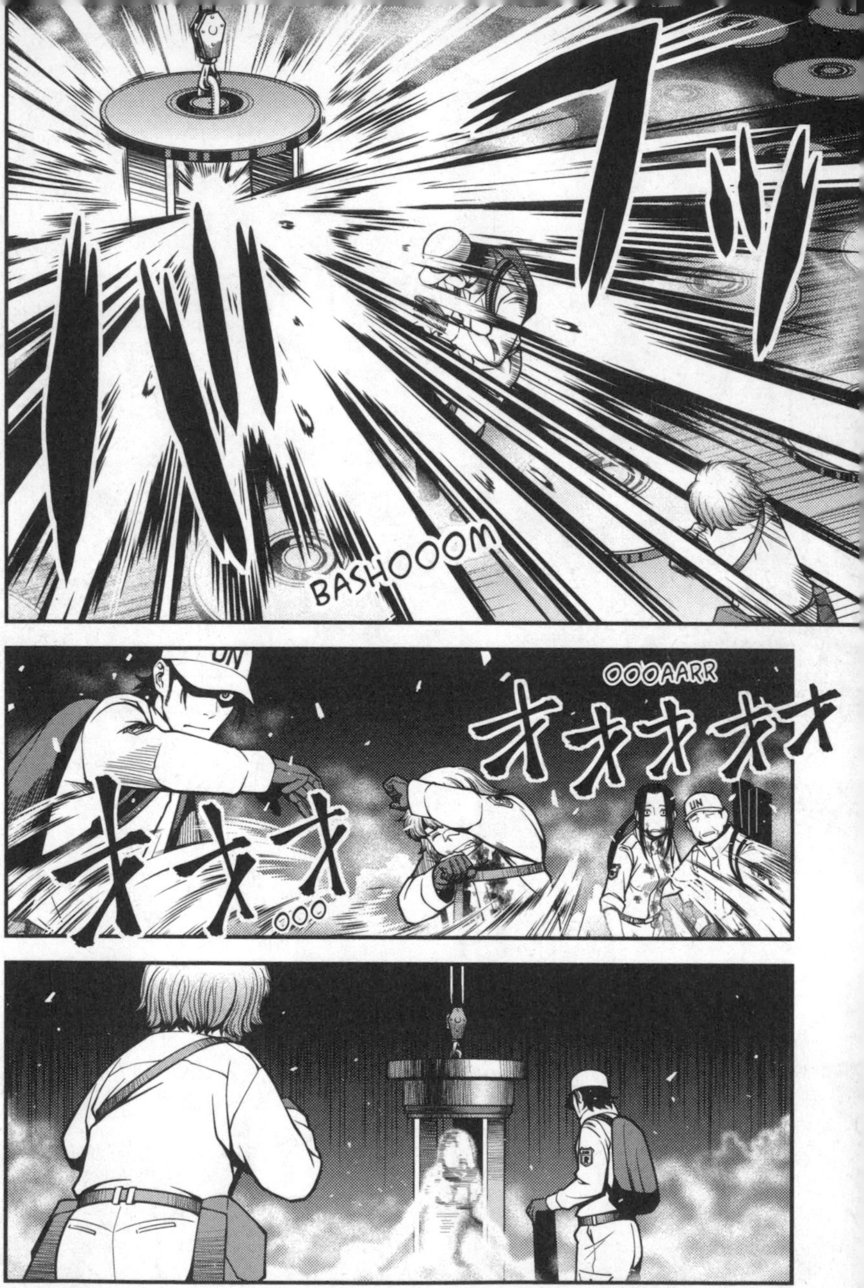
BASHOOOM
OOOAARR
オオオオオ
オオオ
OOO

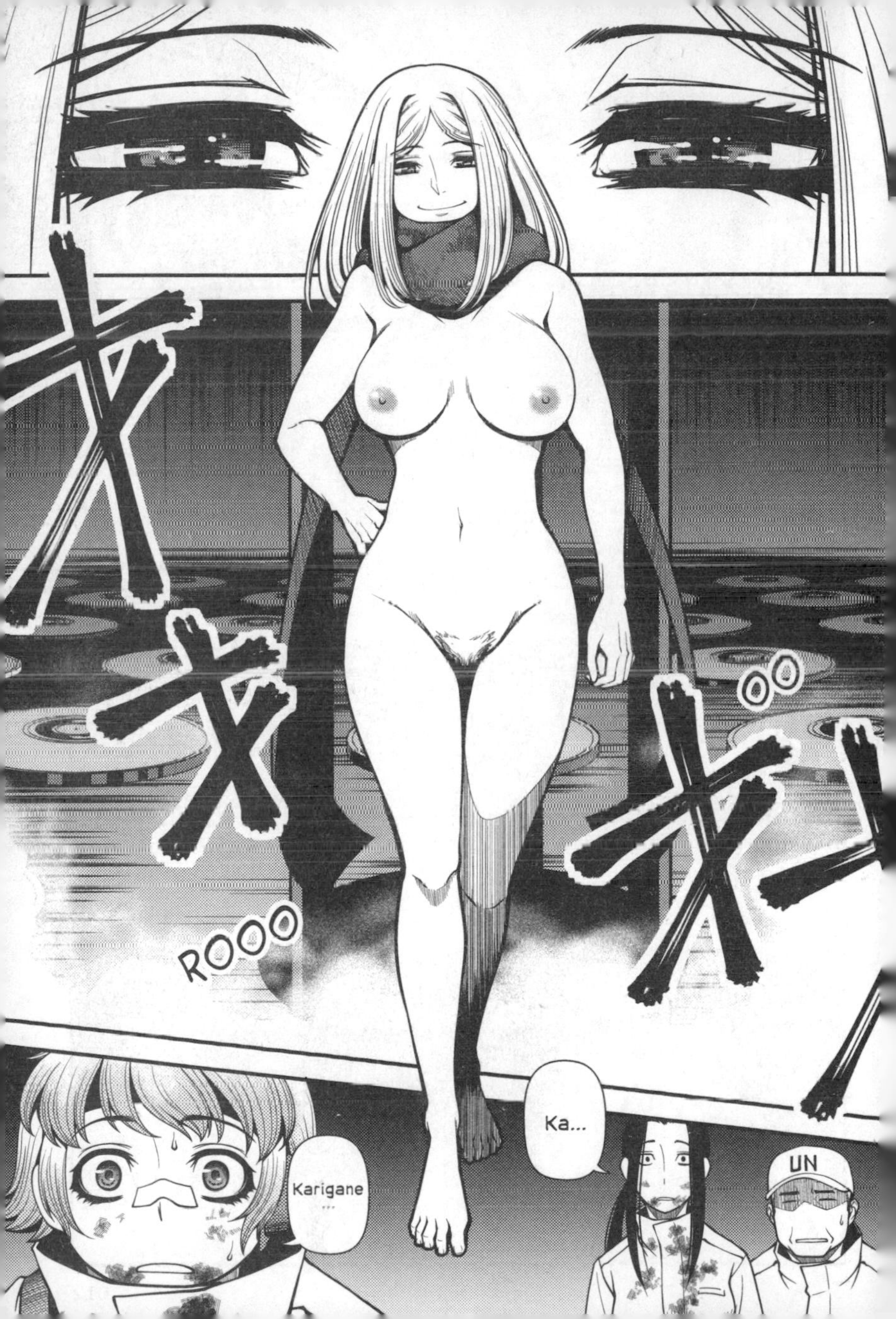
ROOO
UN
Ka...
Karigane
...

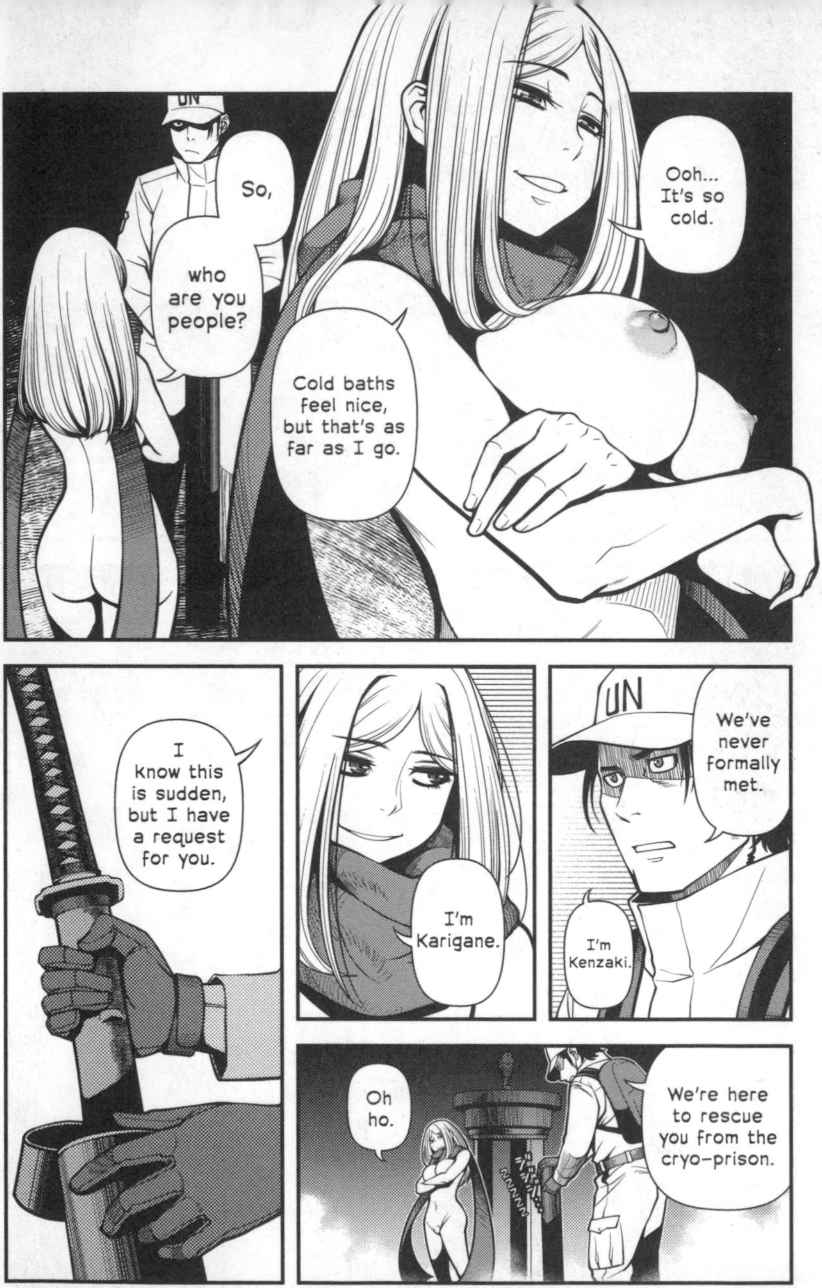
Ooh... It's so cold.
Cold baths feel nice, but that's as far as I go.
So,
who are you people?
We've never formally met.
I'm Kenzaki.
I'm Karigane.
We're here to rescue you from the cryo-prison.
Oh ho.
I know this is sudden, but I have a request for you.

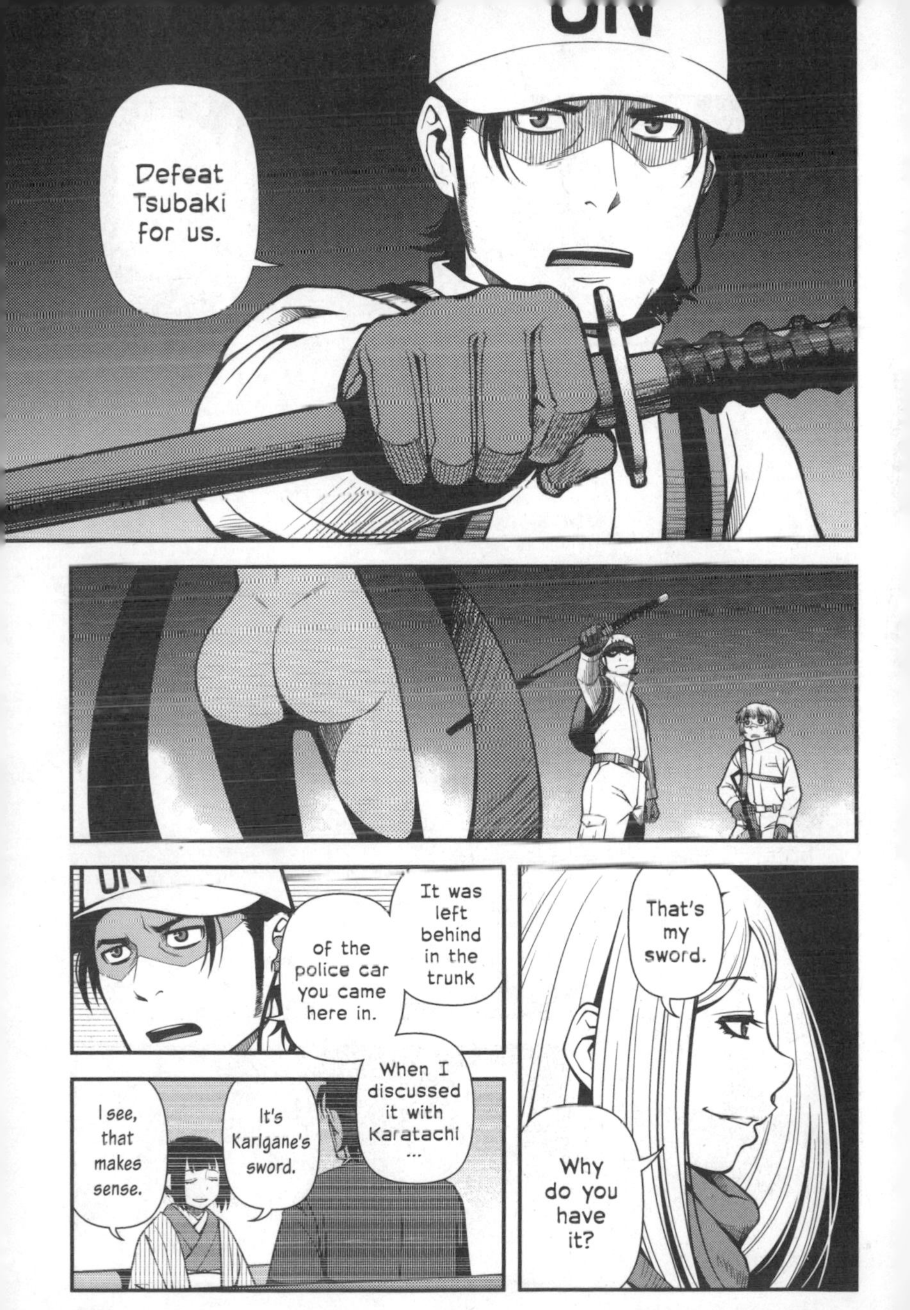
UN
Defeat Tsubaki for us.
That's my sword.
Why do you have it?
UN
It was left behind in the trunk
of the police car you came here in.
When I discussed it with Karatachi ...
It's Karigane's sword.
I see, that makes sense.

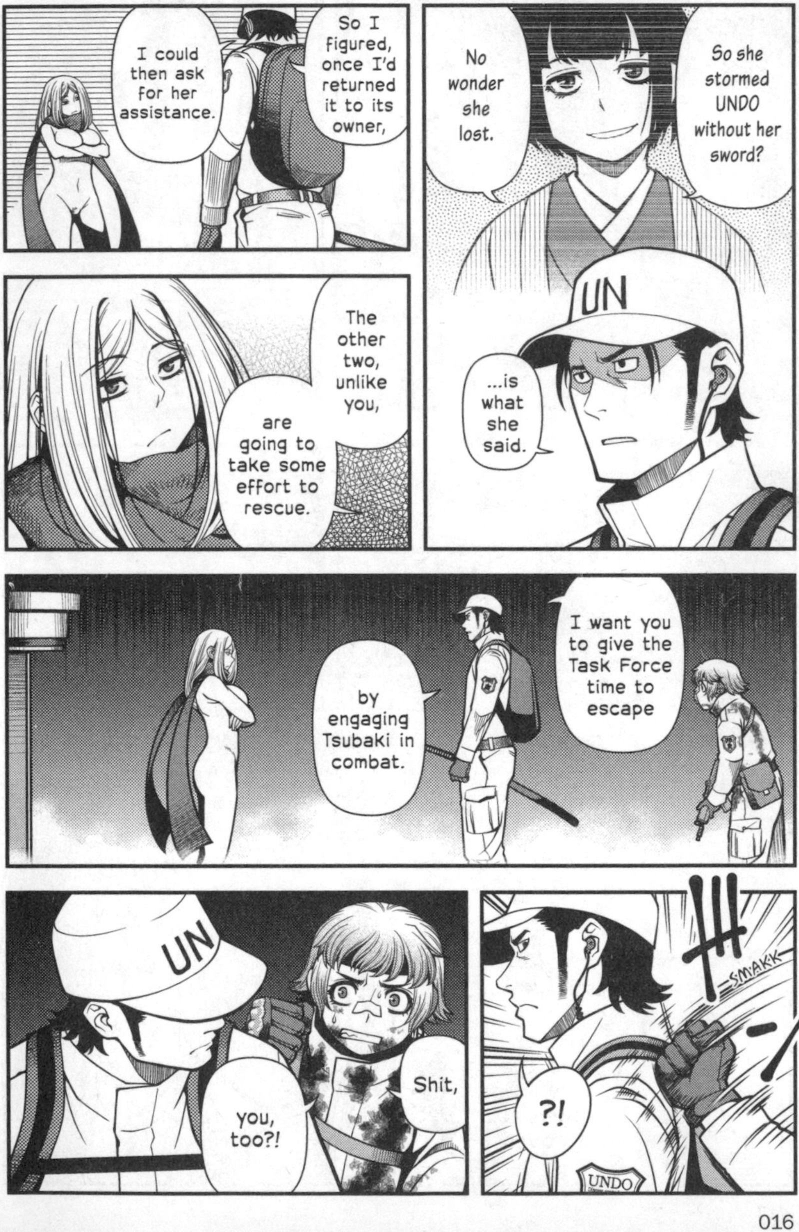
So she stormed UNDO without her sword?
No wonder she lost.
...is what she said.
So I figured, once I'd returned it to its owner,
I could then ask for her assistance.
The other two, unlike you,
are going to take some effort to rescue.
I want you to give the Task Force time to escape
by engaging Tsubaki in combat.
SMAKK
?!
Shit,
you, too?!

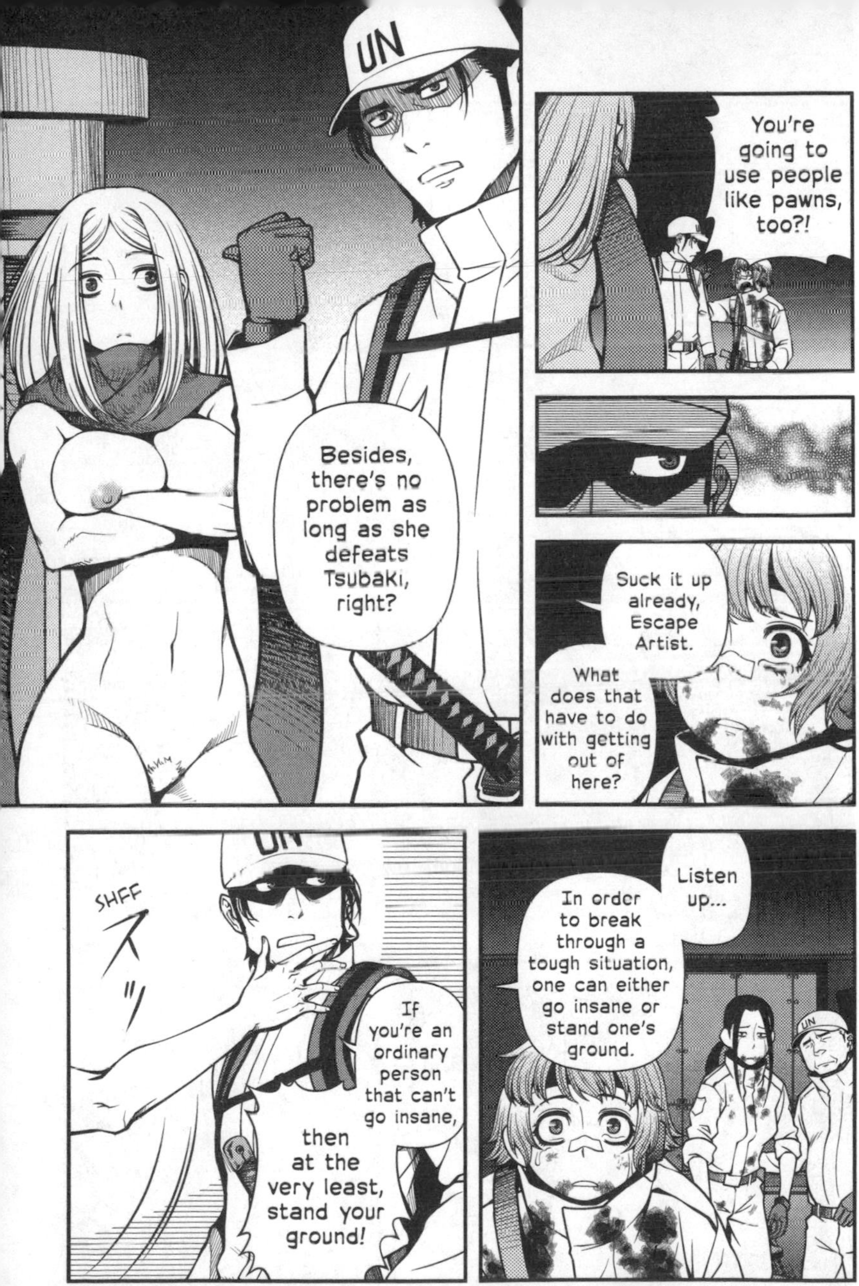
You're going to use people like pawns, too?!
Suck it up already, Escape Artist.
What does that have to do with getting out of here?
Besides, there's no problem as long as she defeats Tsubaki, right?
Listen up...
In order to break through a tough situation, one can either go insane or stand one's ground.
SHFF
If you're an ordinary person that can't go insane,
then at the very least, stand your ground!

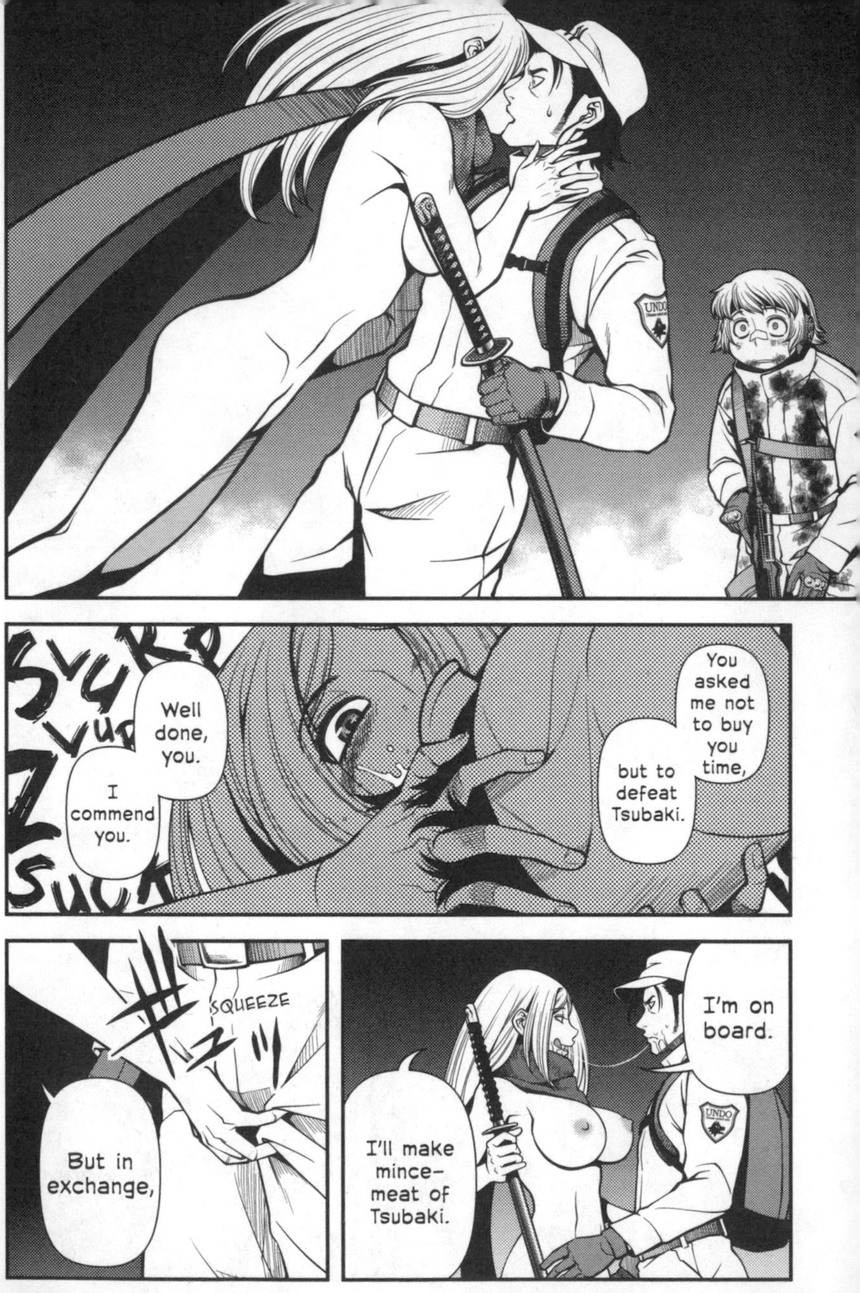
You asked me not to buy you time,
but to defeat Tsubaki.
Well done, you.
I commend you.
I'm on board.
I'll make mince-meat of Tsubaki.
SQUEEZE
But in exchange,

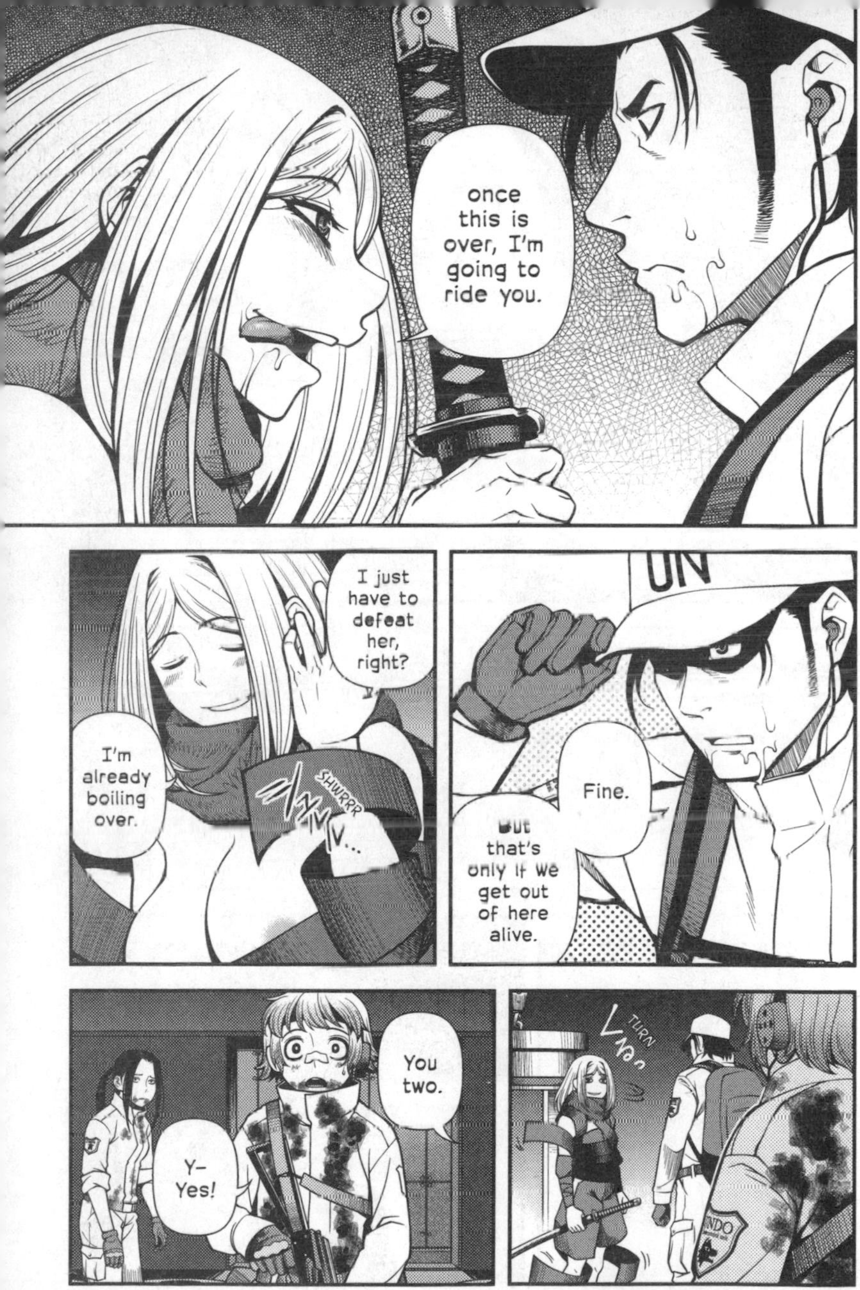
once this is over, I'm going to ride you.
Fine.
But that's only if we get out of here alive.
I just have to defeat her, right?
SHWRRR
I'm already boiling over.
TURN
You two.
Y– Yes!

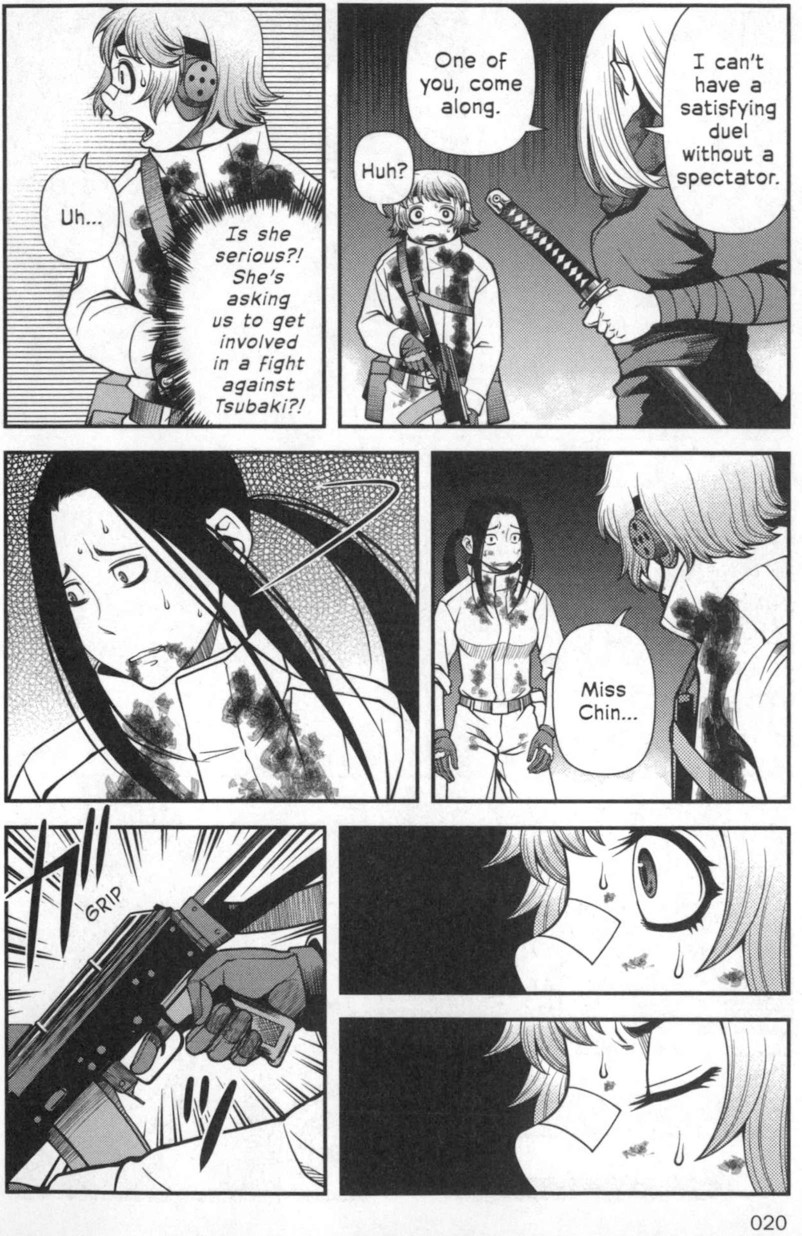
I can't have a satisfying duel without a spectator.
One of you, come along.
Huh?
Is she serious?! She's asking us to get involved in a fight against Tsubaki?!
Uh...
Miss Chin...
GRIP

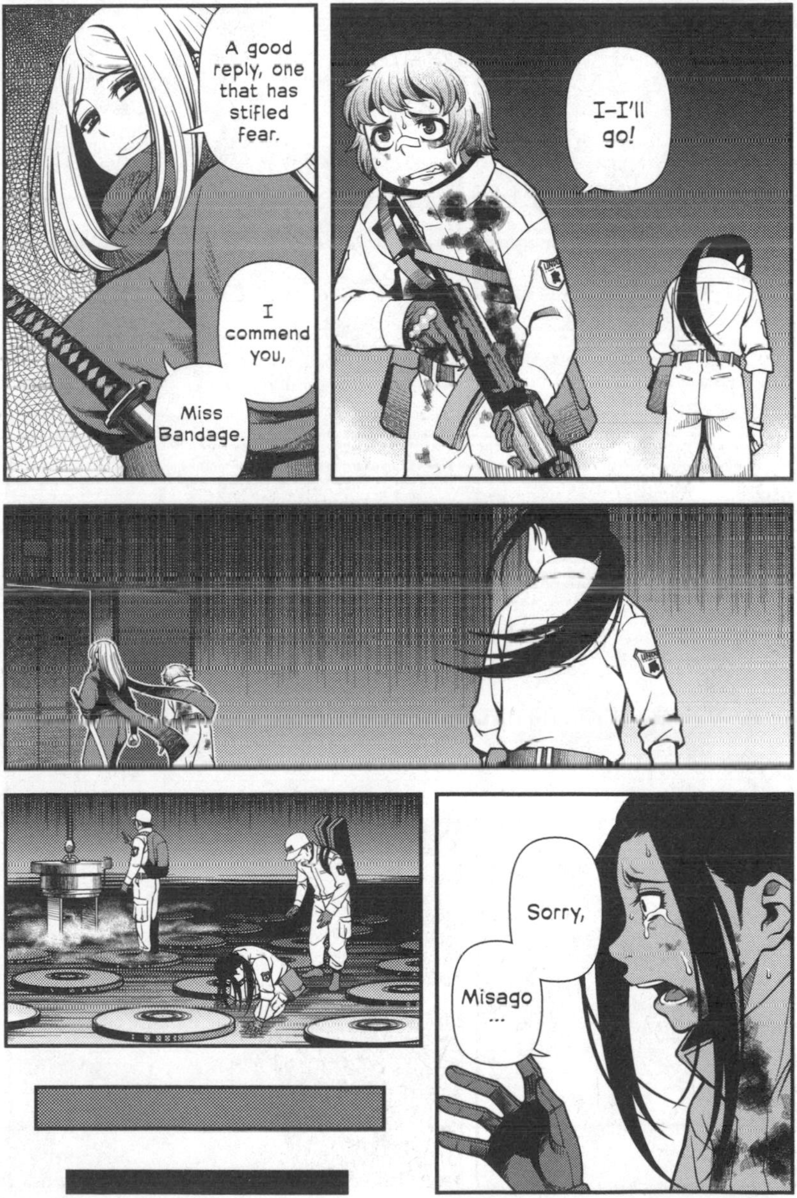
I-I'll go!
A good reply, one that has stifled fear.
I commend you,
Miss Bandage.
Sorry,
Misago ...

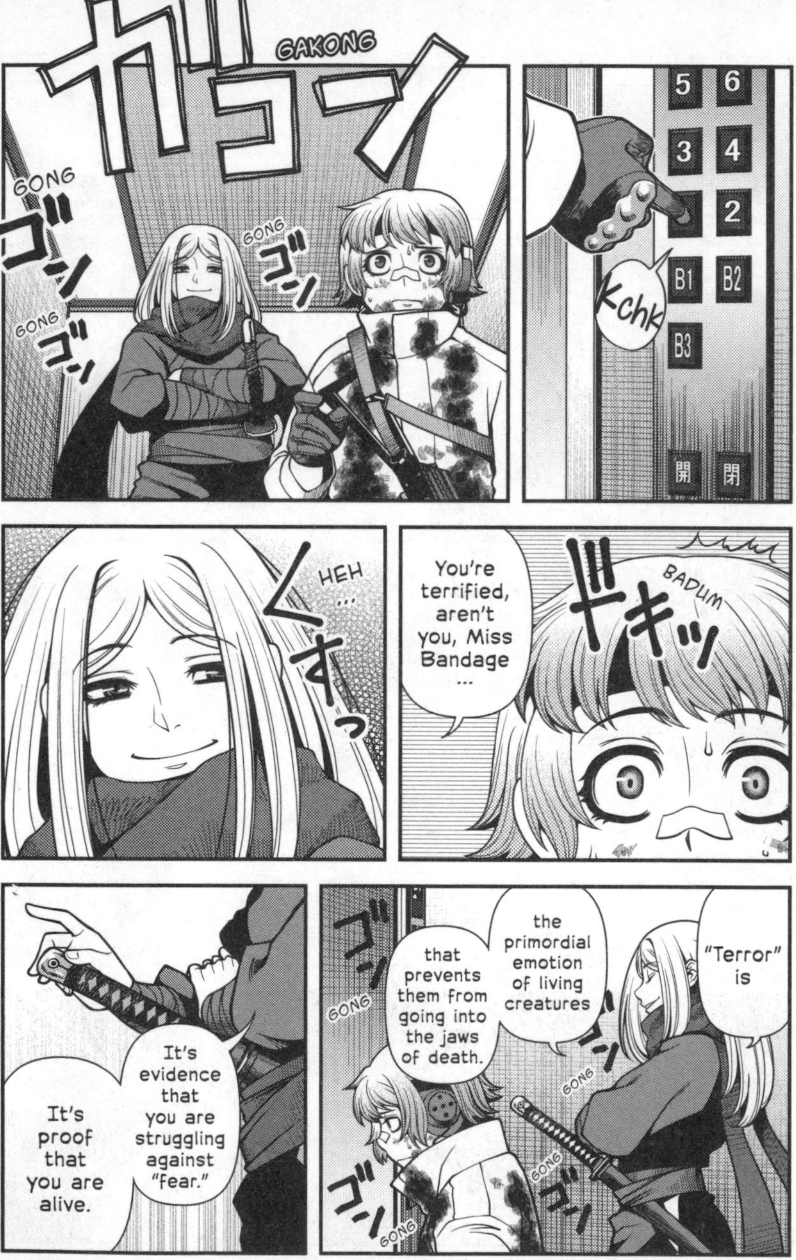
5
6
3
4
2
B1
B2
B3
開
閉
Kchk
ガコン
GAKONG
ゴン
GONG
ゴン
GONG
ゴン
GONG
ドキッ
BADUM
You're terrified, aren't you, Miss Bandage ...
くすっ
HEH ...
"Terror" is
the primordial emotion of living creatures
that prevents them from going into the jaws of death.
ゴン
GONG
ゴン
GONG
ゴン
GONG
ゴン
GONG
It's evidence that you are struggling against "fear."
It's proof that you are alive.

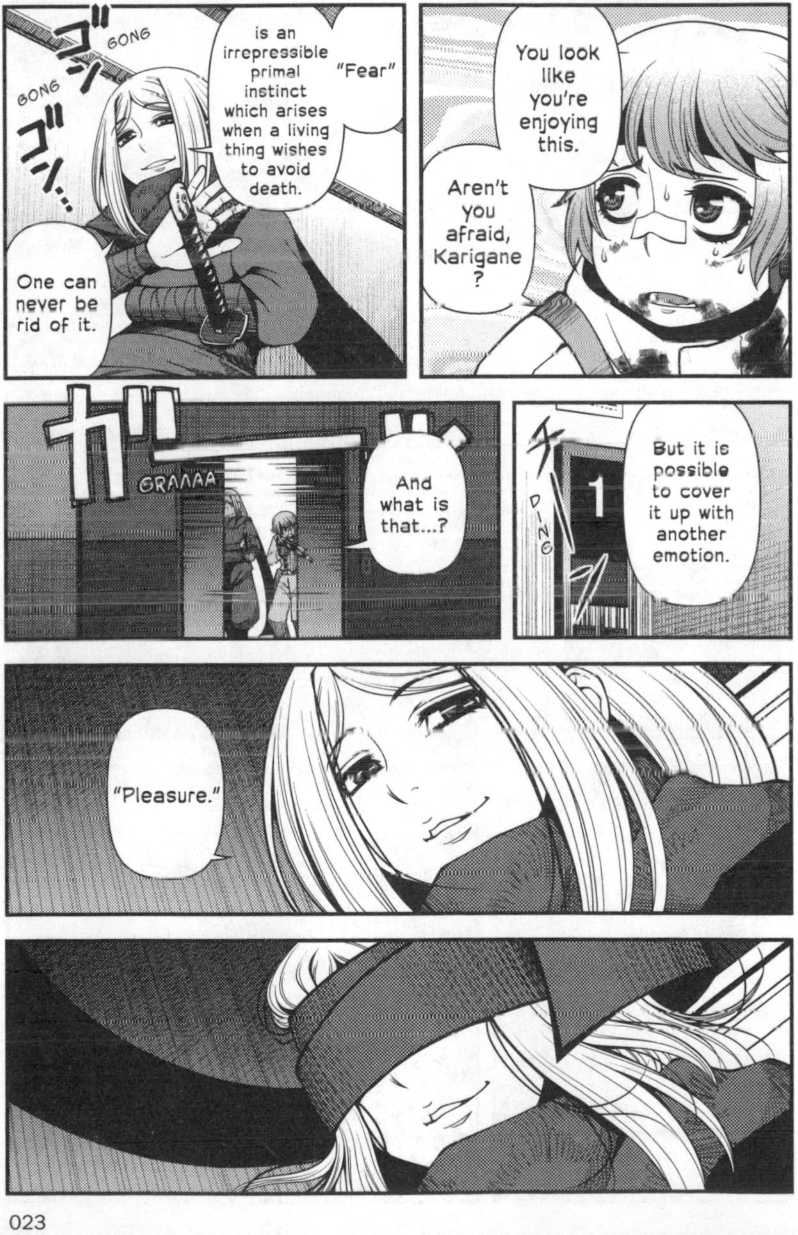
You look like you're enjoying this.
Aren't you afraid, Karigane?
"Fear"
is an irrepressible primal instinct which arises when a living thing wishes to avoid death.
GONG
GONG
One can never be rid of it.
DING
But it is possible to cover it up with another emotion.
GRAAAA
And what is that...?
"Pleasure."

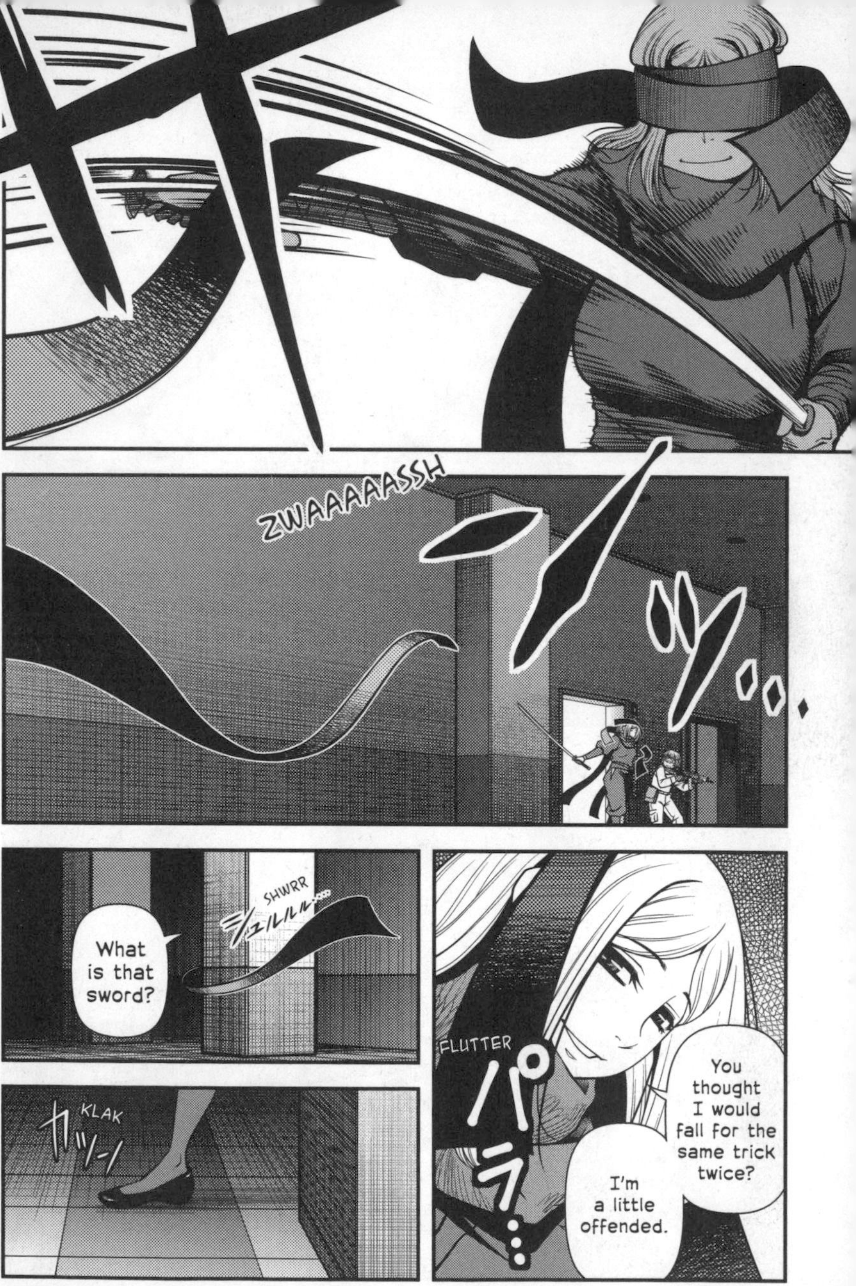
ZWAAAAAASSH
FLUTTER
You thought I would fall for the same trick twice?
I'm a little offended.
SHWRR
シュルルル...
What is that sword?
KLAK

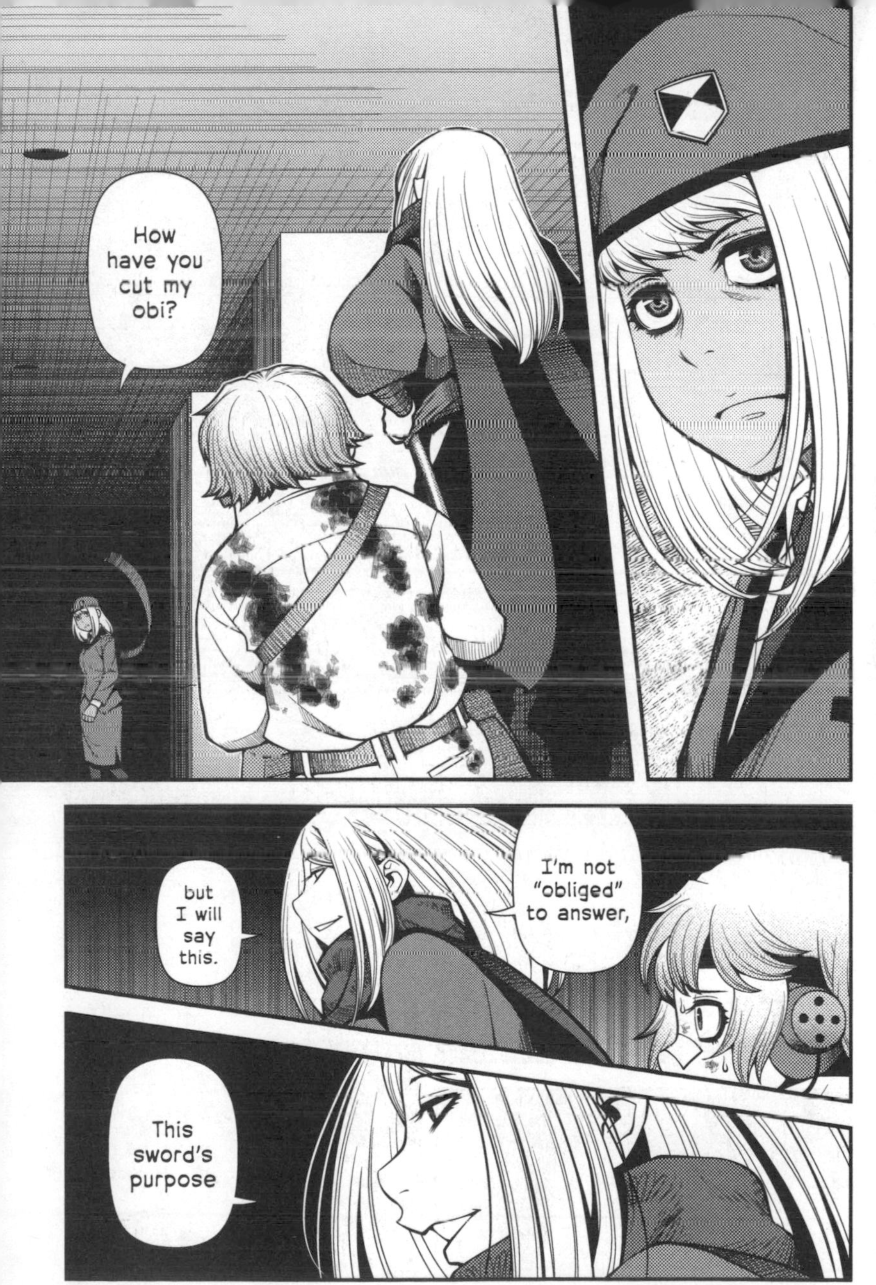
How have you cut my obi?
I'm not "obliged" to answer,
but I will say this.
This sword's purpose

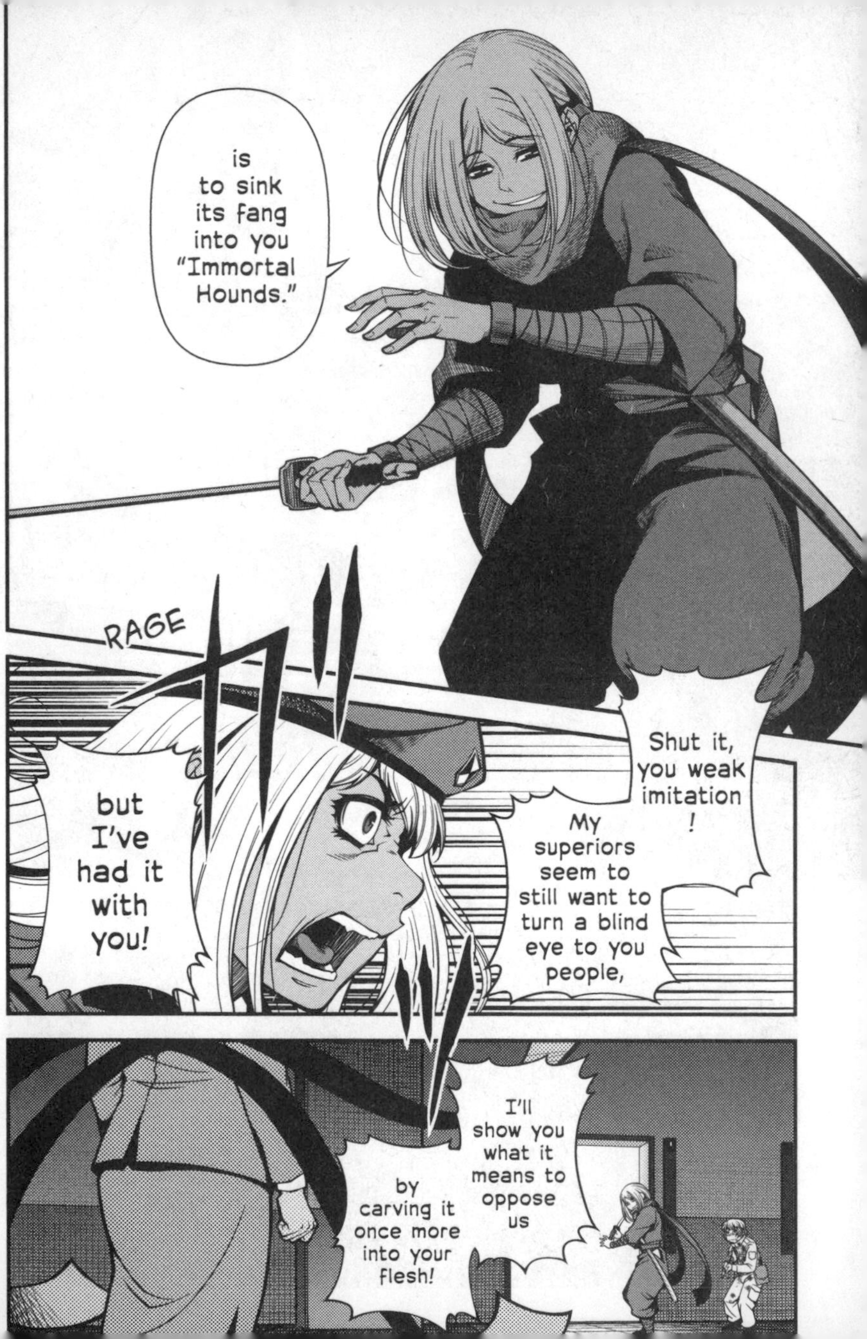
is to sink its fang into you "Immortal Hounds."
RAGE
Shut it, you weak imitation!
My superiors seem to still want to turn a blind eye to you people,
but I've had it with you!
I'll show you what it means to oppose us
by carving it once more into your flesh!

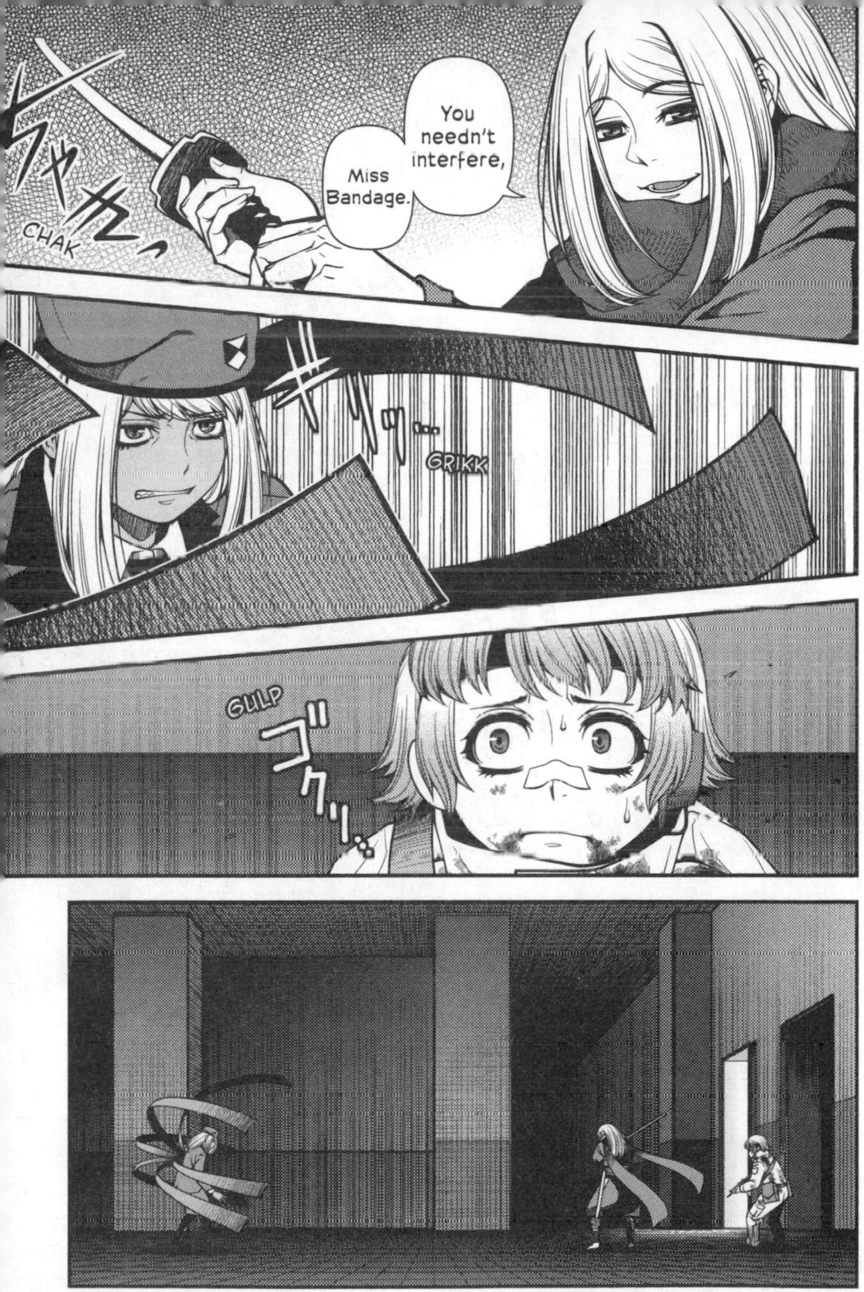
You needn't interfere,
Miss Bandage.
CHAK
GRIKK
GULP

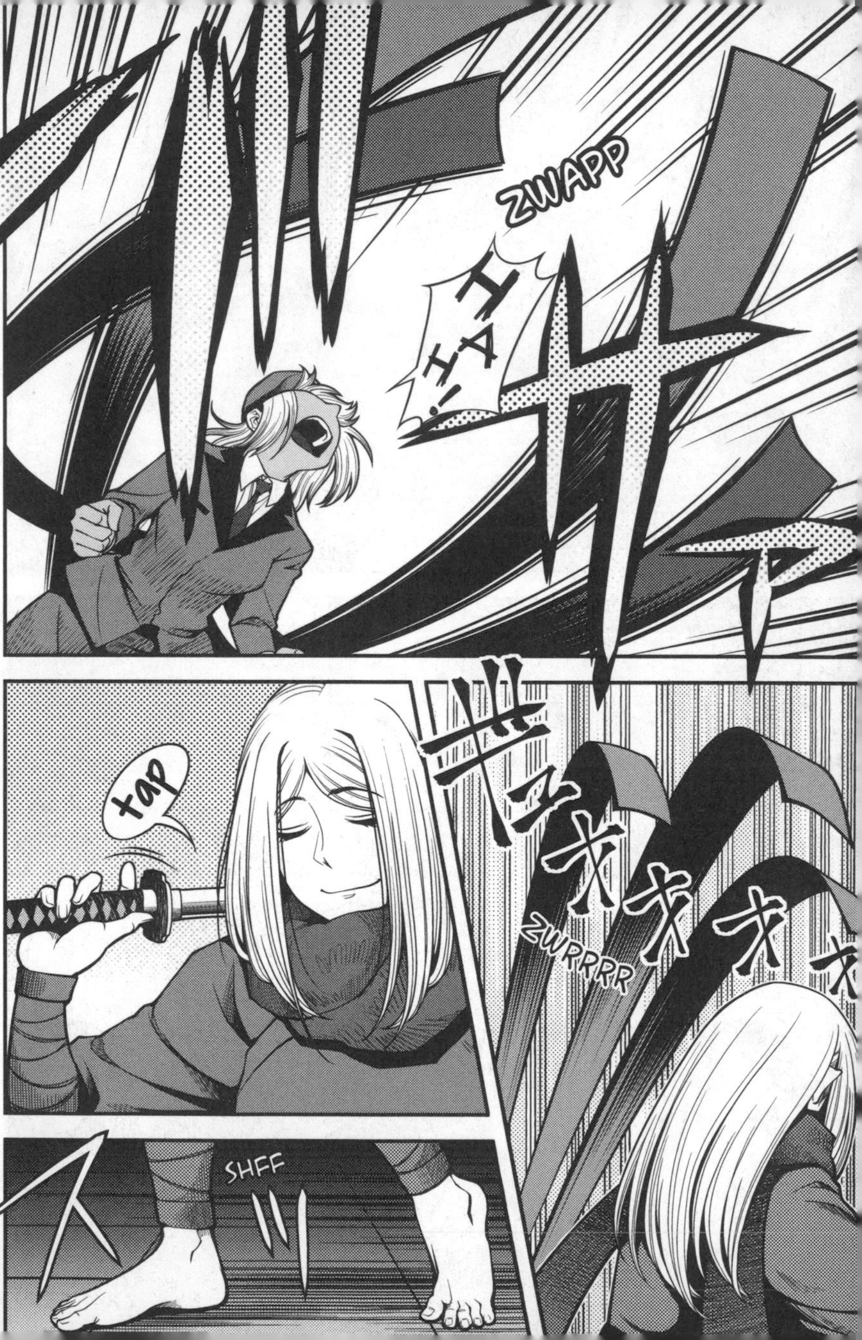
ZWAPP
HA!!
ZWRRRRR
tap
SHFF

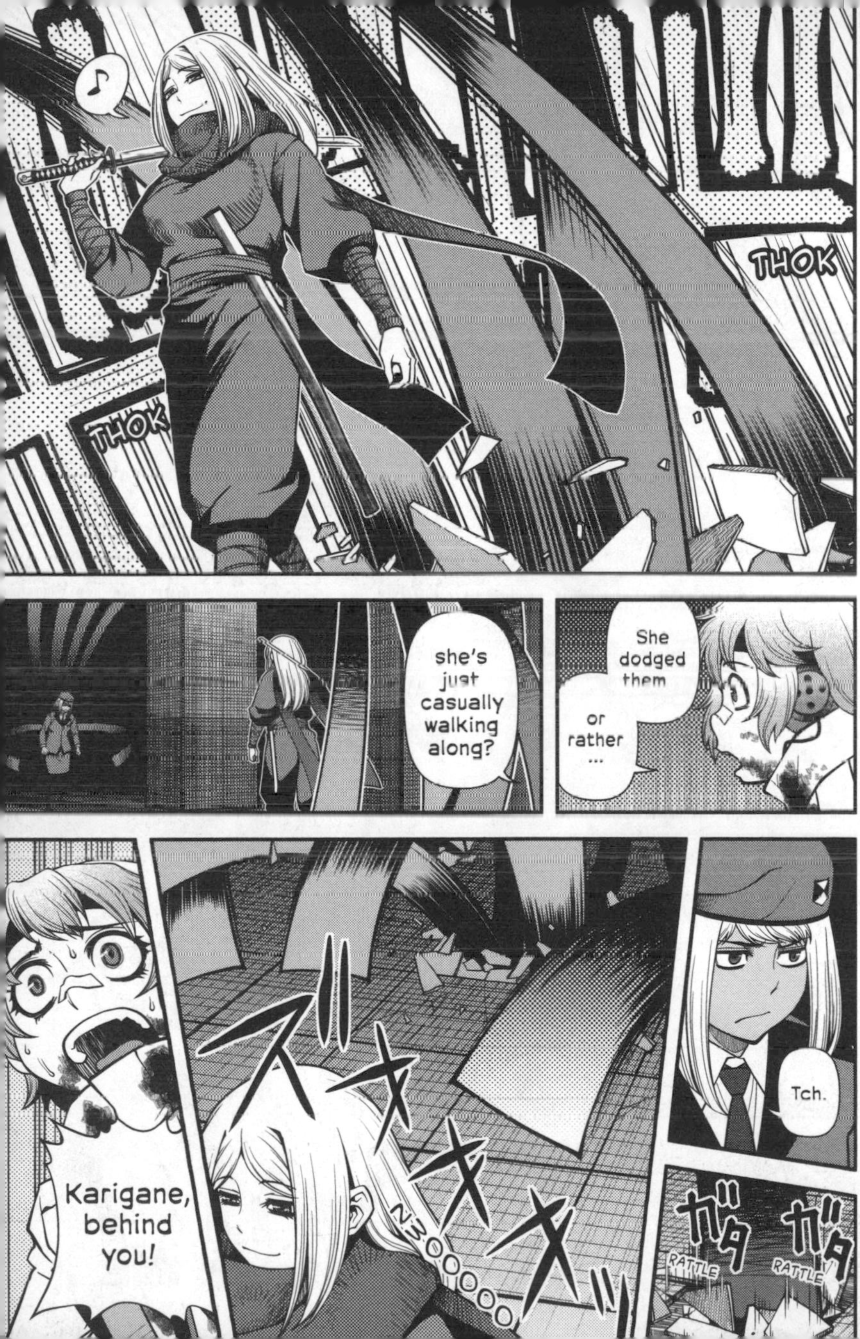
♪
THOK
THOK
She dodged them
or rather ...
she's just casually walking along?
Tch.
ガタ ガタ
RATTLE RATTLE
ZOOOOOOO
Karigane, behind you!

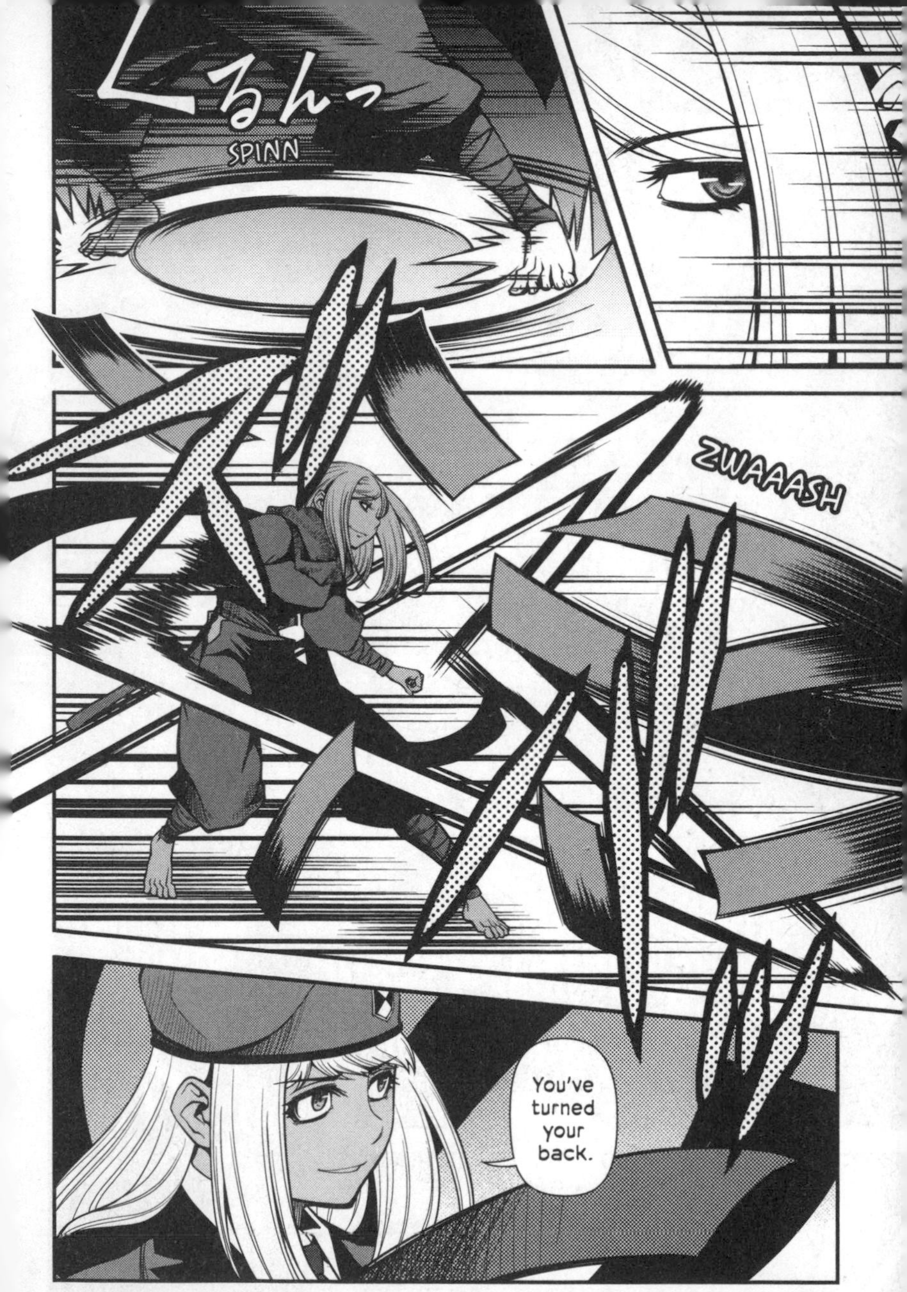
くるんっ
SPINN
ZWAAASH
You've turned your back.

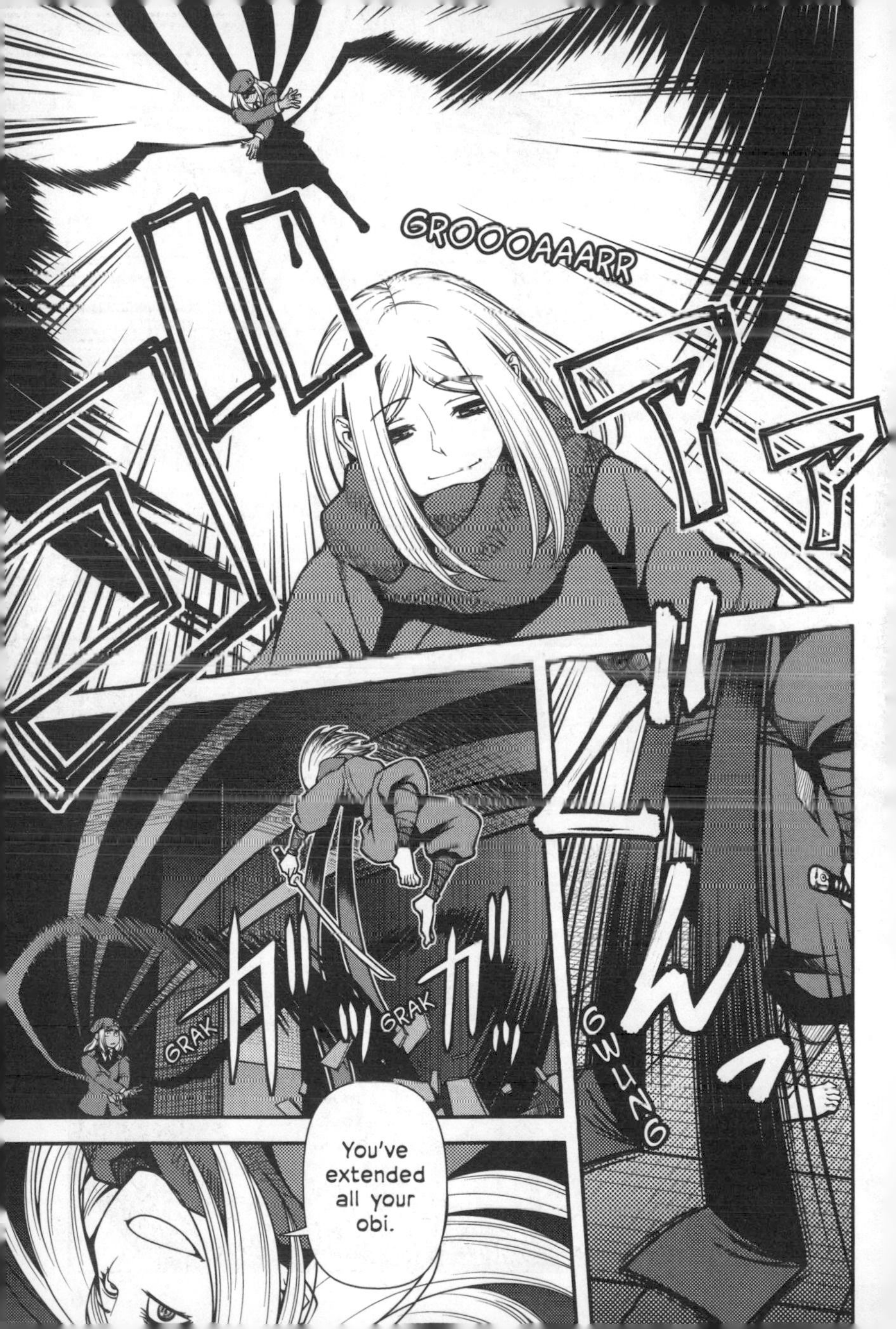
GROOOAAARR
GWUNG
GRAK
GRAK
You've extended all your obi.

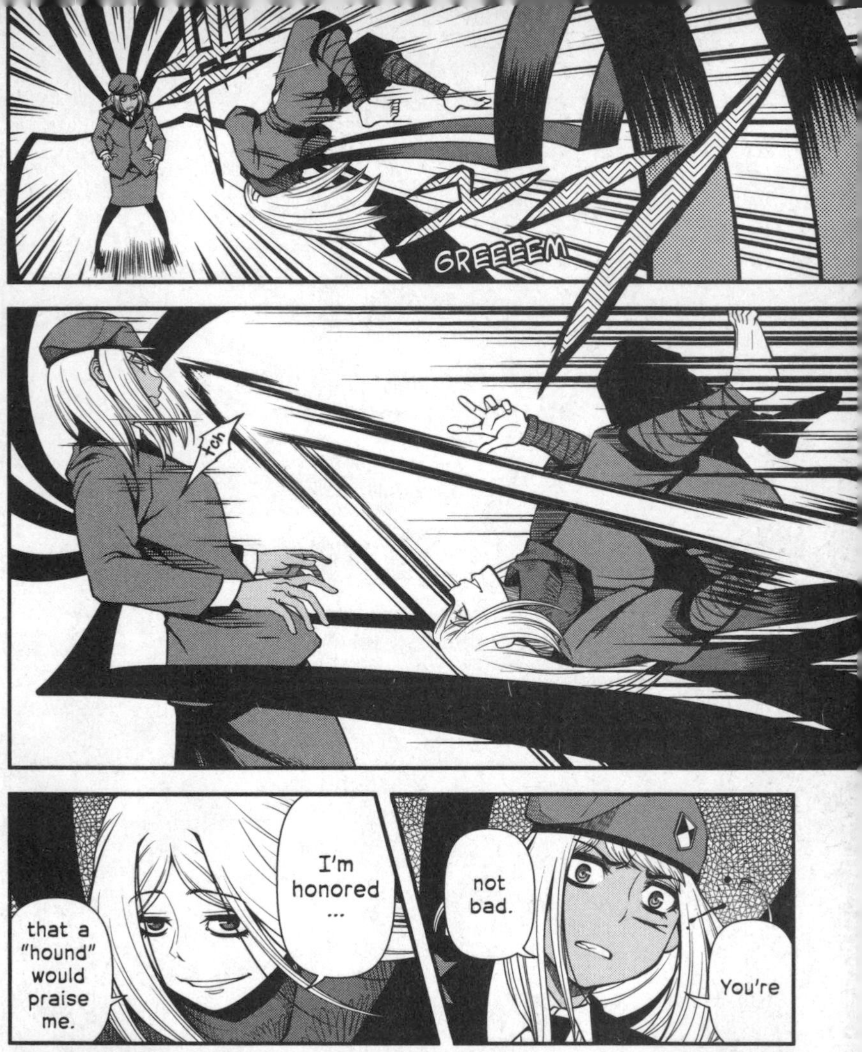
GREEEEEM
tch
You're
not bad.
I'm honored ...
that a "hound" would praise me.
S...
So cool ...

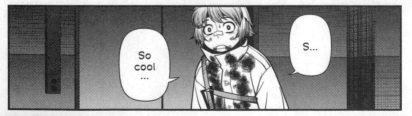

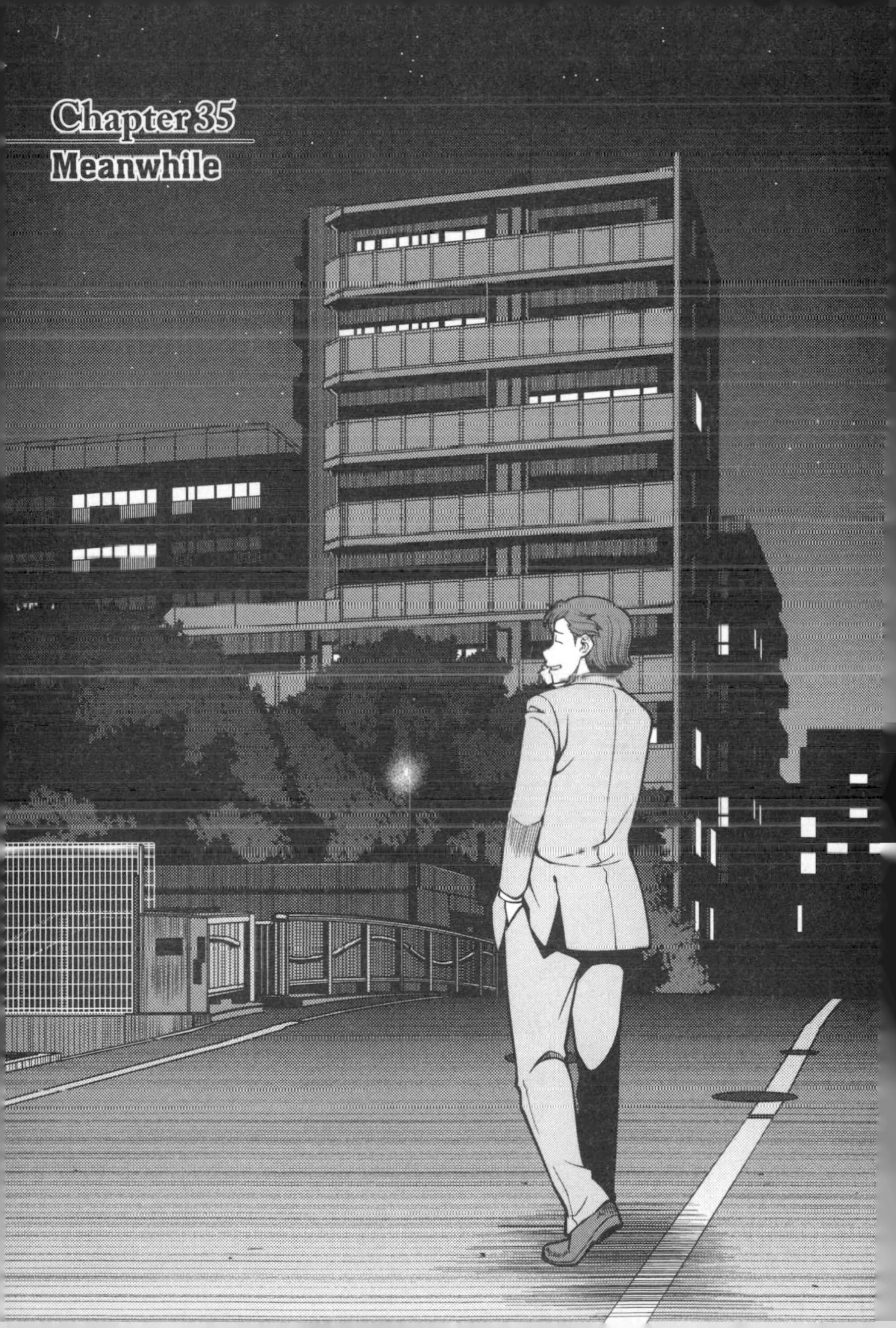
Chapter 35
Meanwhile

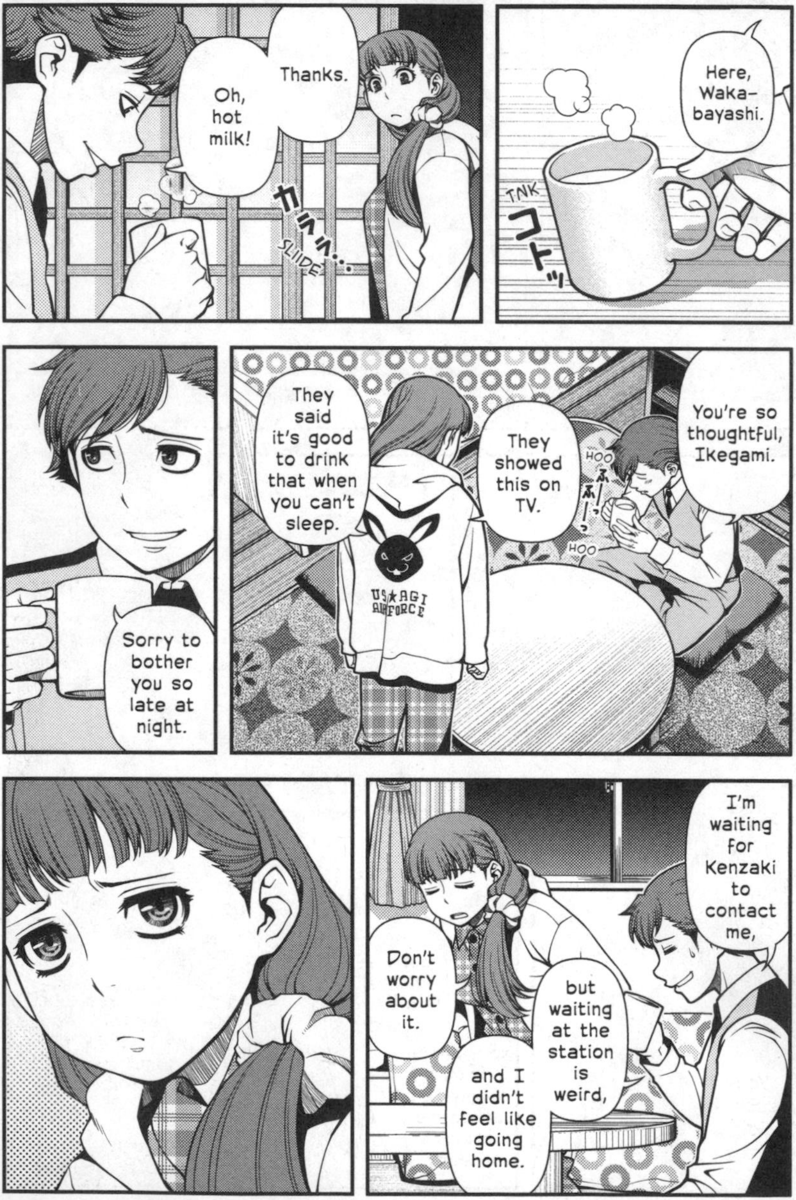
Here, Waka-bayashi.
TNK
コトッ
Thanks.
Oh, hot milk!
SLIIDE
You're so thoughtful, Ikegami.
They showed this on TV.
They said it's good to drink that when you can't sleep.
HOO
HOO
Sorry to bother you so late at night.
I'm waiting for Kenzaki to contact me,
but waiting at the station is weird,
and I didn't feel like going home.
Don't worry about it.

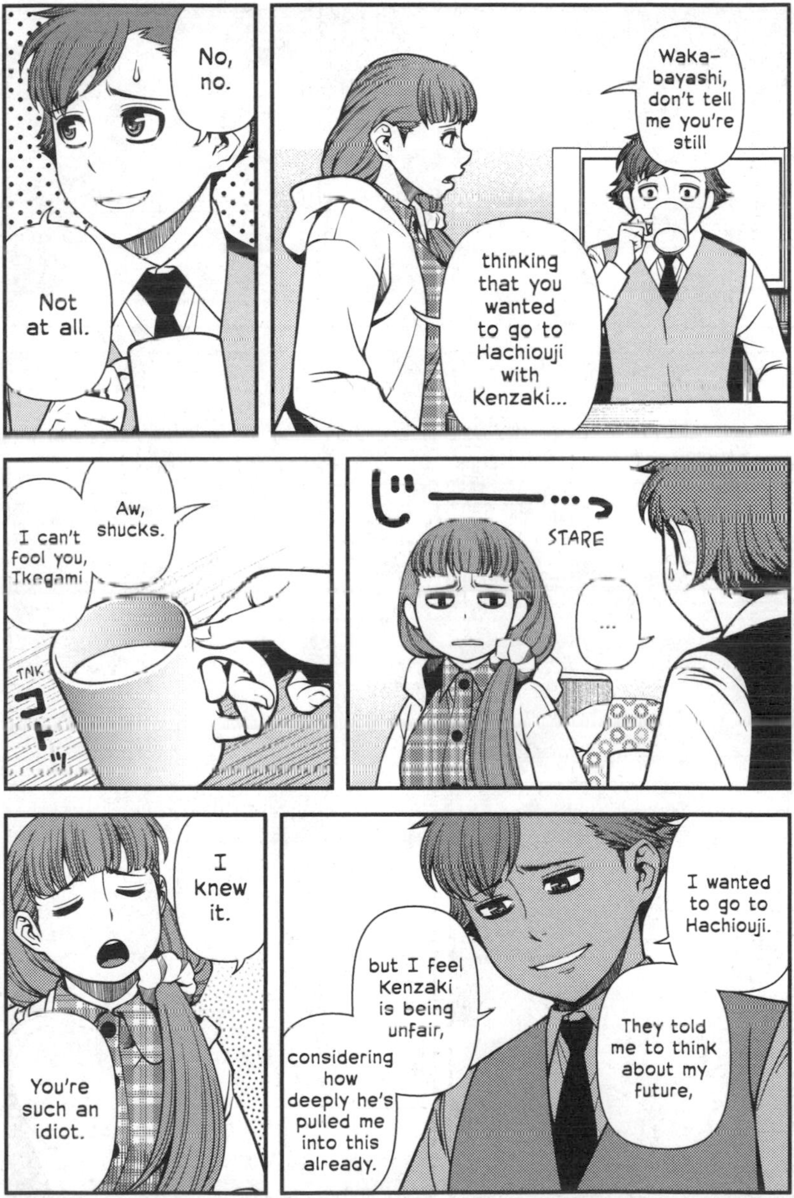
Waka-bayashi, don't tell me you're still
thinking that you wanted to go to Hachiouji with Kenzaki...
No, no.
Not at all.
じーー…っ
STARE
...
Aw, shucks.
I can't fool you, Tkegami
TNK
コトッ
I wanted to go to Hachiouji.
They told me to think about my future,
but I feel Kenzaki is being unfair,
considering how deeply he's pulled me into this already.
I knew it.
You're such an idiot.

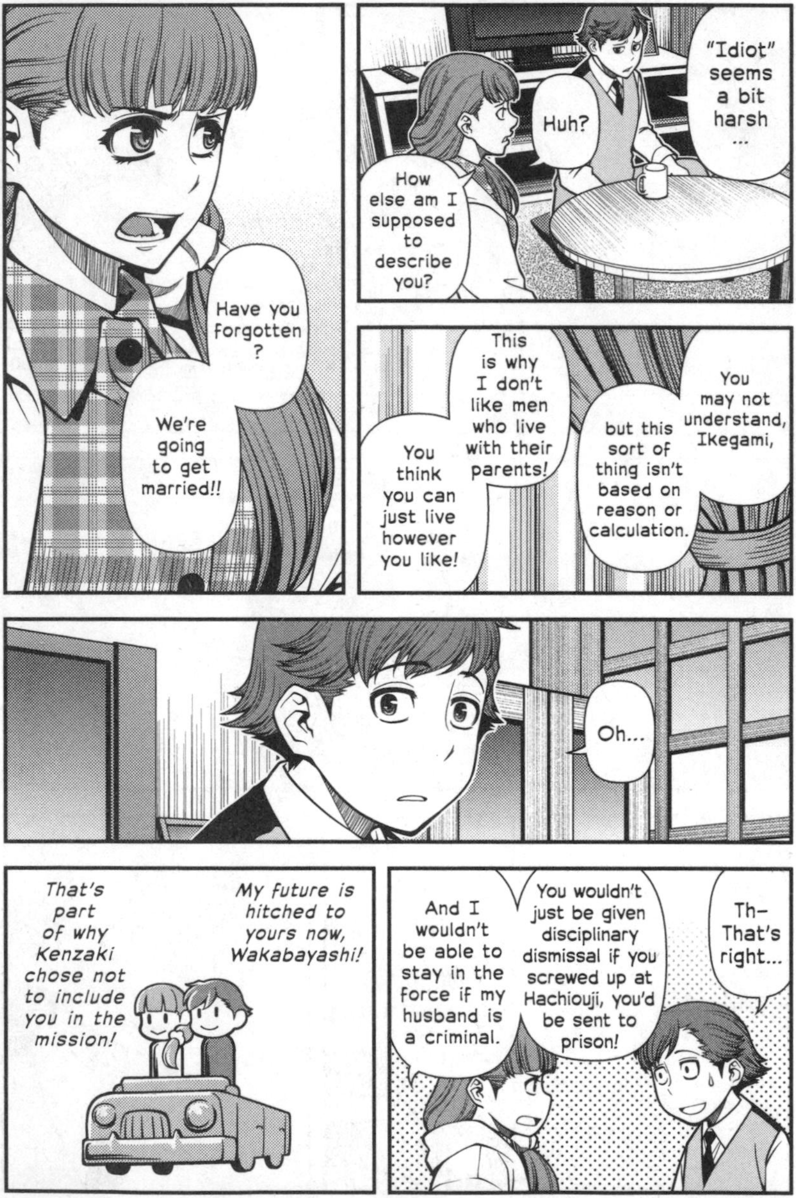
"Idiot" seems a bit harsh ...
Huh?
How else am I supposed to describe you?
You may not understand, Ikegami,
but this sort of thing isn't based on reason or calculation.
This is why I don't like men who live with their parents!
You think you can just live however you like!
Have you forgotten ?
We're going to get married!!
Oh...
Th— That's right...
You wouldn't just be given disciplinary dismissal if you screwed up at Hachiouji, you'd be sent to prison!
And I wouldn't be able to stay in the force if my husband is a criminal.
My future is hitched to yours now, Wakabayashi!
That's part of why Kenzaki chose not to include you in the mission!

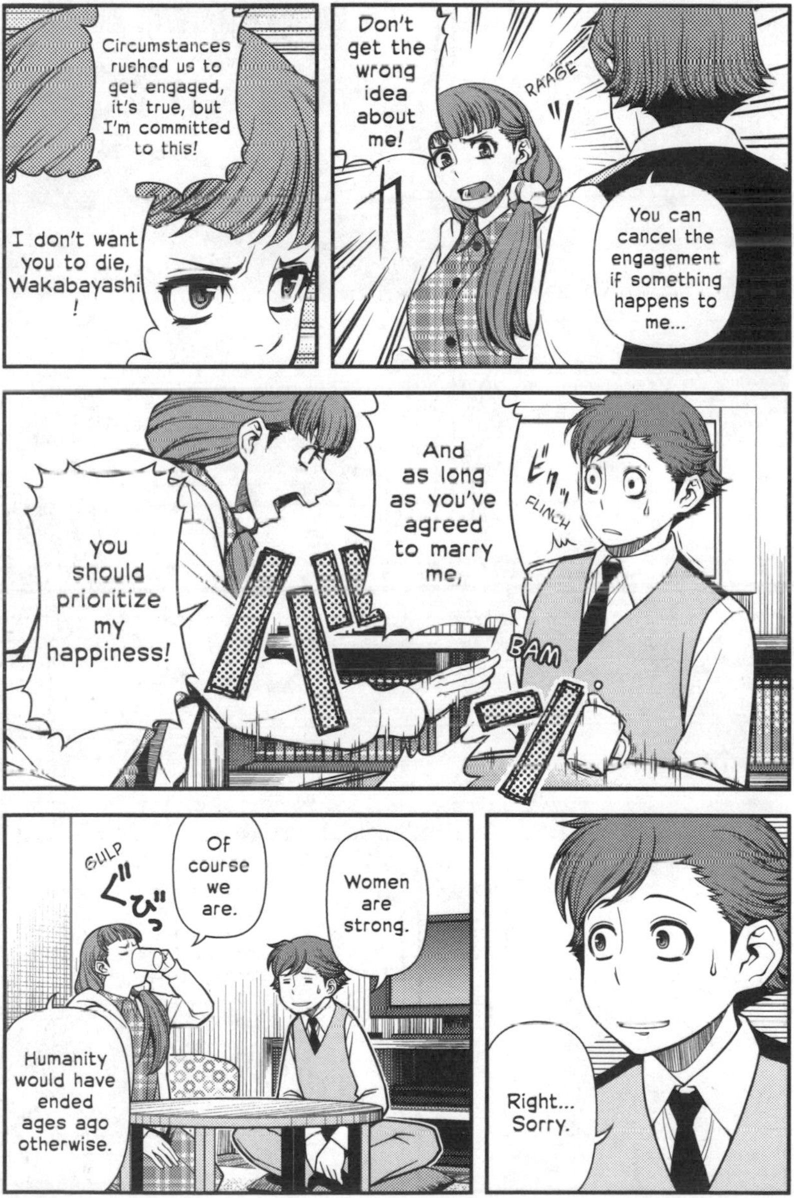
Don't get the wrong idea about me!
RAAGE
You can cancel the engagement if something happens to me...
Circumstances rushed us to get engaged, it's true, but I'm committed to this!
I don't want you to die, Wakabayashi!
And as long as you've agreed to marry me,
FLINCH
BAM
you should prioritize my happiness!
Right... Sorry.
Women are strong.
Of course we are.
GULP
Humanity would have ended ages ago otherwise.

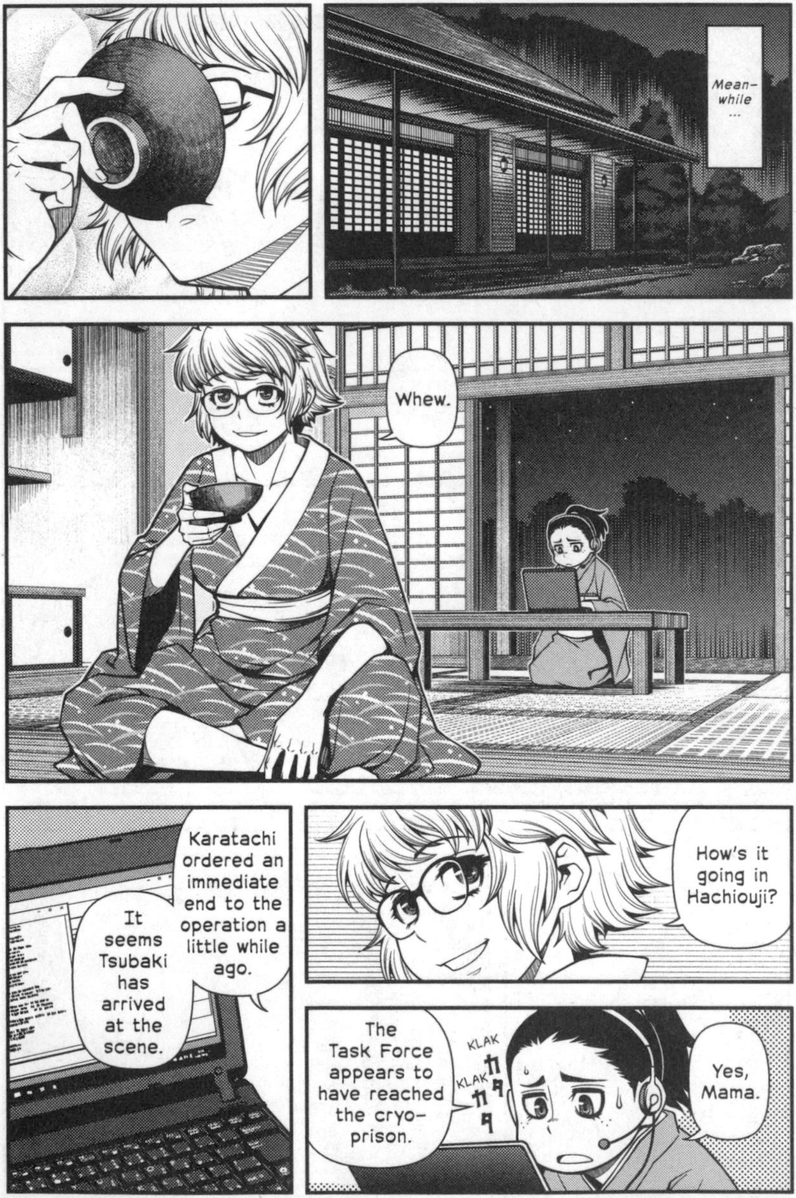
Mean-while ...
Whew.
How's it going in Hachiouji?
Yes, Mama.
KLAK カタ
KLAK カタ
The Task Force appears to have reached the cryo-prison.
Karatachi ordered an immediate end to the operation a little while ago.
It seems Tsubaki has arrived at the scene.

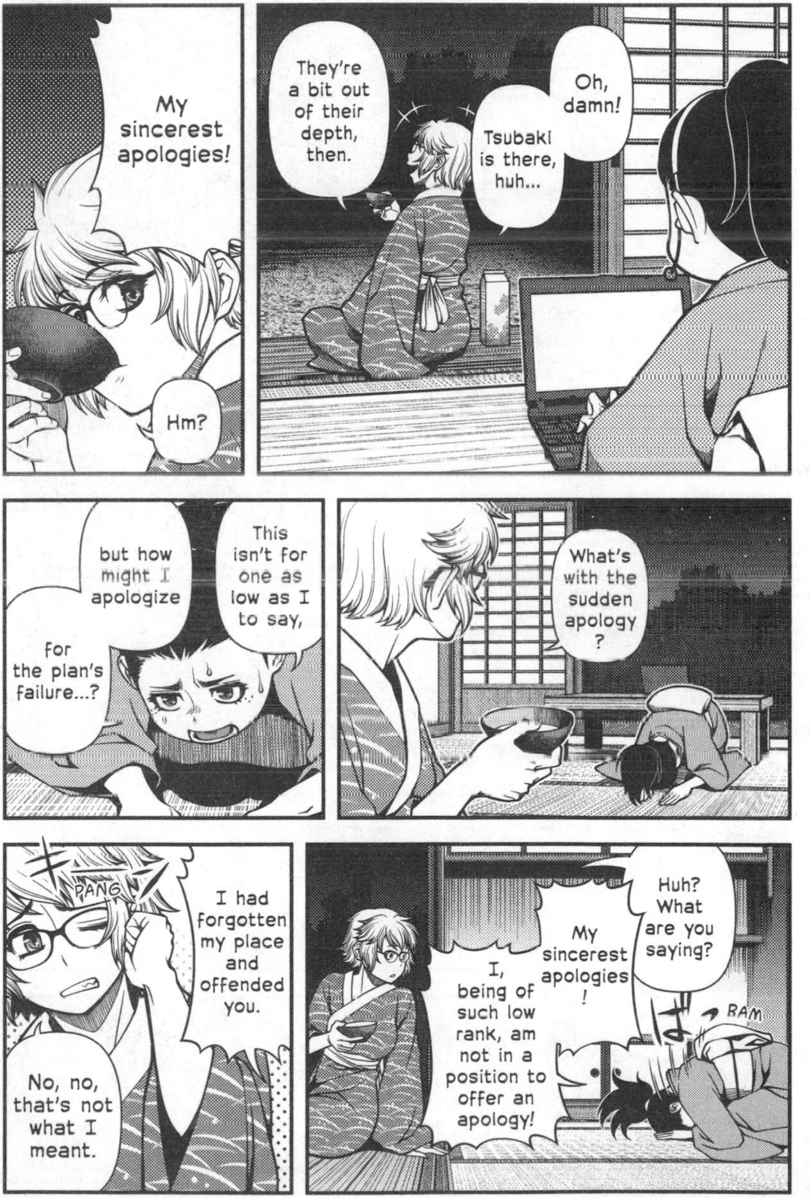
Oh, damn!
Tsubaki is there, huh...
They're a bit out of their depth, then.
My sincerest apologies!
Hm?
What's with the sudden apology?
This isn't for one as low as I to say,
but how might I apologize
for the plan's failure...?
Huh? What are you saying?
My sincerest apologies!
I, being of such low rank, am not in a position to offer an apology!
BAM
PANG
I had forgotten my place and offended you.
No, no, that's not what I meant.

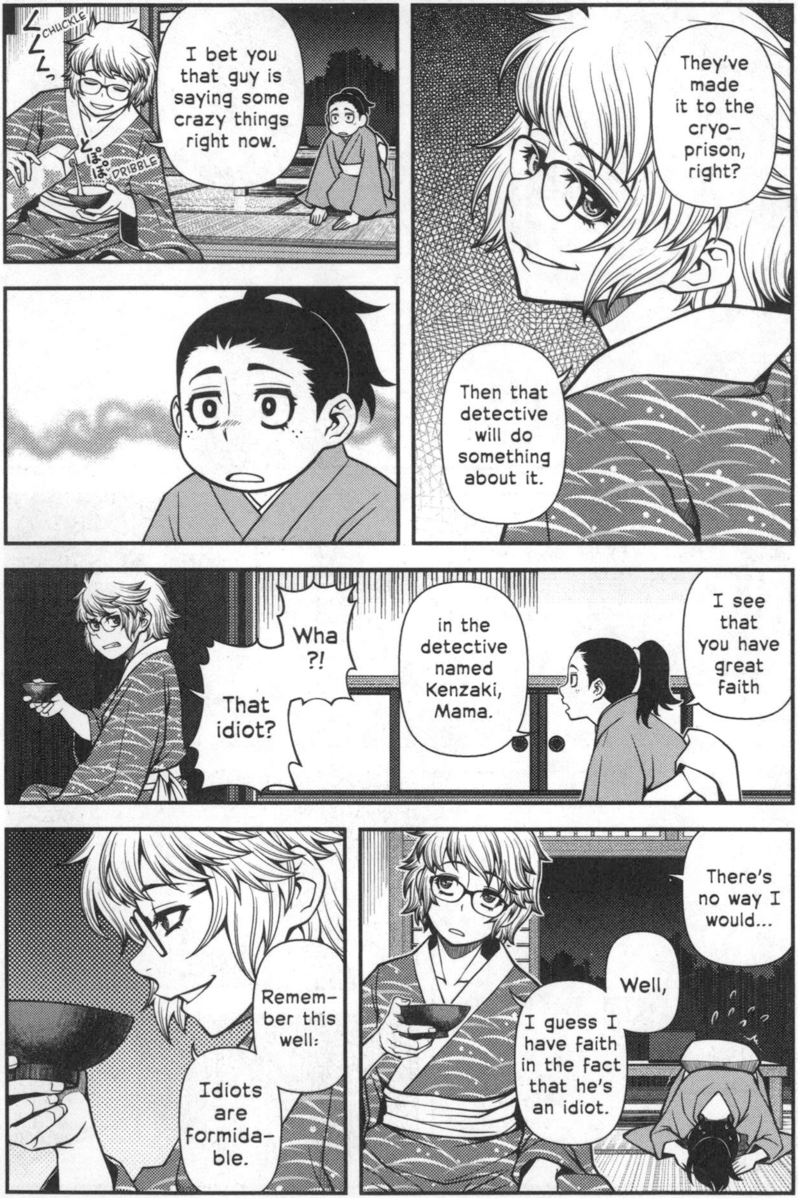
They've made it to the cryo-prison, right?
Then that detective will do something about it.
くくくっ CHUCKLE
I bet you that guy is saying some crazy things right now.
とぽぽ DRIBBLE
I see that you have great faith
in the detective named Kenzaki, Mama.
Wha ?!
That idiot?
There's no way I would...
Well,
I guess I have faith in the fact that he's an idiot.
Remember this well:
Idiots are formidable.

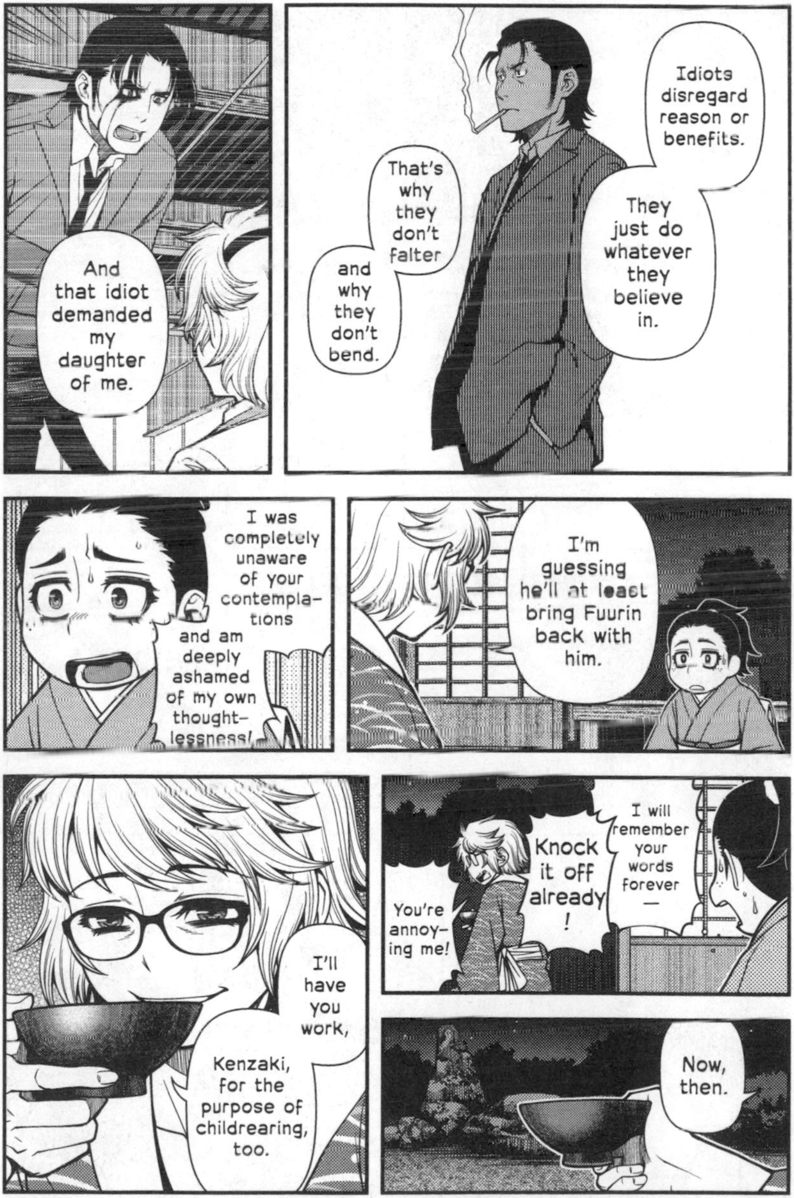
Idiots disregard reason or benefits.
They just do whatever they believe in.
That's why they don't falter
and why they don't bend.
And that idiot demanded my daughter of me.
I'm guessing he'll at least bring Fuurin back with him.
I was completely unaware of your contempla-tions
and am deeply ashamed of my own thought-lessness!
I will remember your words forever —
Knock it off already!
You're annoy-ing me!
Now, then.
I'll have you work,
Kenzaki, for the purpose of childrearing, too.

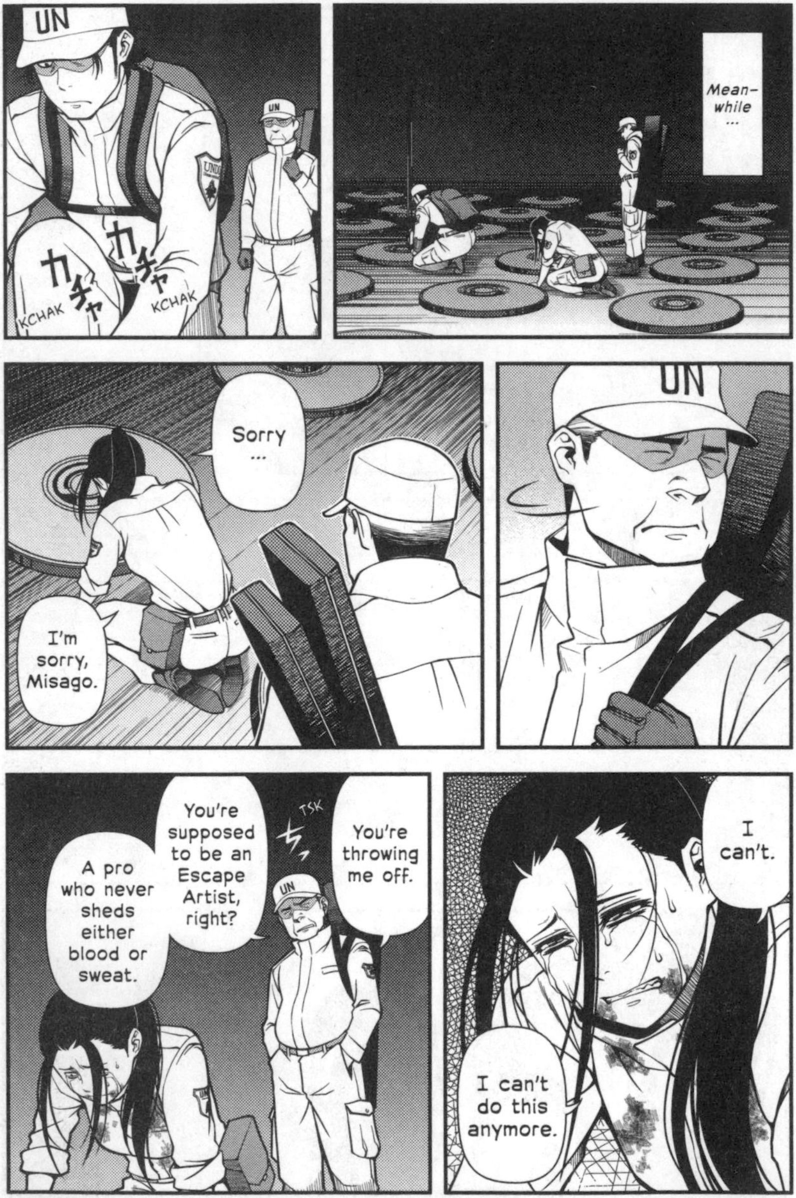
Mean-while ...
カチャ
KCHAK
カチャ
KCHAK
Sorry ...
I'm sorry, Misago.
I can't.
I can't do this anymore.
TSK
You're throwing me off.
You're supposed to be an Escape Artist, right?
A pro who never sheds either blood or sweat.

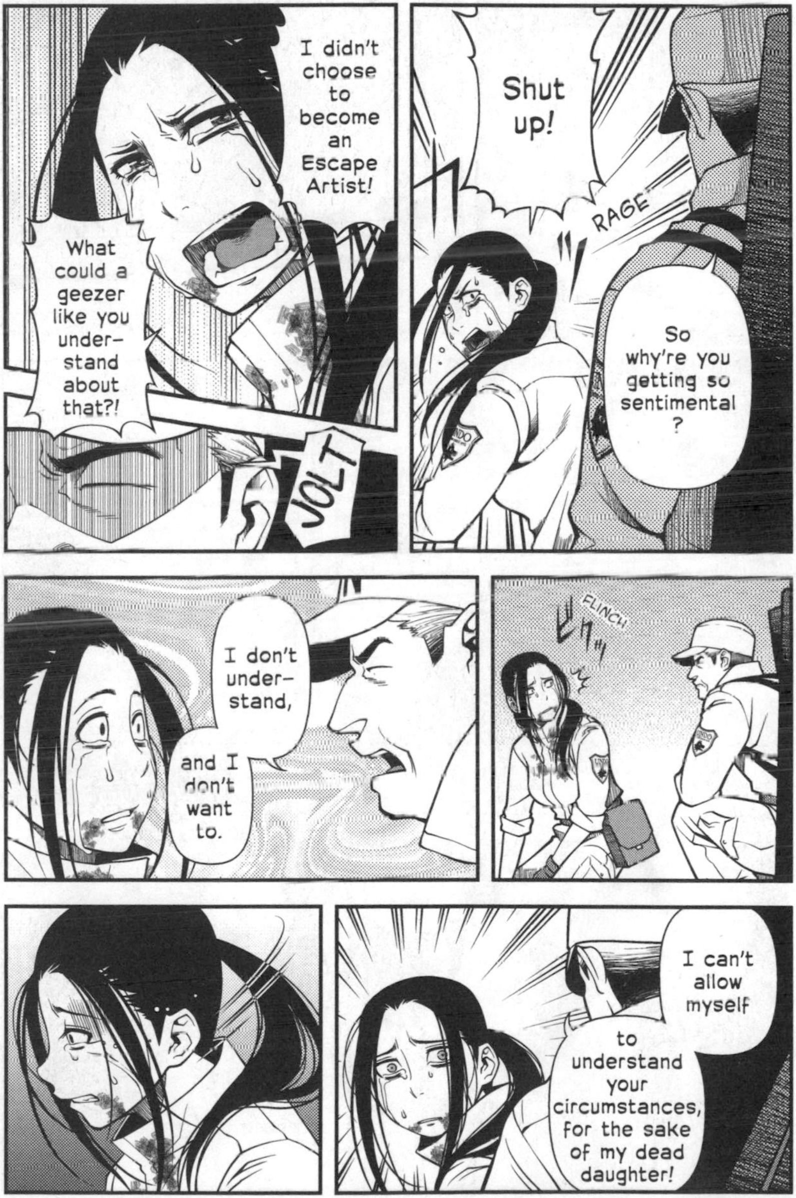
Shut up!
RAGE
So why're you getting so sentimental?
I didn't choose to become an Escape Artist!
What could a geezer like you under-stand about that?!
JOLT
FLINCH
I don't under-stand,
and I don't want to.
I can't allow myself
to understand your circumstances, for the sake of my dead daughter!

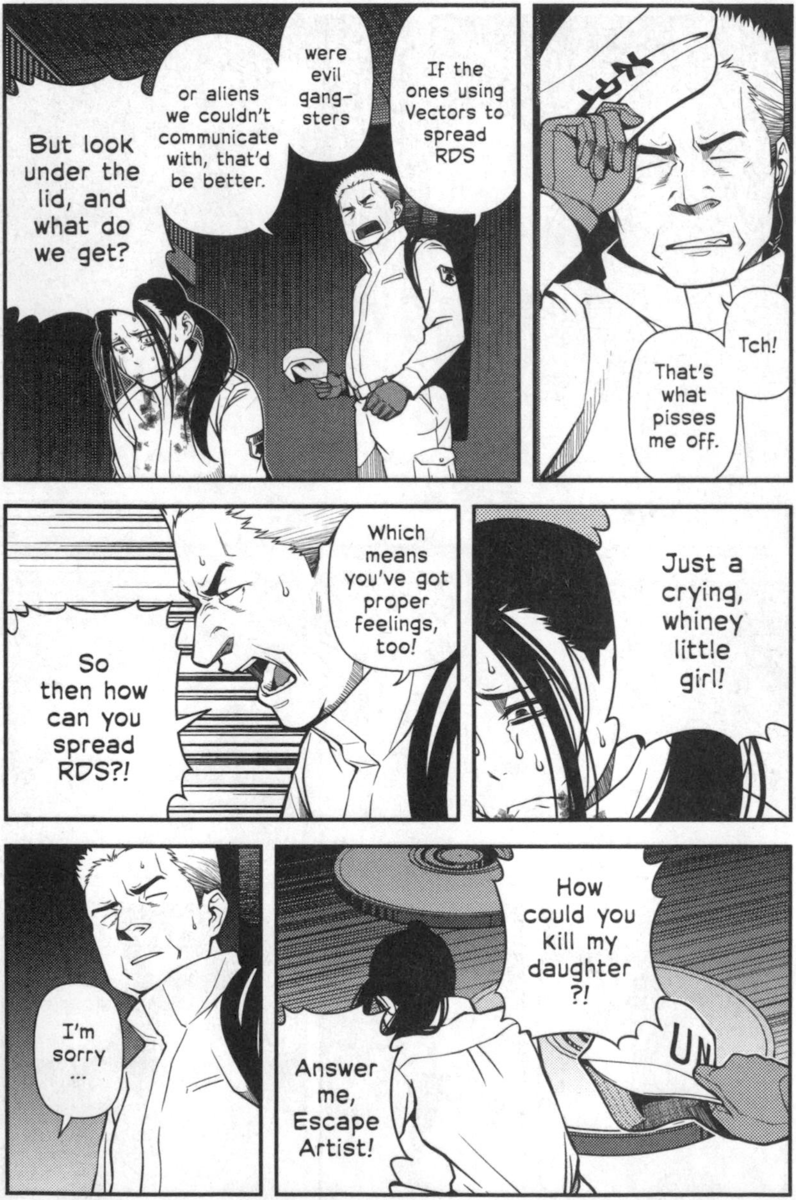
Tch!
That's what pisses me off.
If the ones using Vectors to spread RDS
were evil gangsters
or aliens we couldn't communicate with, that'd be better.
But look under the lid, and what do we get?
Just a crying, whiney little girl!
Which means you've got proper feelings, too!
So then how can you spread RDS?!
How could you kill my daughter ?!
UN
Answer me, Escape Artist!
I'm sorry ...

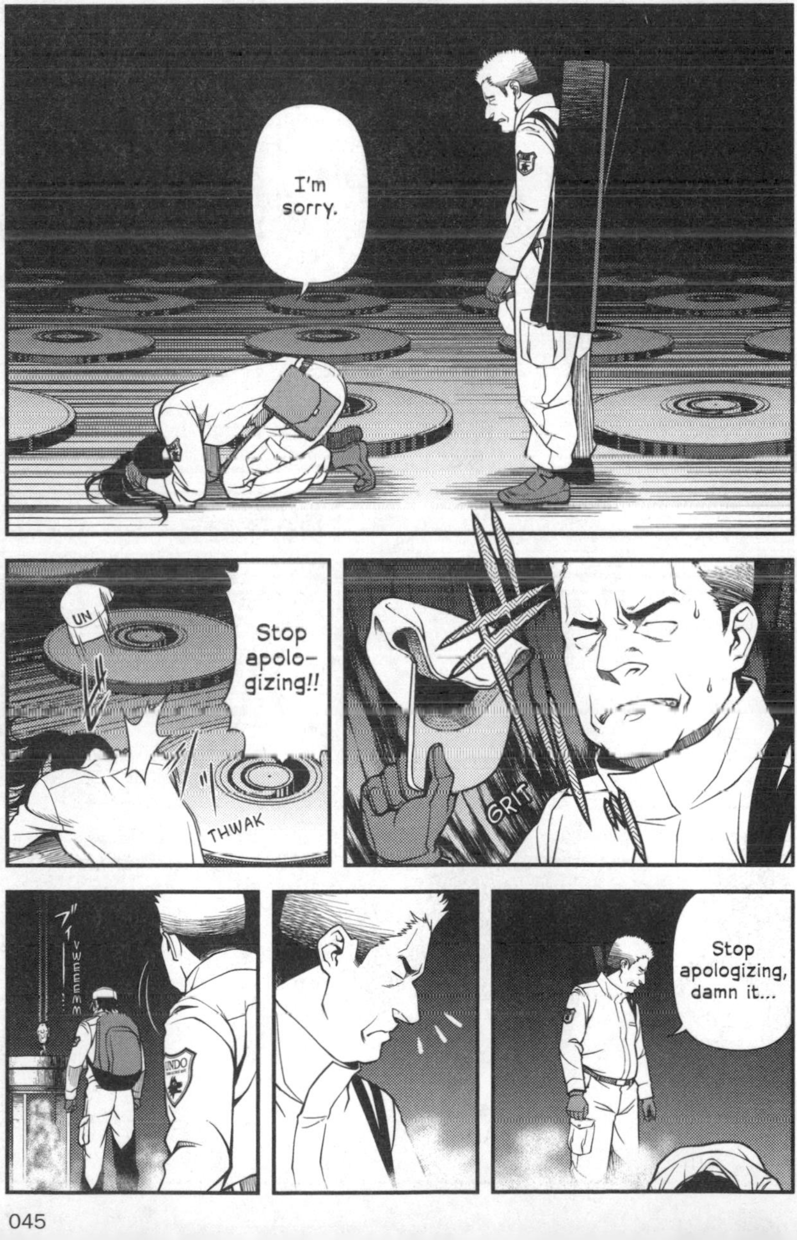
I'm sorry.
GRIT
Stop apolo-gizing!!
THWAK
Stop apologizing, damn it...
VWEEEMM

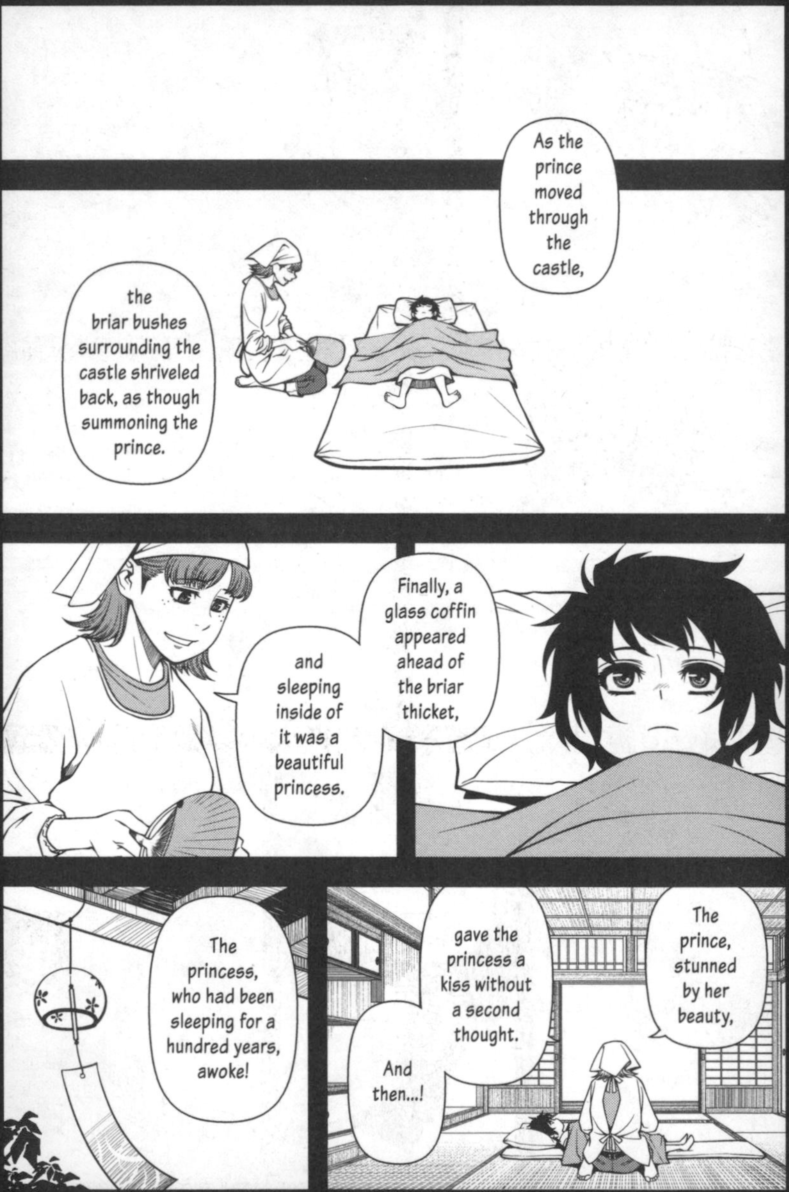
As the prince moved through the castle,
the briar bushes surrounding the castle shriveled back, as though summoning the prince.
Finally, a glass coffin appeared ahead of the briar thicket,
and sleeping inside of it was a beautiful princess.
The prince, stunned by her beauty,
gave the princess a kiss without a second thought.
And then...!
The princess, who had been sleeping for a hundred years, awoke!

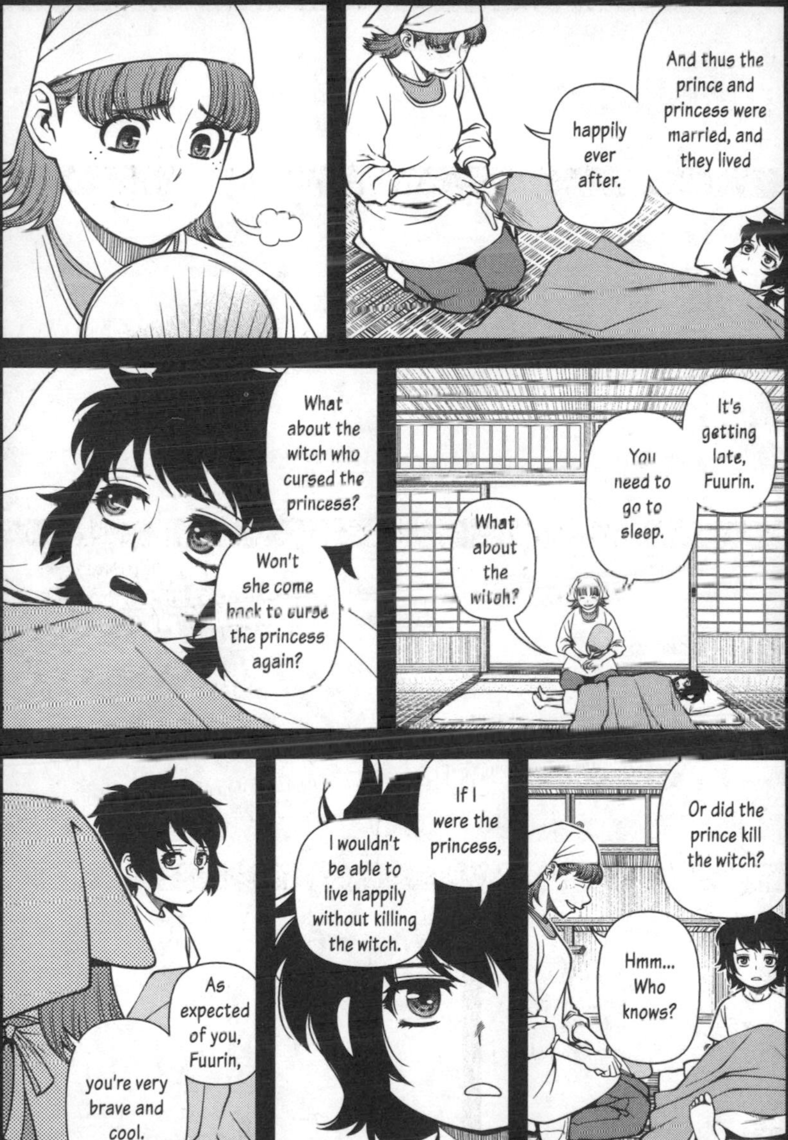
And thus the prince and princess were married, and they lived
happily ever after.
It's getting late, Fuurin.
You need to go to sleep.
What about the witch?
What about the witch who cursed the princess?
Won't she come back to curse the princess again?
Or did the prince kill the witch?
Hmm... Who knows?
If I were the princess,
I wouldn't be able to live happily without killing the witch.
As expected of you, Fuurin,
you're very brave and cool.

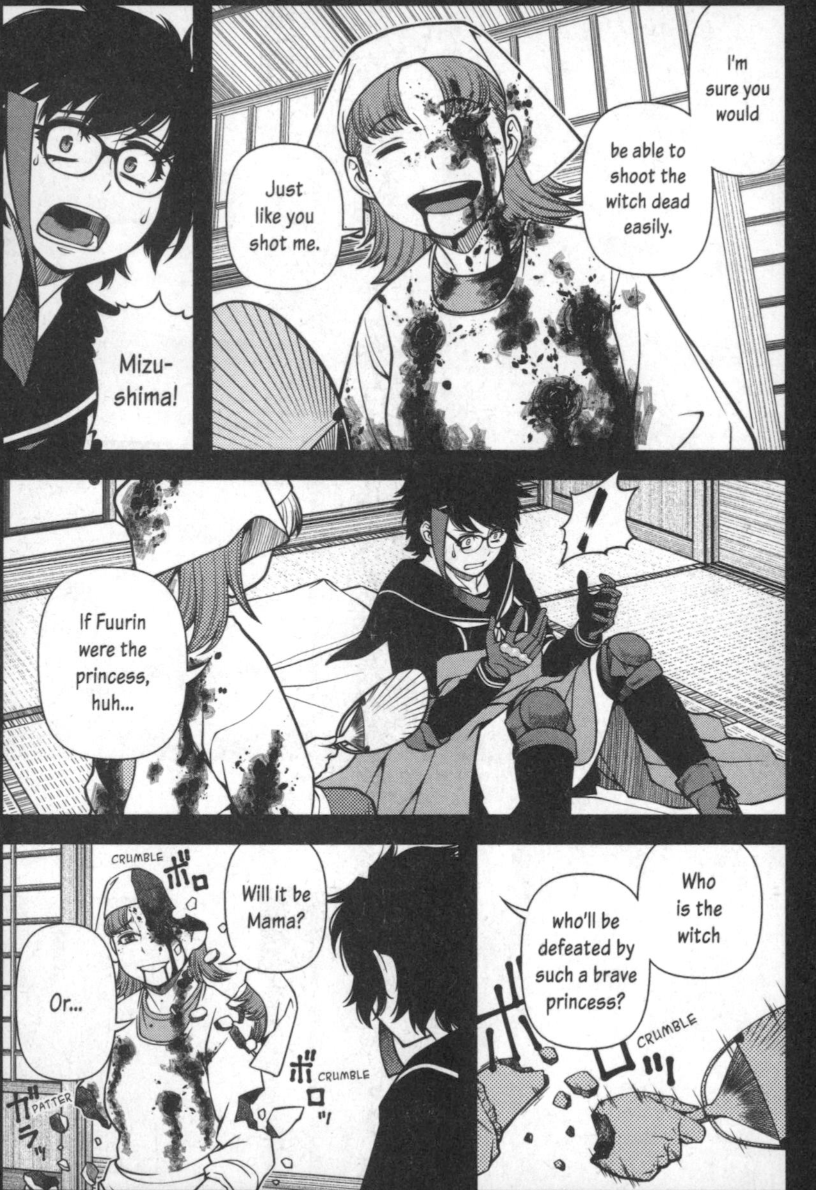
I'm sure you would
be able to shoot the witch dead easily.
Just like you shot me.
Mizu-shima!
!
If Fuurin were the princess, huh...
Who is the witch
who'll be defeated by such a brave princess?
CRUMBLE
Will it be Mama?
CRUMBLE
Or...
CRUMBLE
PATTER

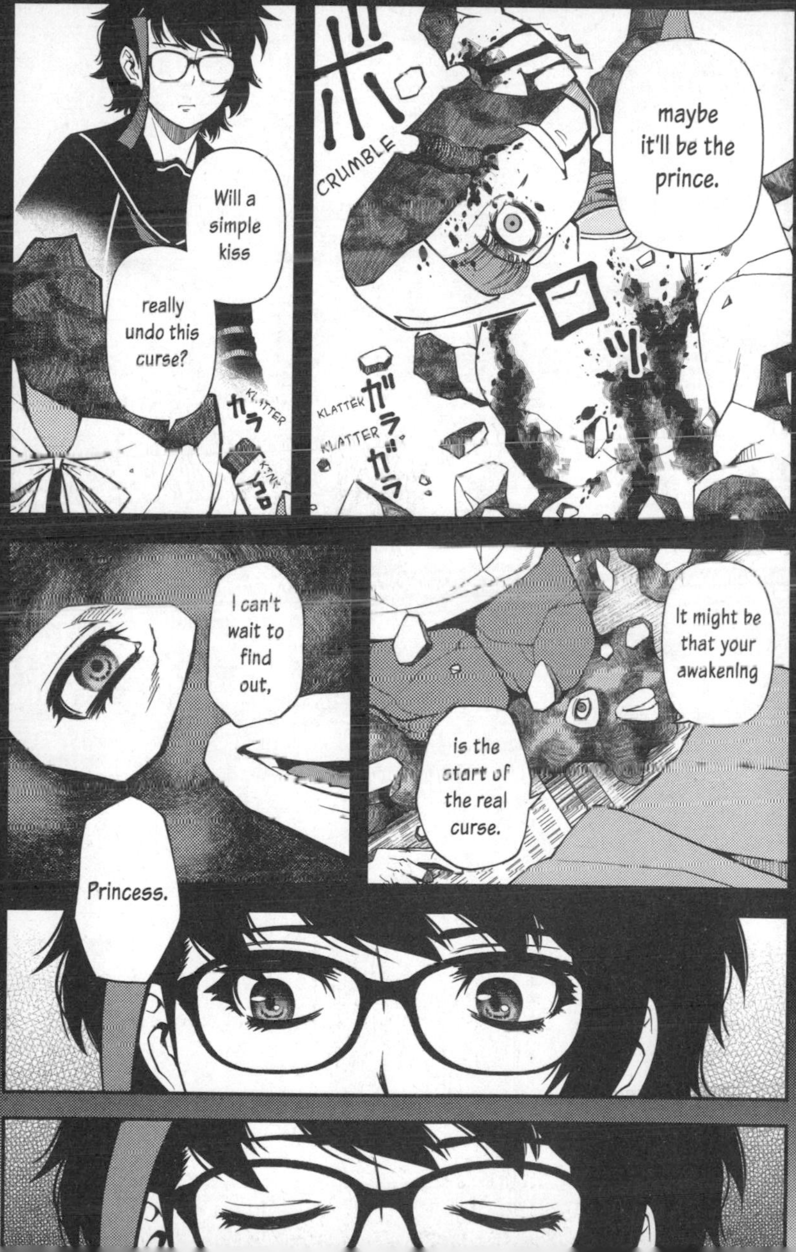
maybe it'll be the prince.
ボロッ
CRUMBLE
ガラ。ガラ
KLATTEK
KLATTER
Will a simple kiss
really undo this curse?
カラ
KLATTER
コロ
It might be that your awakening
is the start of the real curse.
I can't wait to find out,
Princess.

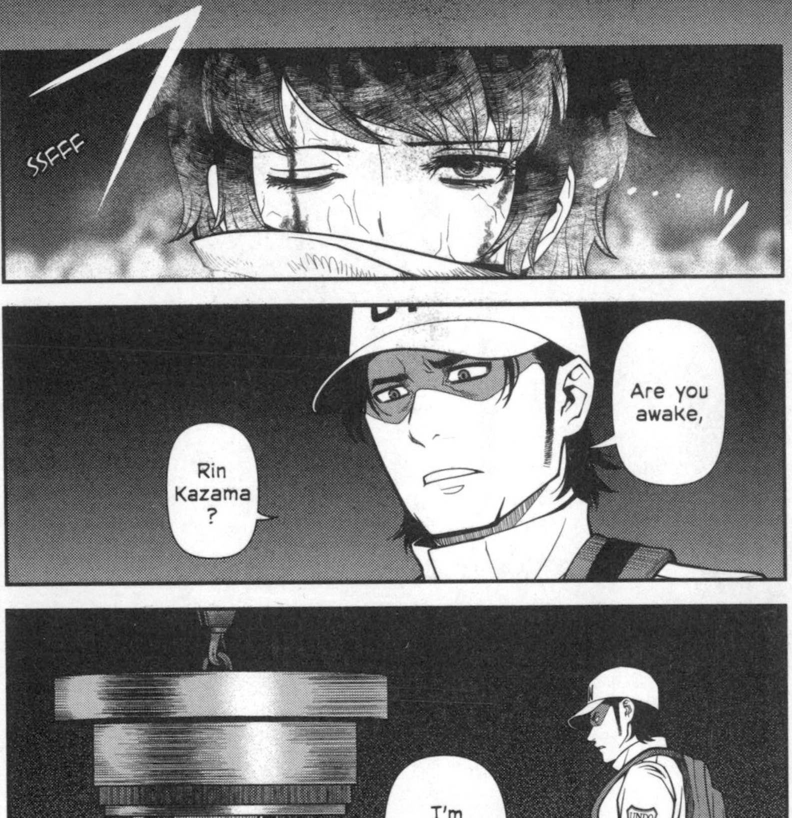
SSFFF
Are you awake,
Rin Kazama ?
I'm here to take you away.

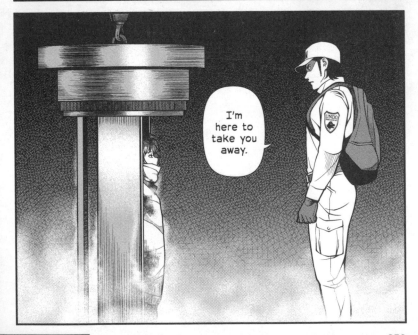

Chapter 36
Karigane vs. Tsubaki

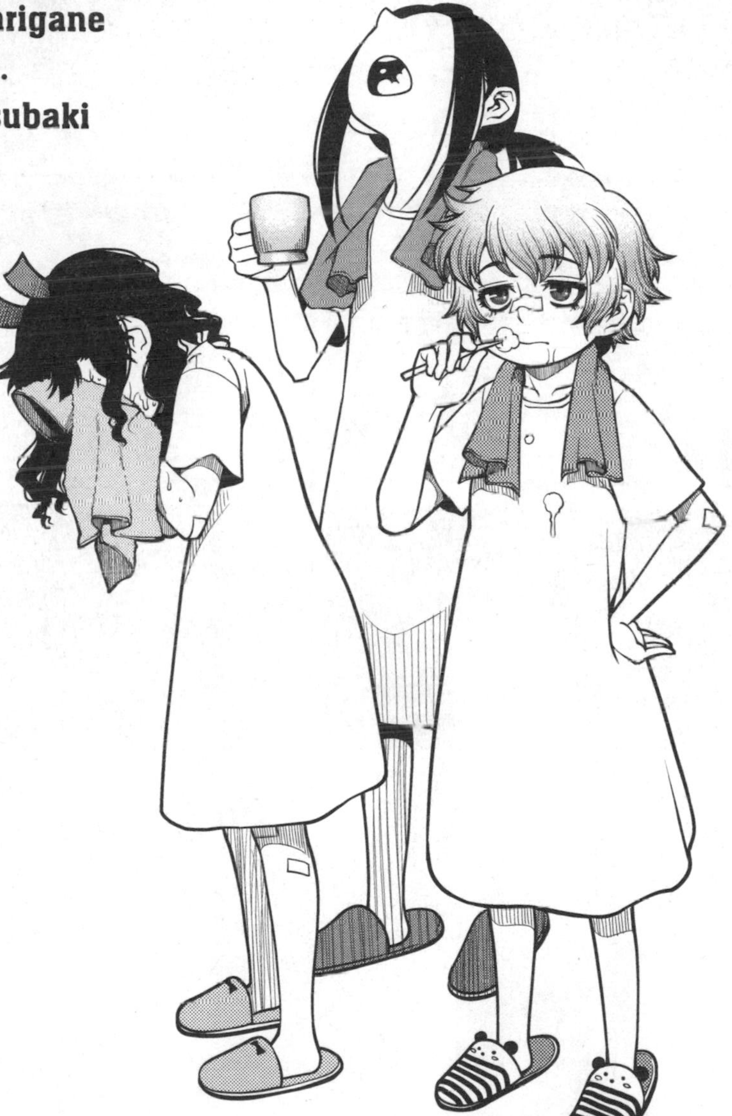

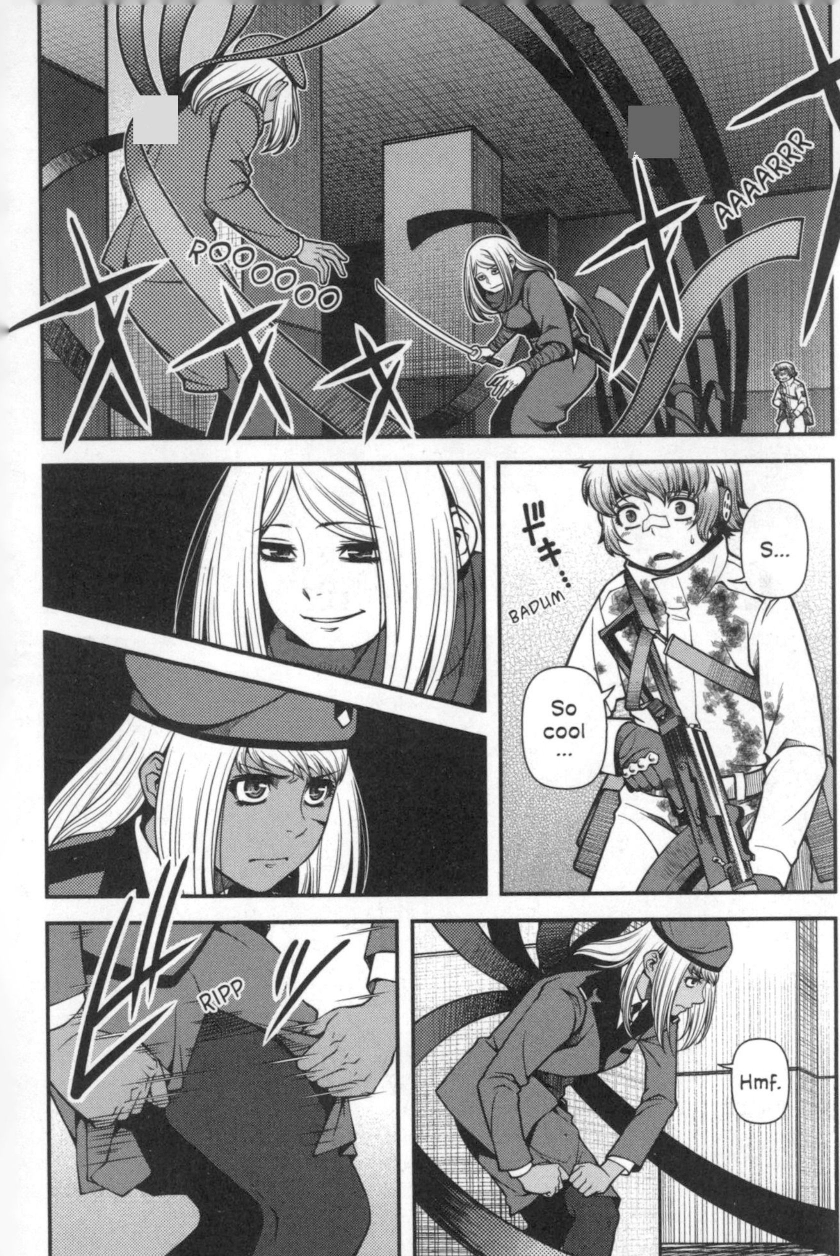
AAAARRR
POOOOOO
ドキ…
BADUM
S...
So cool ...
Hmf.
RIPP

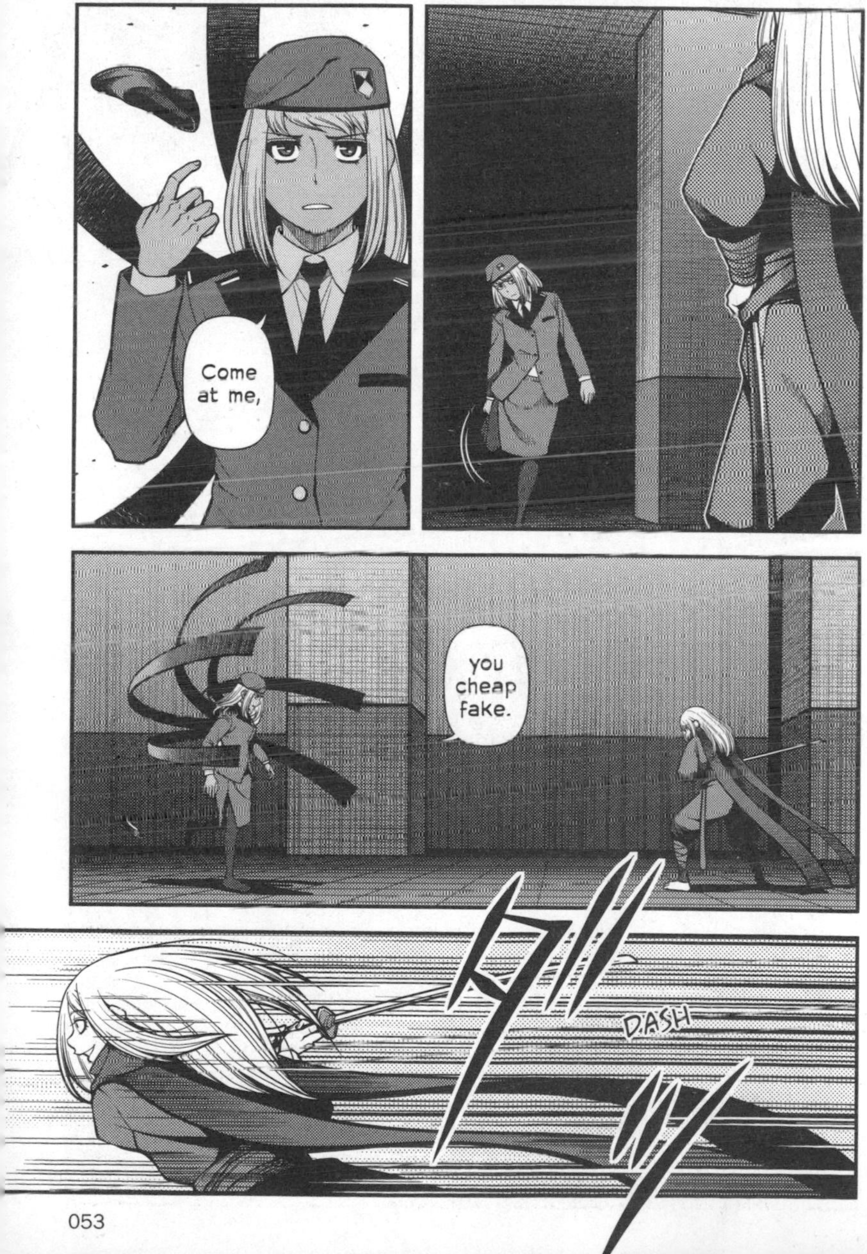
Come at me,
you cheap fake.
DASH

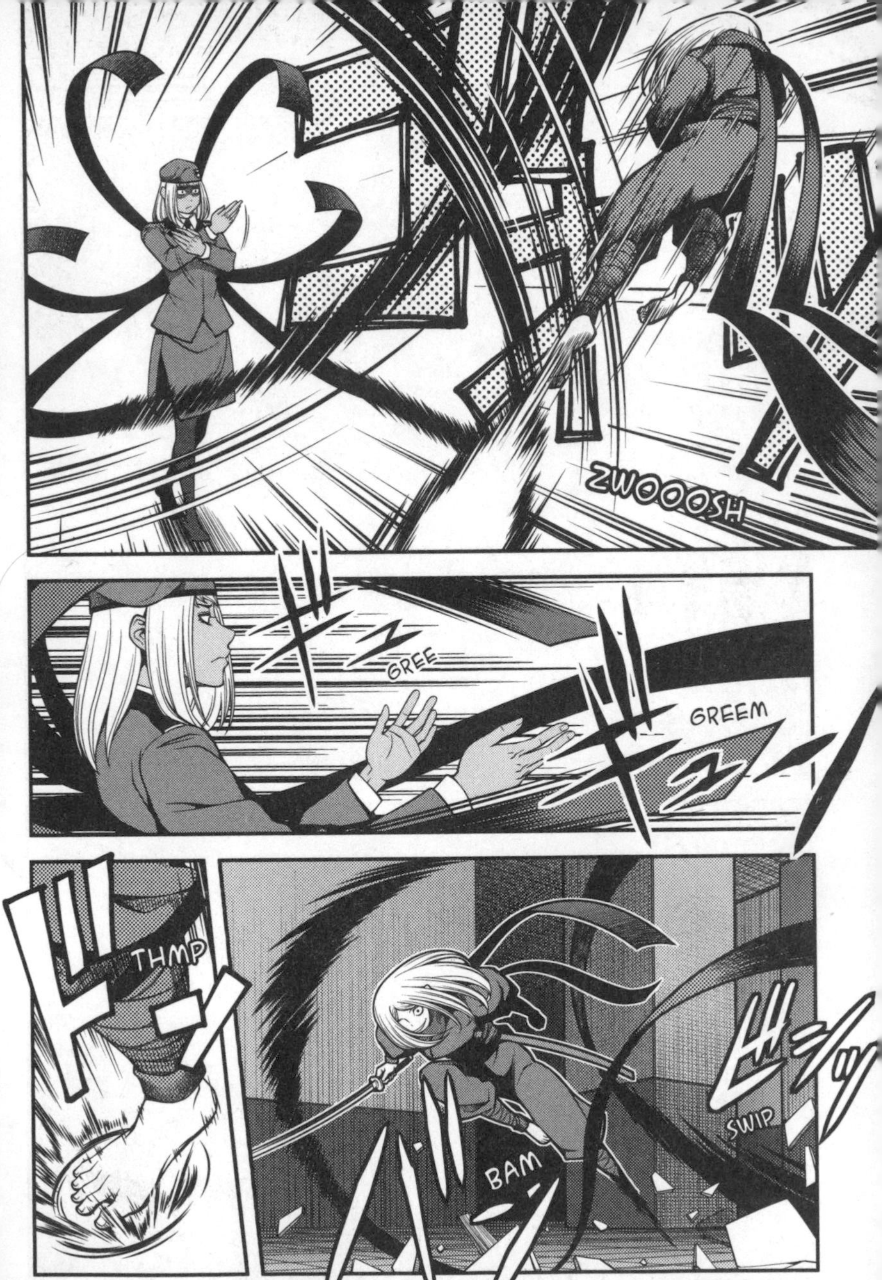
ZWOOOSH
GREE
GREEM
SWIP
BAM
THMP

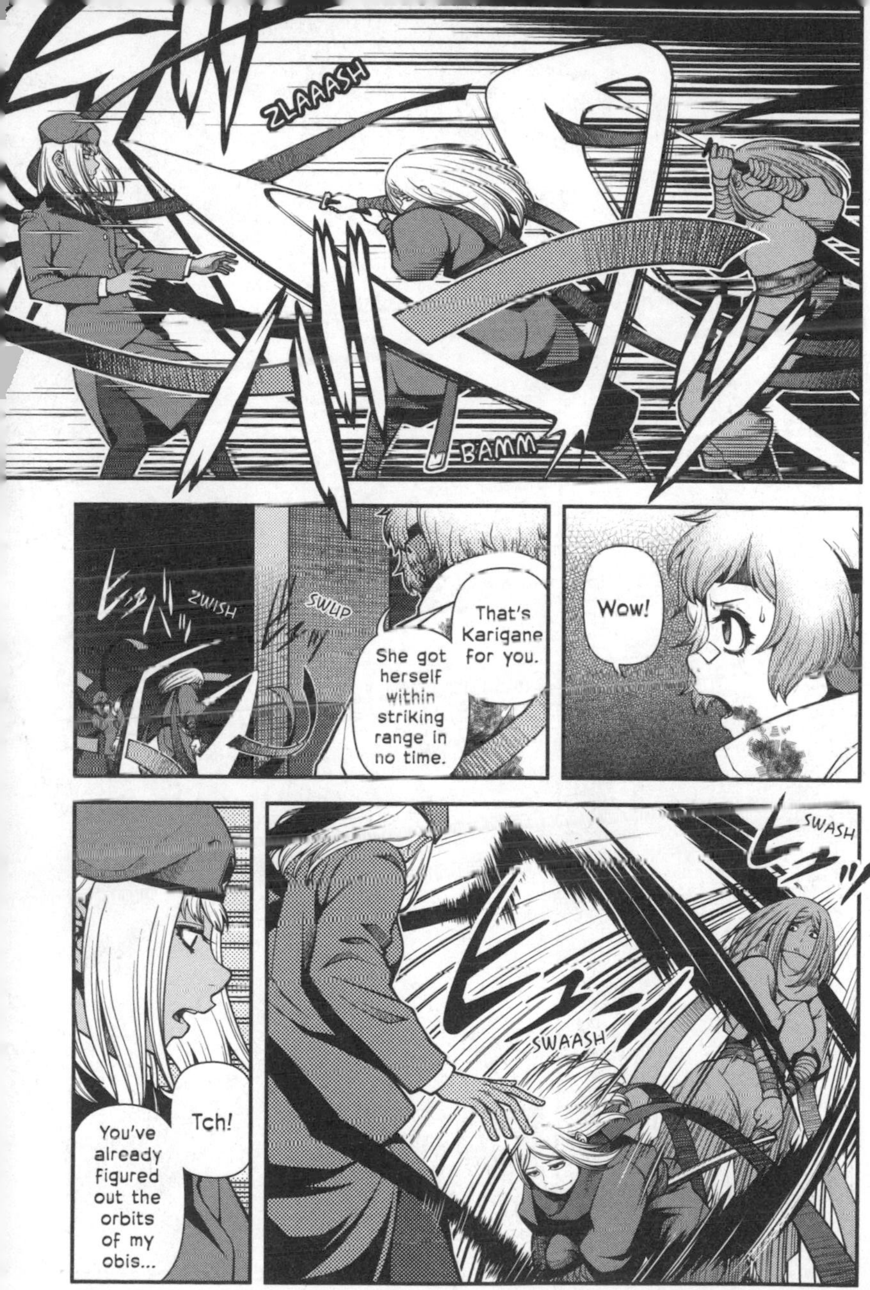
ZLAAASH
BAMM
Wow!
That's Karigane for you.
She got herself within striking range in no time.
SWUP
ZWISH
SWASH
SWAASH
Tch!
You've already figured out the orbits of my obis...

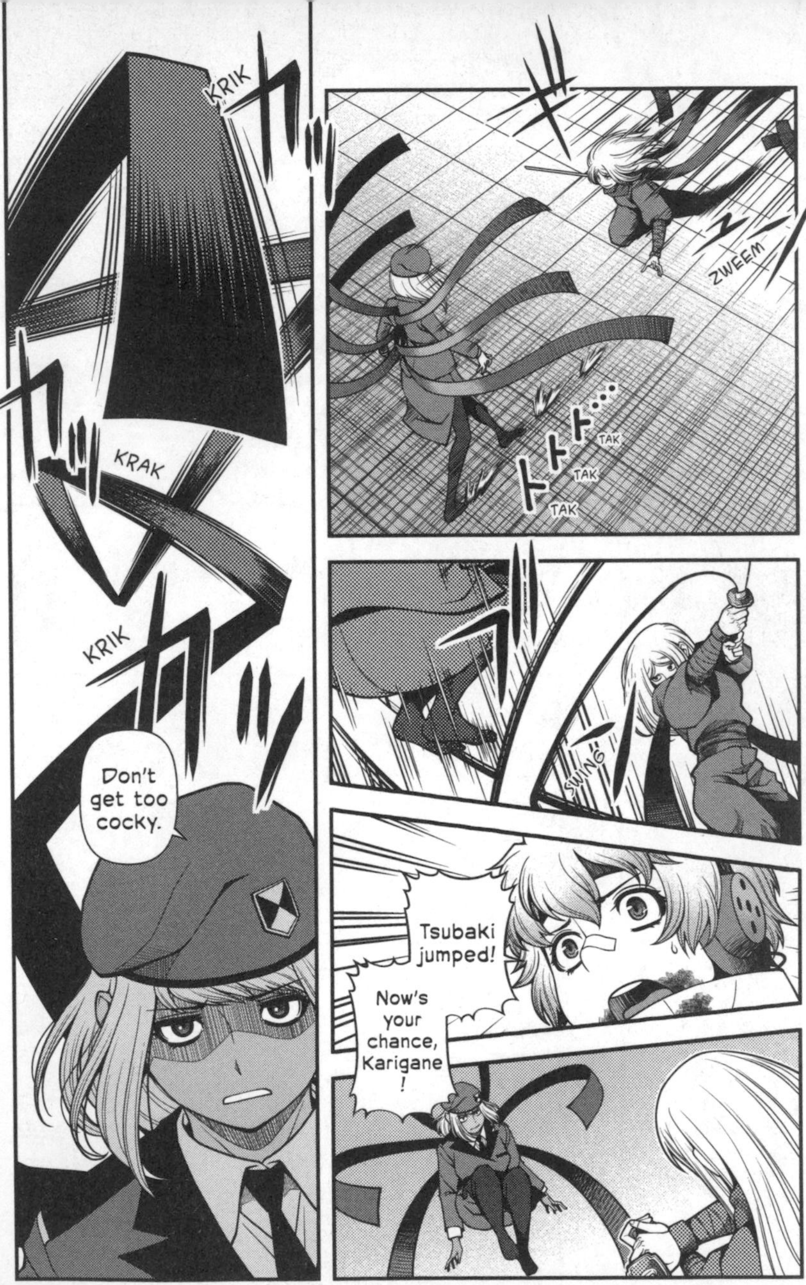
ZWEEM
TAK
TAK
TAK
SWING
Tsubaki jumped!
Now's your chance, Karigane!
KRIK
KRAK
KRIK
Don't get too cocky.

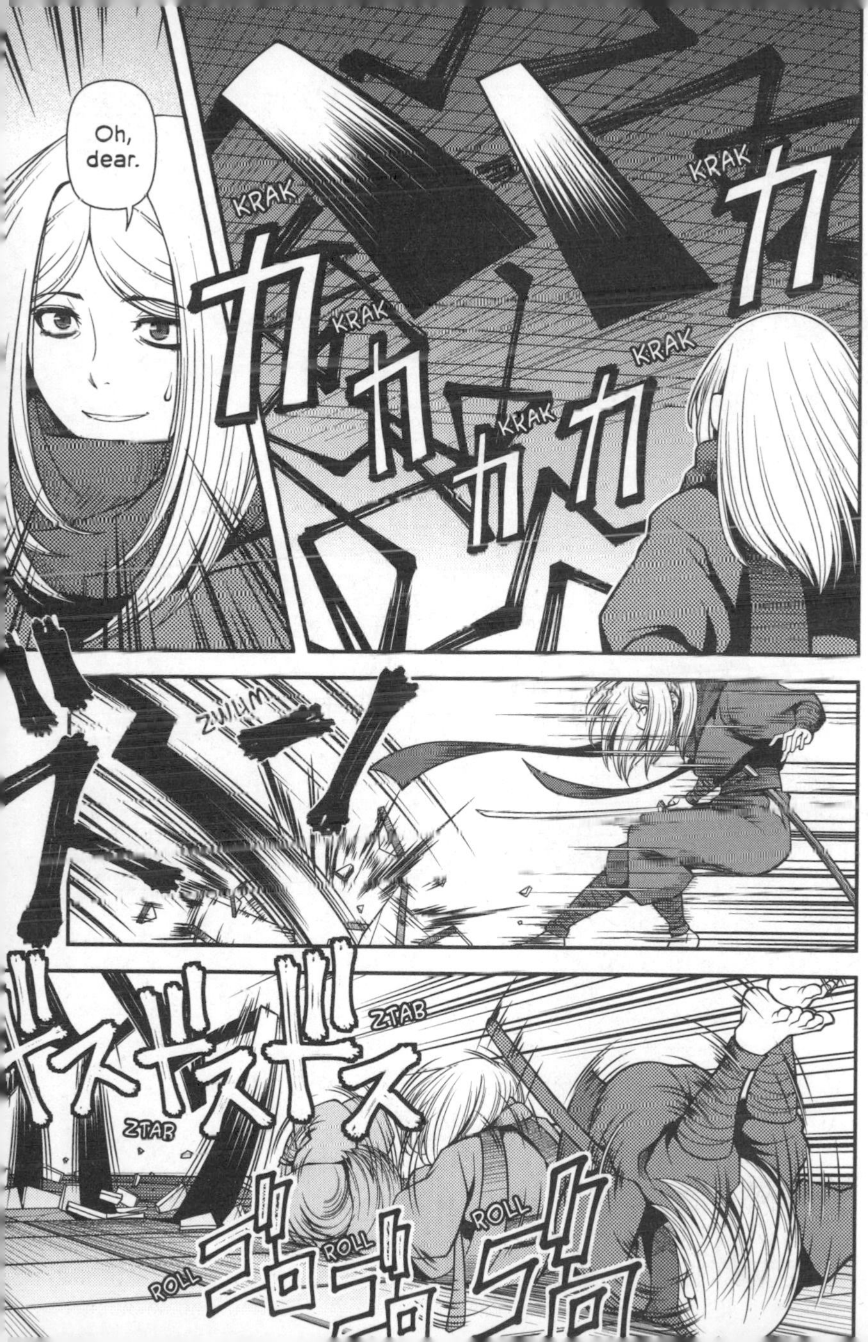
KRAK
KRAK
KRAK
KRAK
KRAK
Oh, dear.
ZWUM
ZTAB
ZTAB
ROLL
ROLL
ROLL

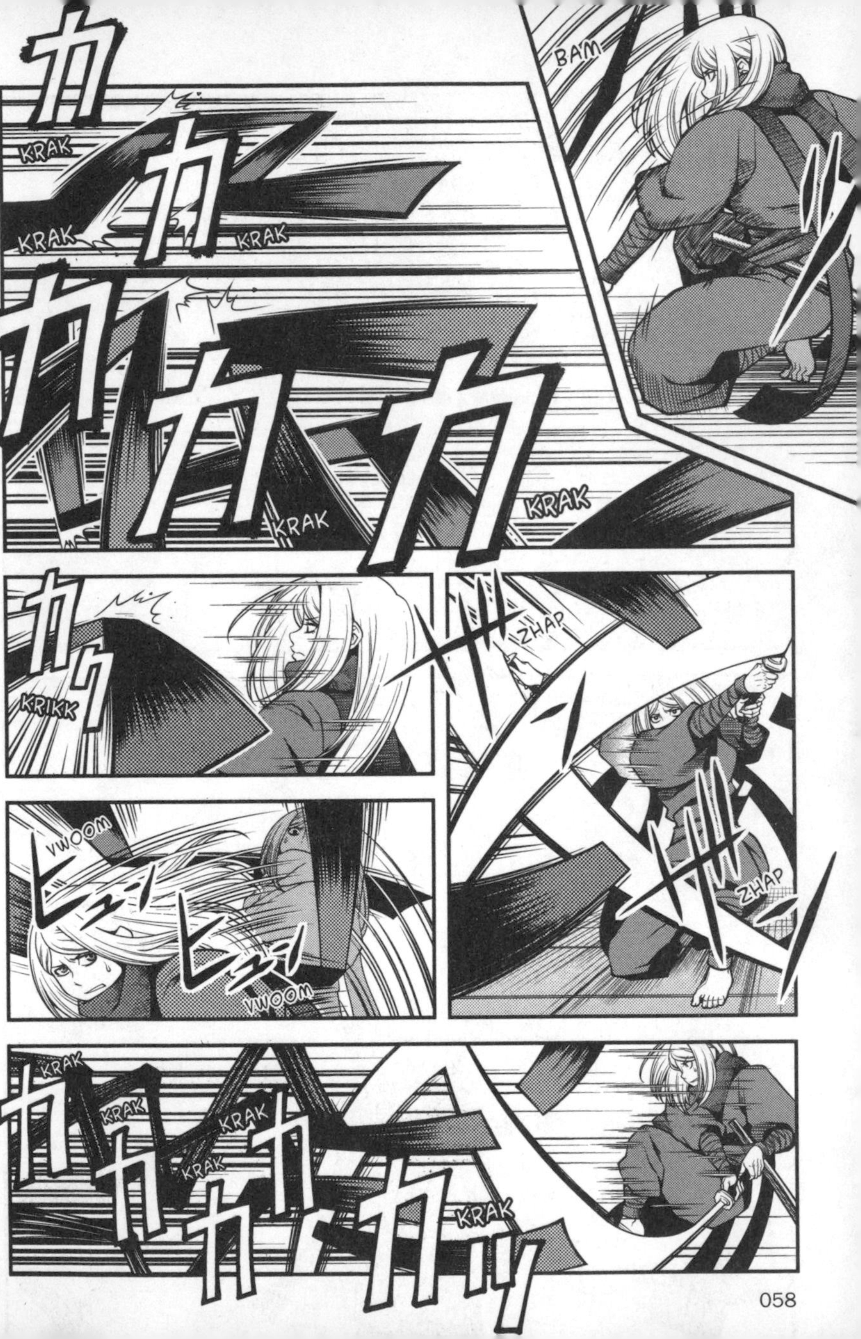
BAM
KRAK
KRAK
KRAK
KRAK
KRAK
ZHAP
ZHAP
KRIKK
VWOOM
VWOOM
KRAK
KRAK
KRAK
KRAK
KRAK
KRAK

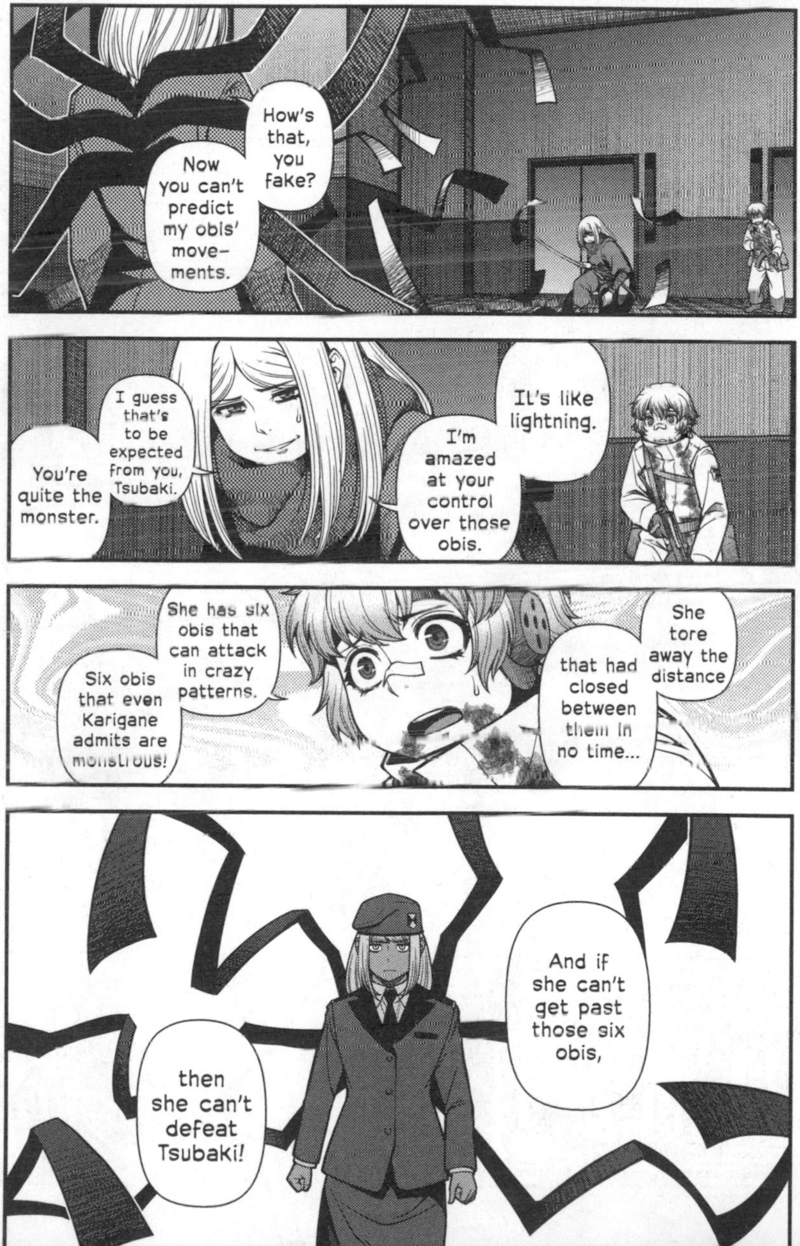
How's that, you fake?
Now you can't predict my obis' movements.
It's like lightning.
I'm amazed at your control over those obis.
I guess that's to be expected from you, Tsubaki.
You're quite the monster.
She tore away the distance
that had closed between them in no time...
She has six obis that can attack in crazy patterns.
Six obis that even Karigane admits are monstrous!
And if she can't get past those six obis,
then she can't defeat Tsubaki!

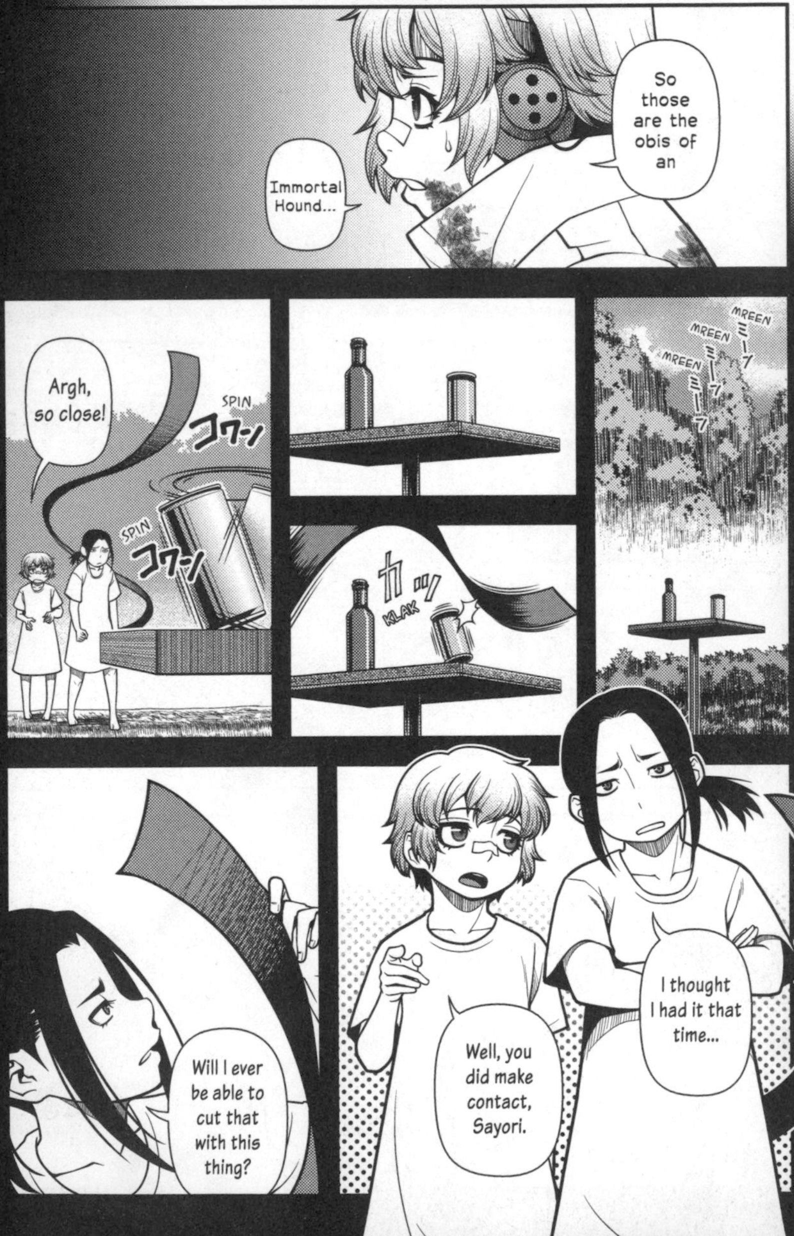
So those are the obis of an
Immortal Hound...
MREEN
MREEN
MREEN
KLAK
Argh, so close!
SPIN
SPIN
I thought I had it that time...
Well, you did make contact, Sayori.
Will I ever be able to cut that with this thing?

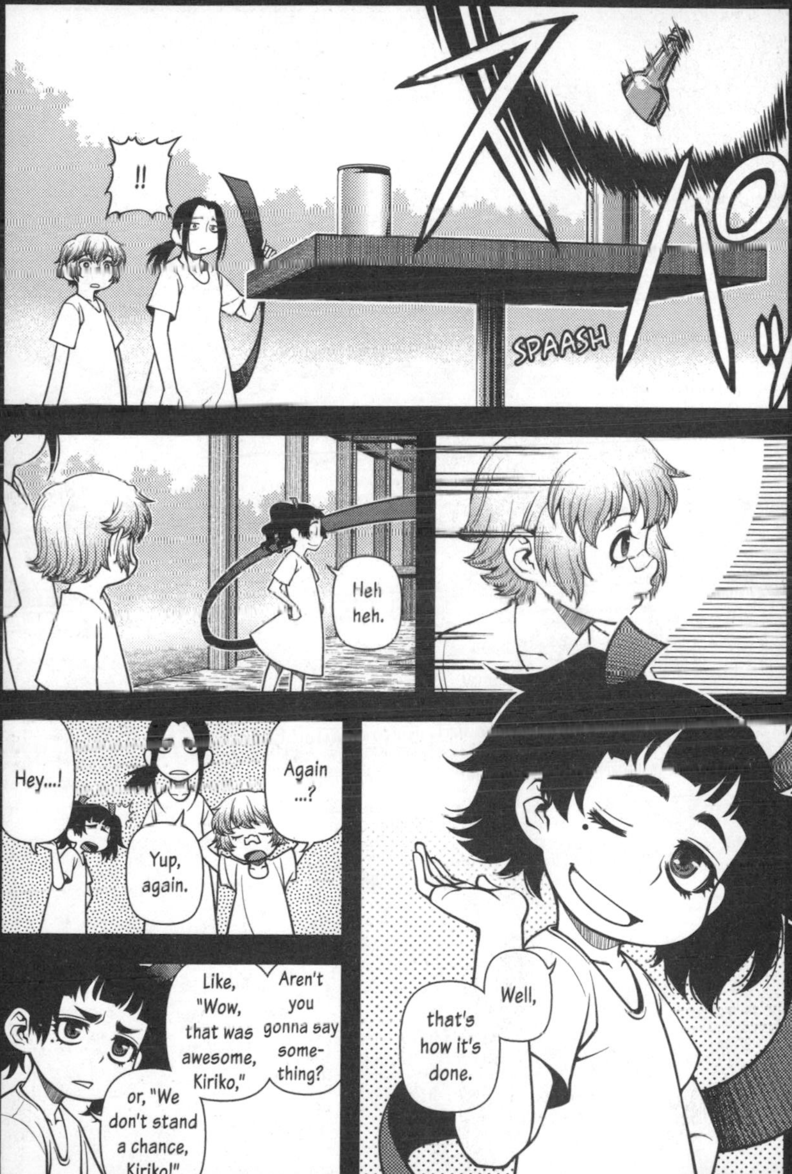
SPAASH
!!
Heh heh.
Well, that's how it's done.
Again ...?
Yup, again.
Hey...!
Aren't you gonna say some-thing?
Like, "Wow, that was awesome, Kiriko,"
or, "We don't stand a chance, Kiriko!"

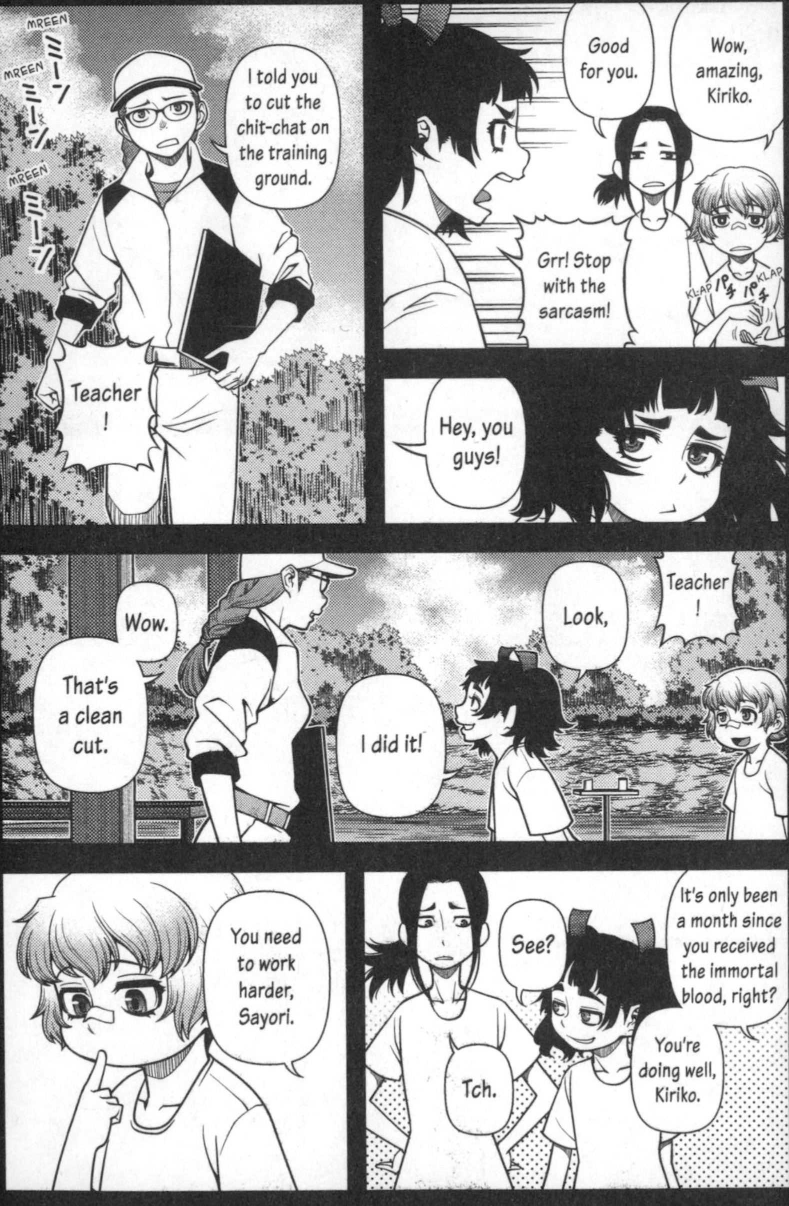

Wow, amazing, Kiriko.
Good for you.
Grr! Stop with the sarcasm!
KLAP パチ KLAP パチ
Hey, you guys!
I told you to cut the chit-chat on the training ground.
MREEN ミーン
MREEN ミーン
MREEN ミーン
Teacher!
Teacher!
Look,
I did it!
Wow.
That's a clean cut.
It's only been a month since you received the immortal blood, right?
See?
You're doing well, Kiriko.
Tch.
You need to work harder, Sayori.

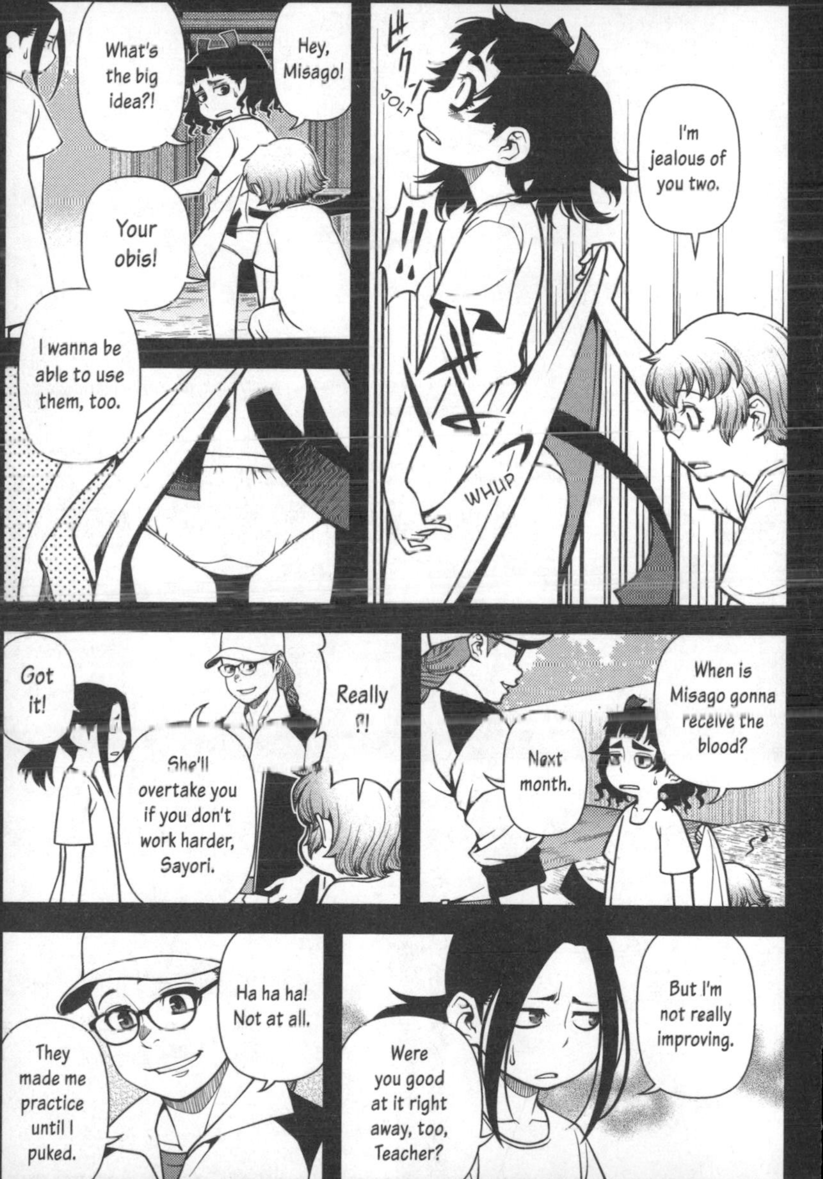
I'm jealous of you two.
JOLT
WHUP
Hey, Misago!
What's the big idea?!
Your obis!
I wanna be able to use them, too.
When is Misago gonna receive the blood?
Next month.
Really ?!
She'll overtake you if you don't work harder, Sayori.
Got it!
But I'm not really improving.
Were you good at it right away, too, Teacher?
Ha ha ha! Not at all.
They made me practice until I puked.

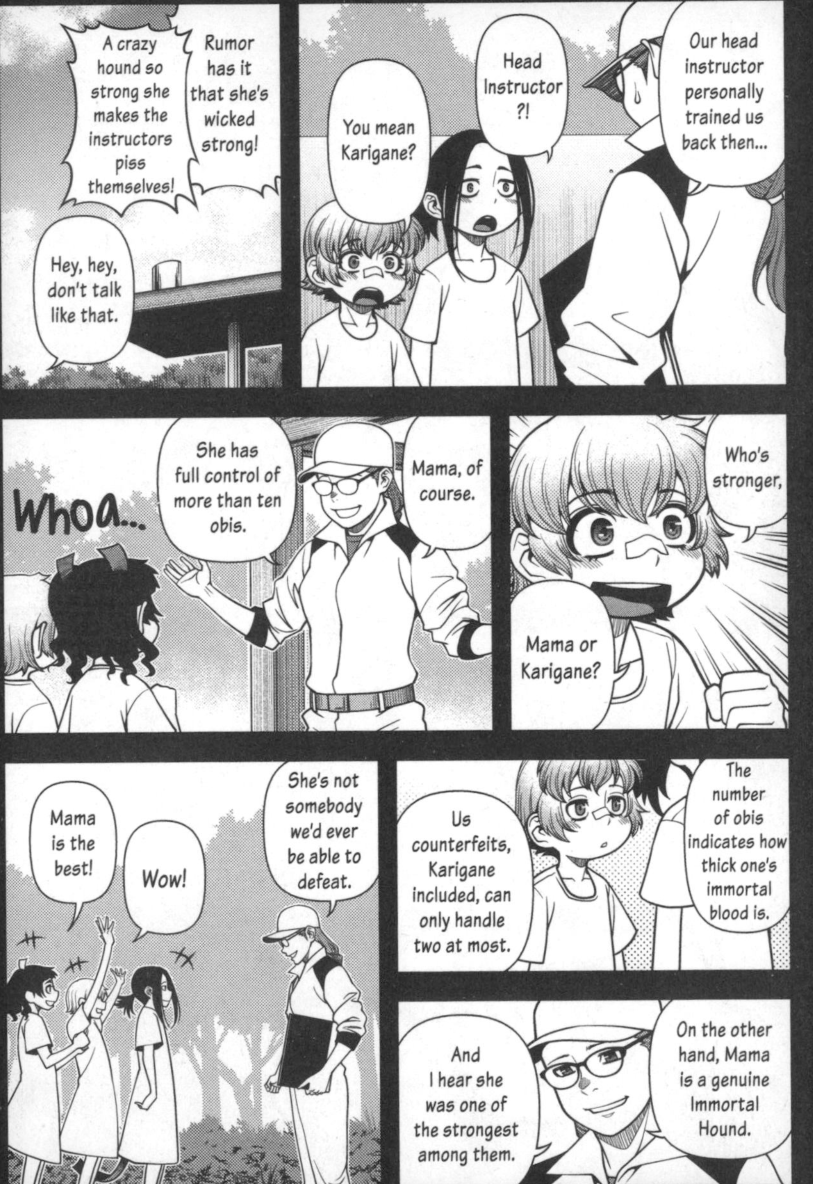
Our head instructor personally trained us back then...
Head Instructor?!
You mean Karigane?
Rumor has it that she's wicked strong!
A crazy hound so strong she makes the instructors piss themselves!
Hey, hey, don't talk like that.
Who's stronger,
Mama or Karigane?
Mama, of course.
She has full control of more than ten obis.
Whoa...
The number of obis indicates how thick one's immortal blood is.
Us counterfeits, Karigane included, can only handle two at most.
On the other hand, Mama is a genuine Immortal Hound.
And I hear she was one of the strongest among them.
She's not somebody we'd ever be able to defeat.
Wow!
Mama is the best!

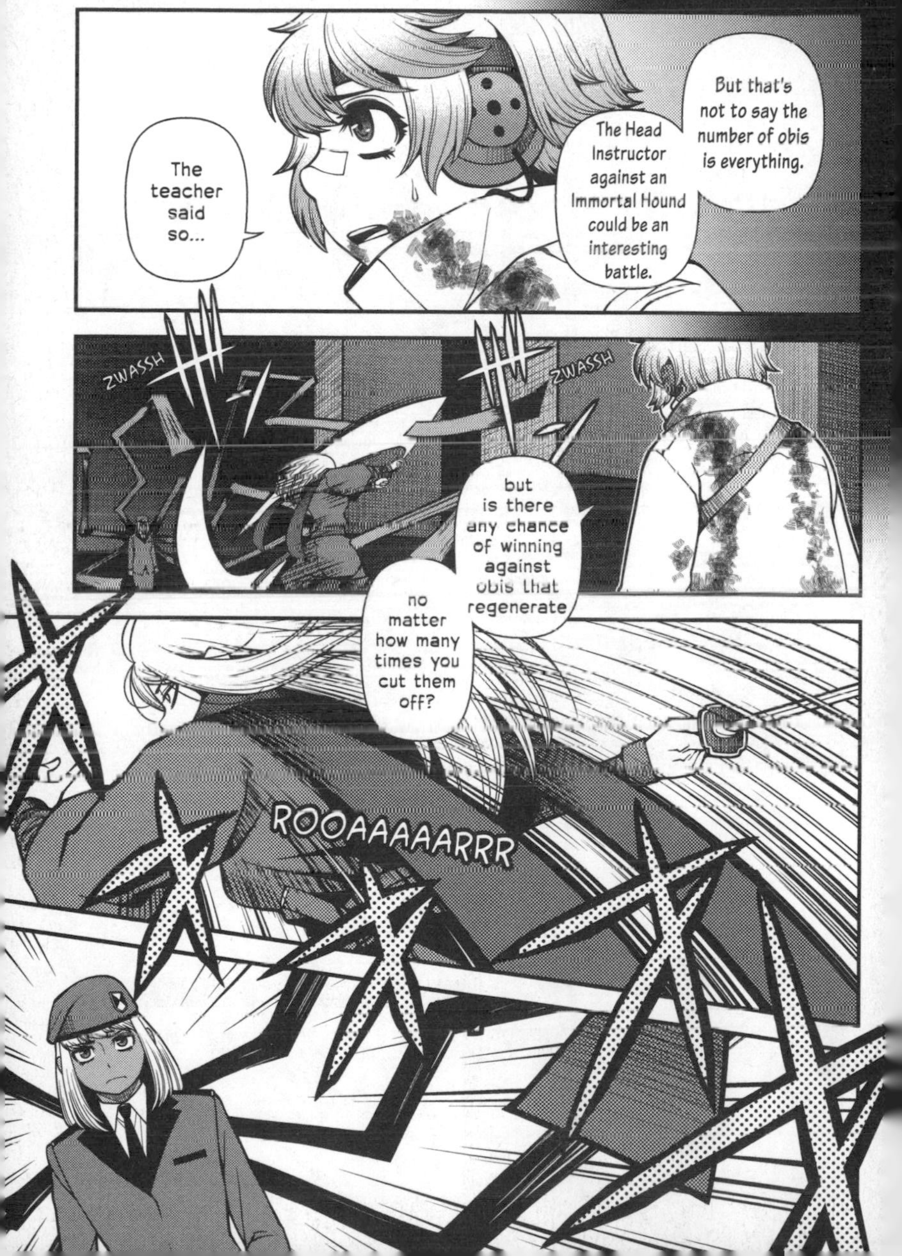

But that's not to say the number of obis is everything.
The Head Instructor against an Immortal Hound could be an interesting battle.
The teacher said so...
ZWASSH
ZWASSH
but is there any chance of winning against obis that regenerate
no matter how many times you cut them off?
ROOAAAAARRR

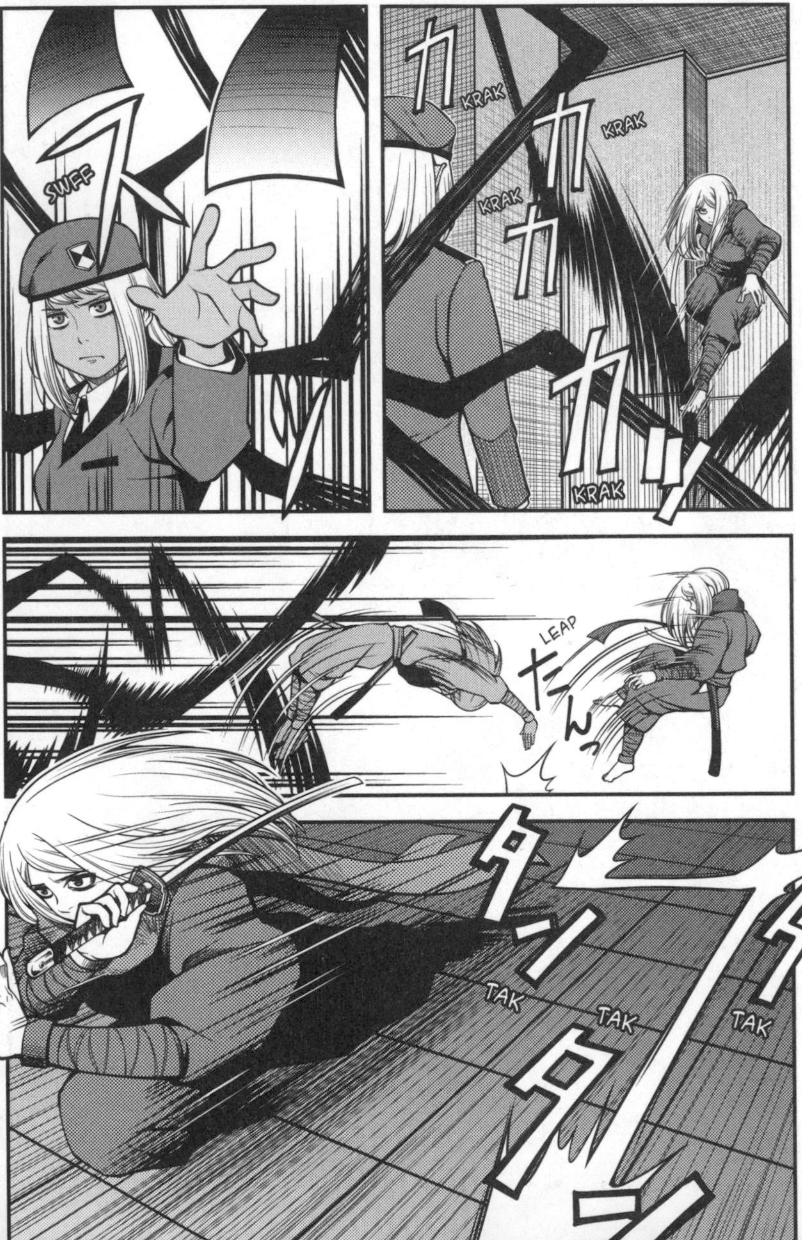
カカカカッ
KRAK
KRAK
KRAK
KRAK
SWFF
LEAP
たんっ
TAK
TAK
TAK

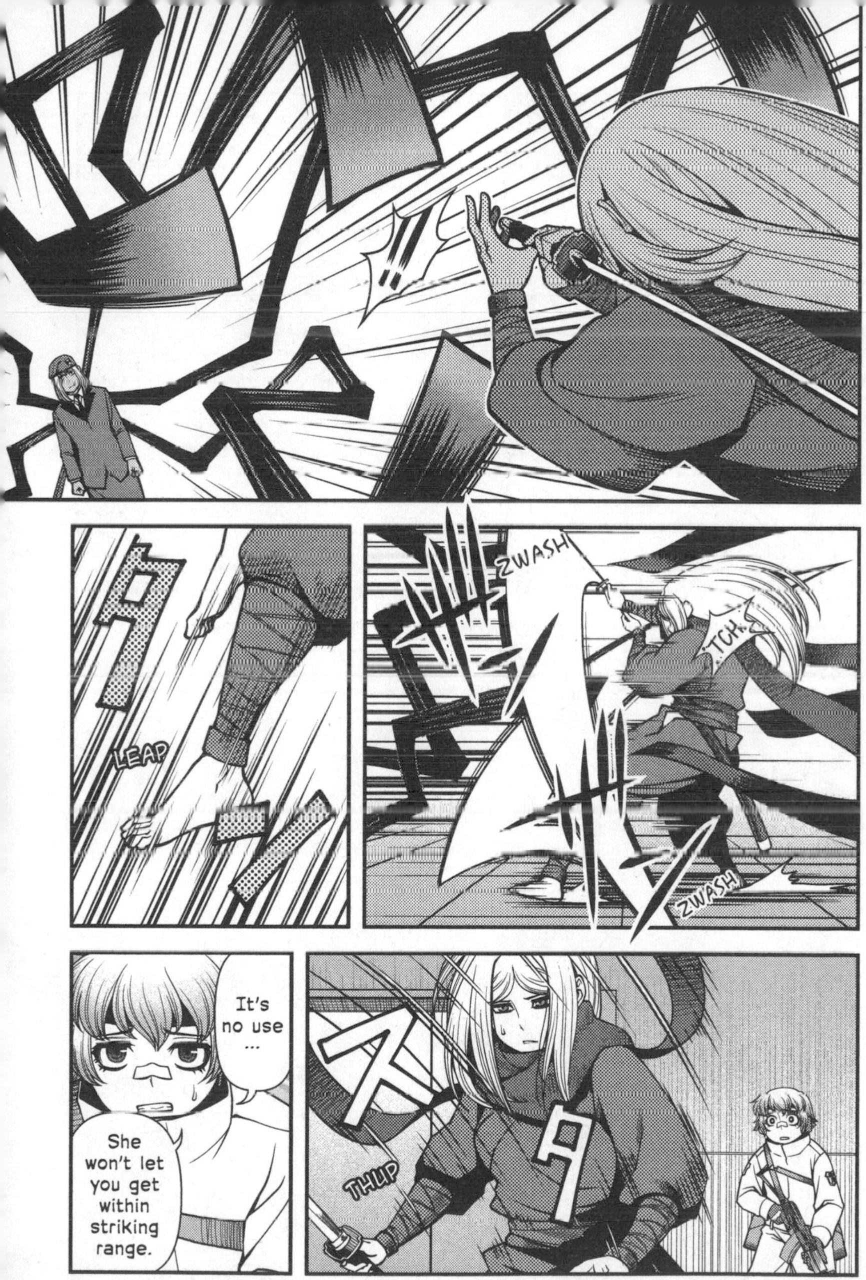
!!
ZWASH
TCH
ZWASH
LEAP
THUP
It's no use ...
She won't let you get within striking range.

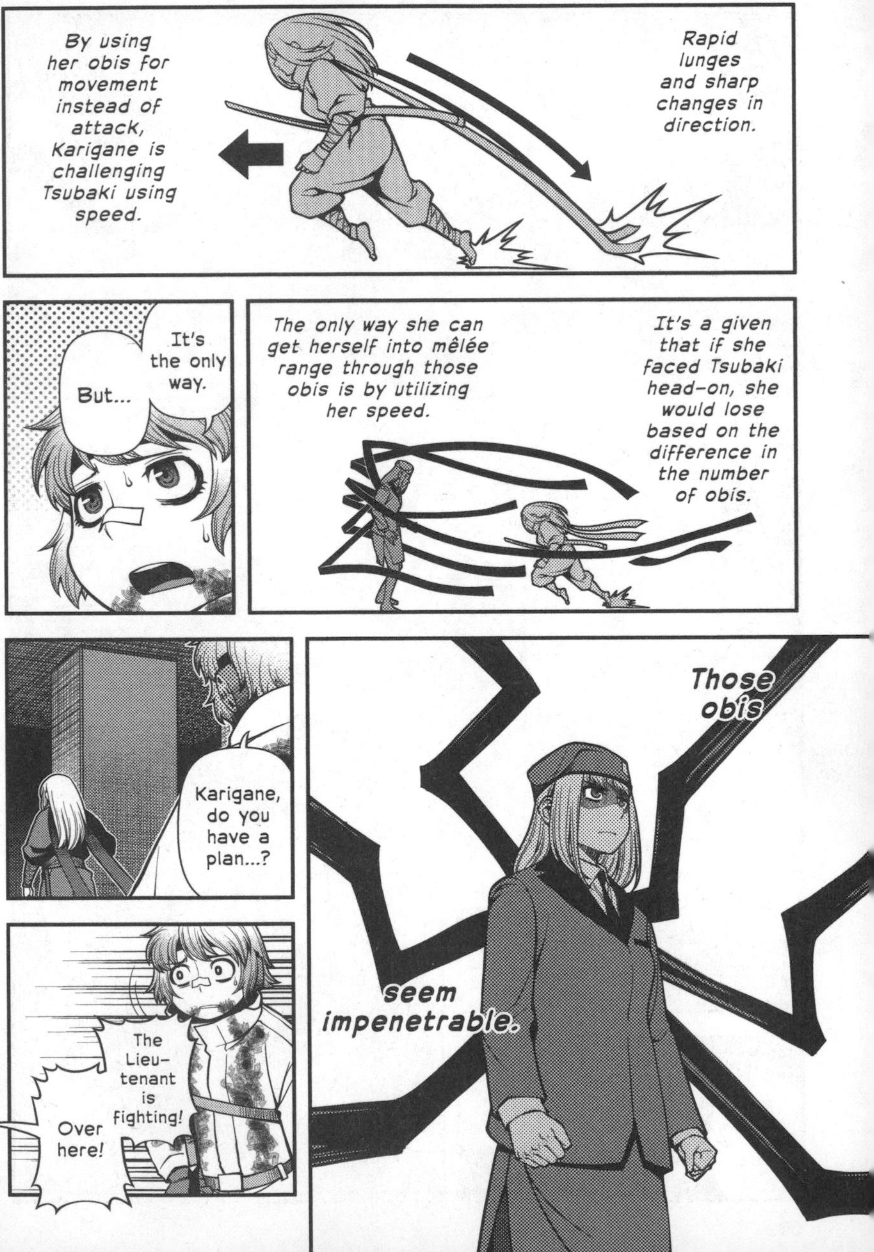

Rapid lunges and sharp changes in direction.
By using her obis for movement instead of attack, Karigane is challenging Tsubaki using speed.
It's a given that if she faced Tsubaki head-on, she would lose based on the difference in the number of obis.
The only way she can get herself into mêlée range through those obis is by utilizing her speed.
It's the only way.
But...
Those obis
seem impenetrable.
Karigane, do you have a plan...?
The Lieutenant is fighting!
Over here!

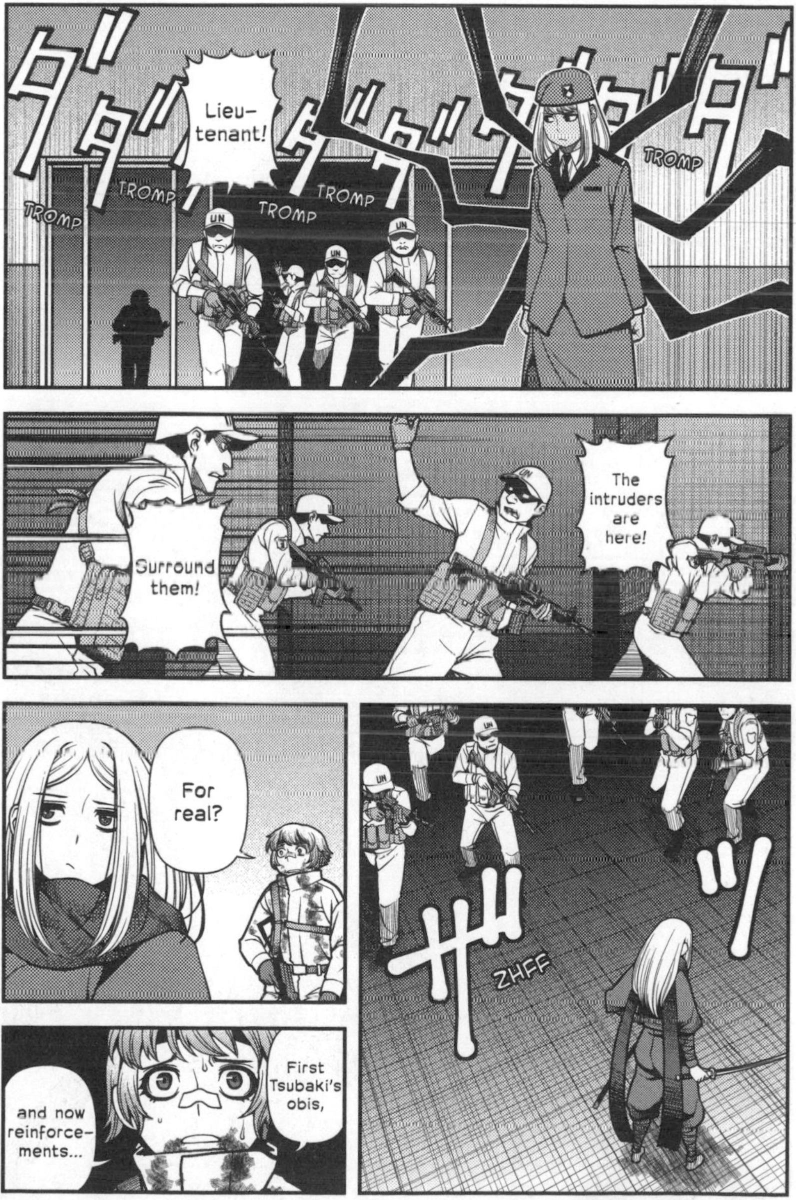
TROMP
Lieu-tenant!
TROMP
TROMP
TROMP
TROMP
The intruders are here!
Surround them!
ZHFF
For real?
First Tsubaki's obis,
and now reinforce-ments...

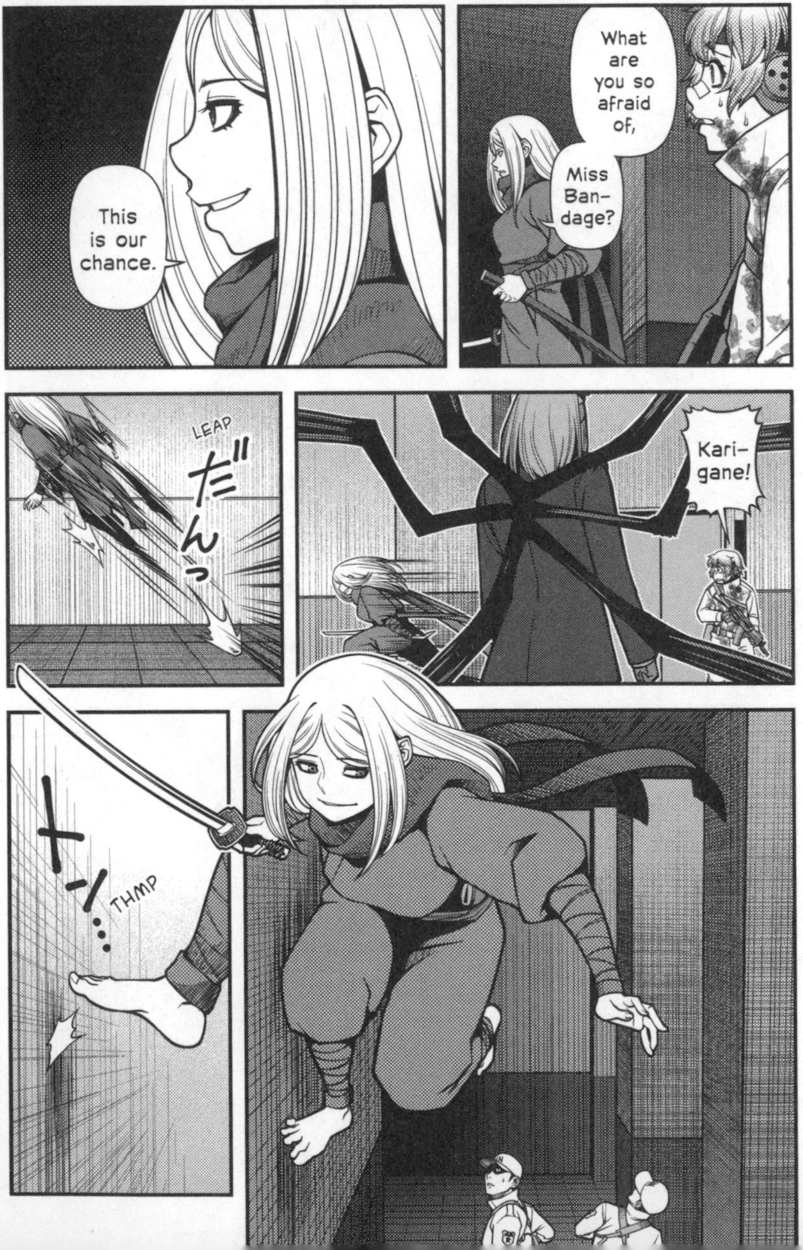
What are you so afraid of,
Miss Ban-dage?
This is our chance.
Kari-gane!
LEAP
だんっ
THMP

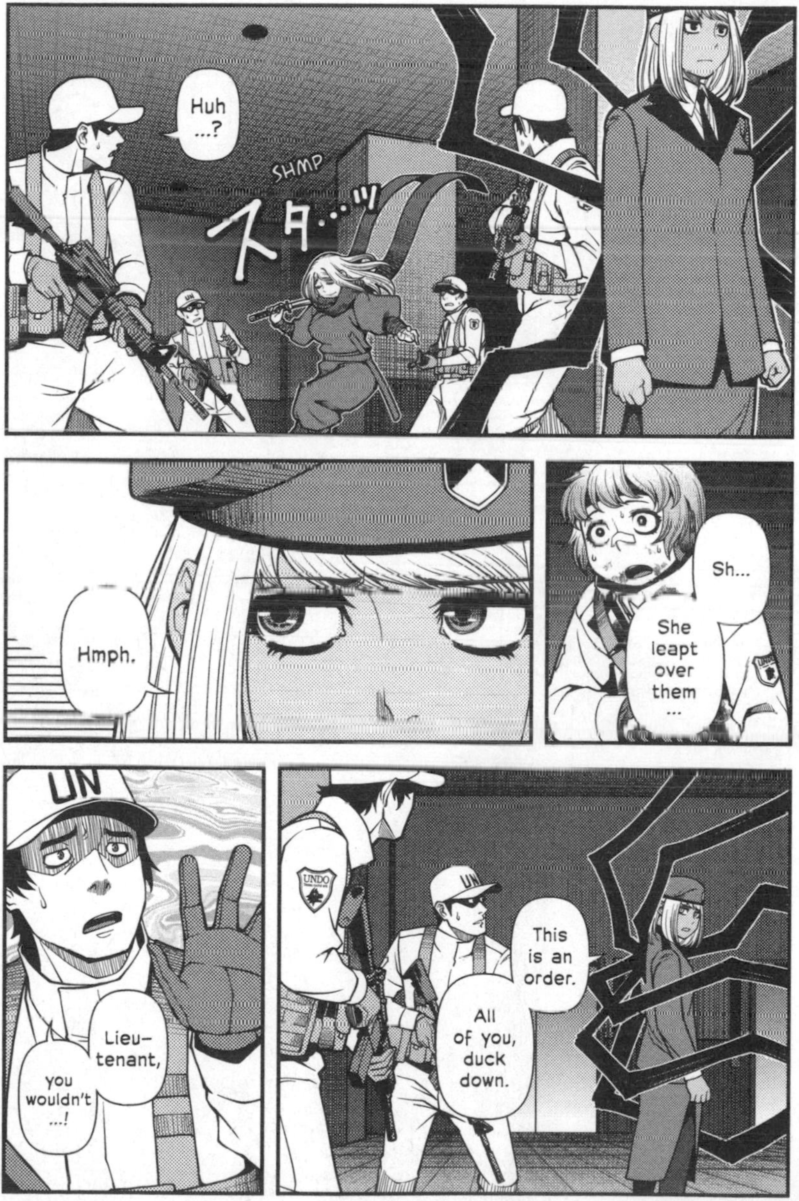
Huh ...?
SHMP
スタ…ッ
Sh...
She leapt over them ...
Hmph.
This is an order.
All of you, duck down.
Lieu-tenant,
you wouldn't ...!

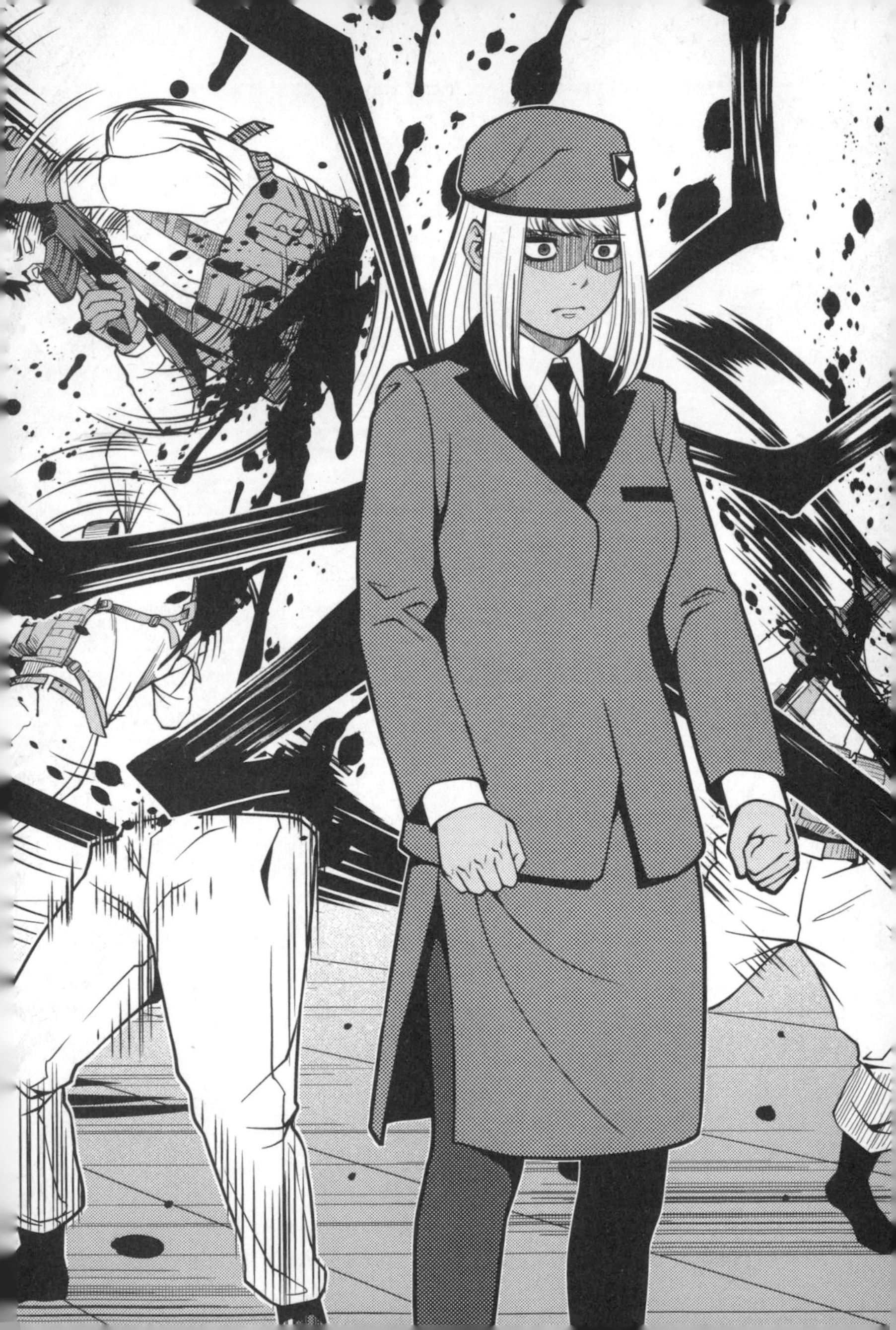

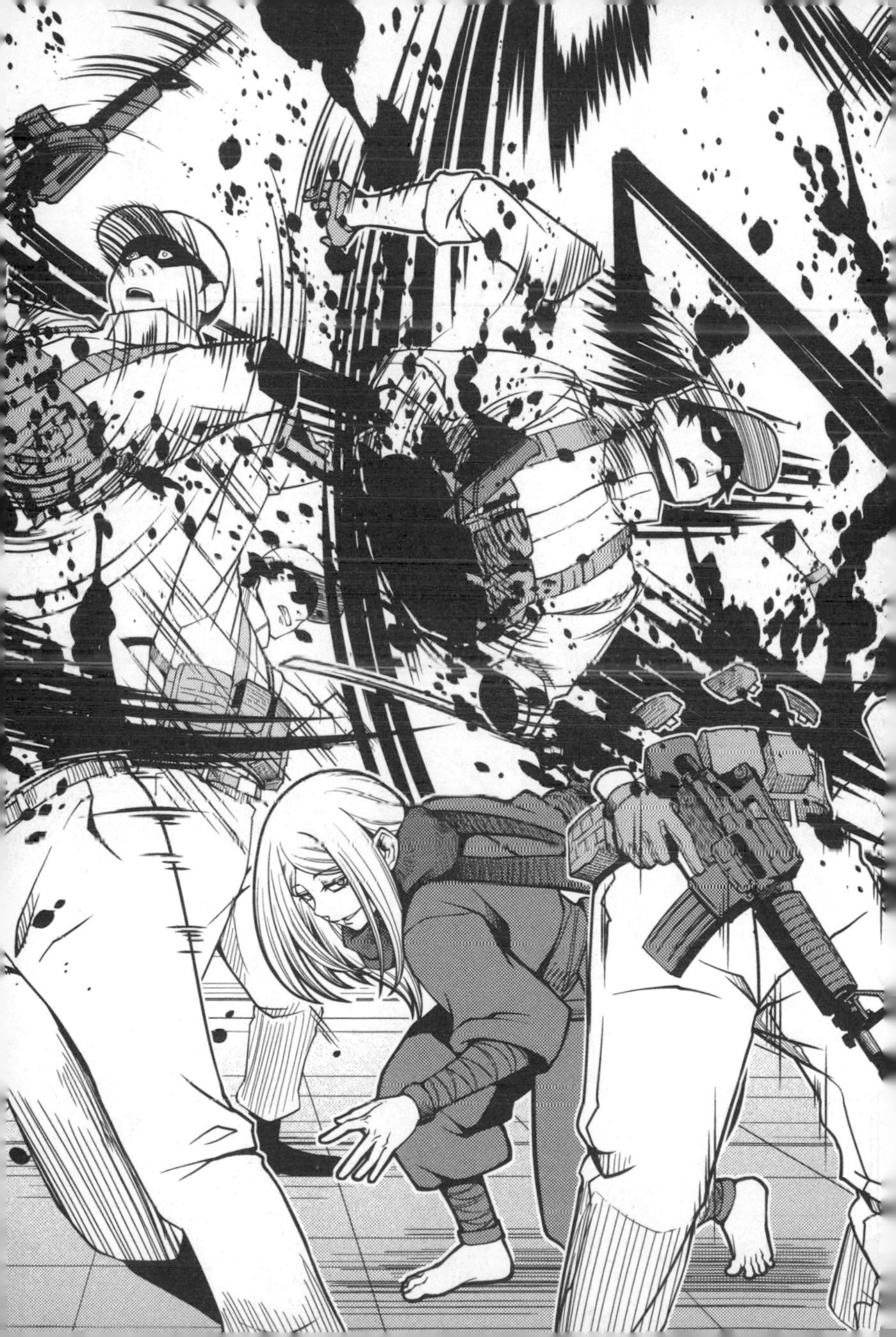

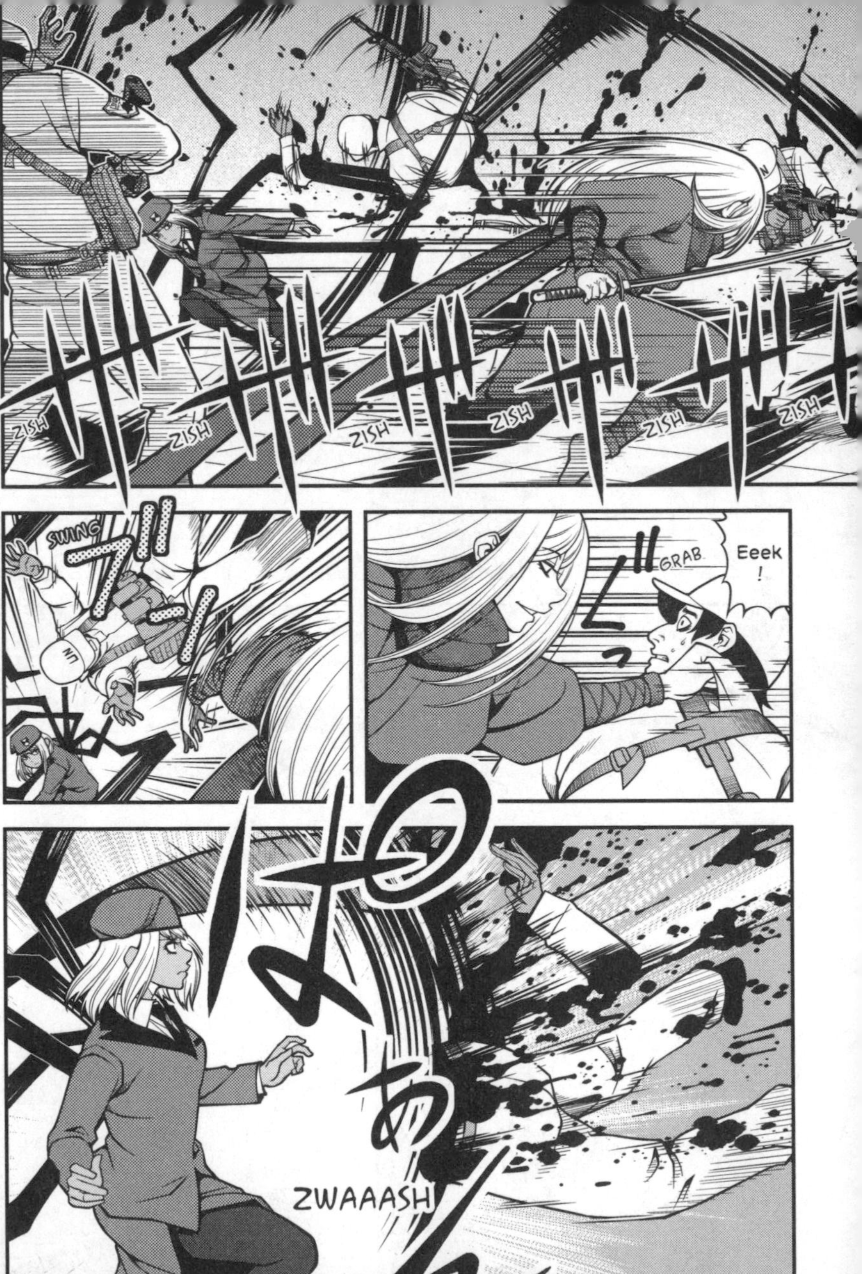
ZISH
ZISH
ZISH
ZISH
ZISH
ZISH
GRAB
Eeek!
SWING
ZWAAASH

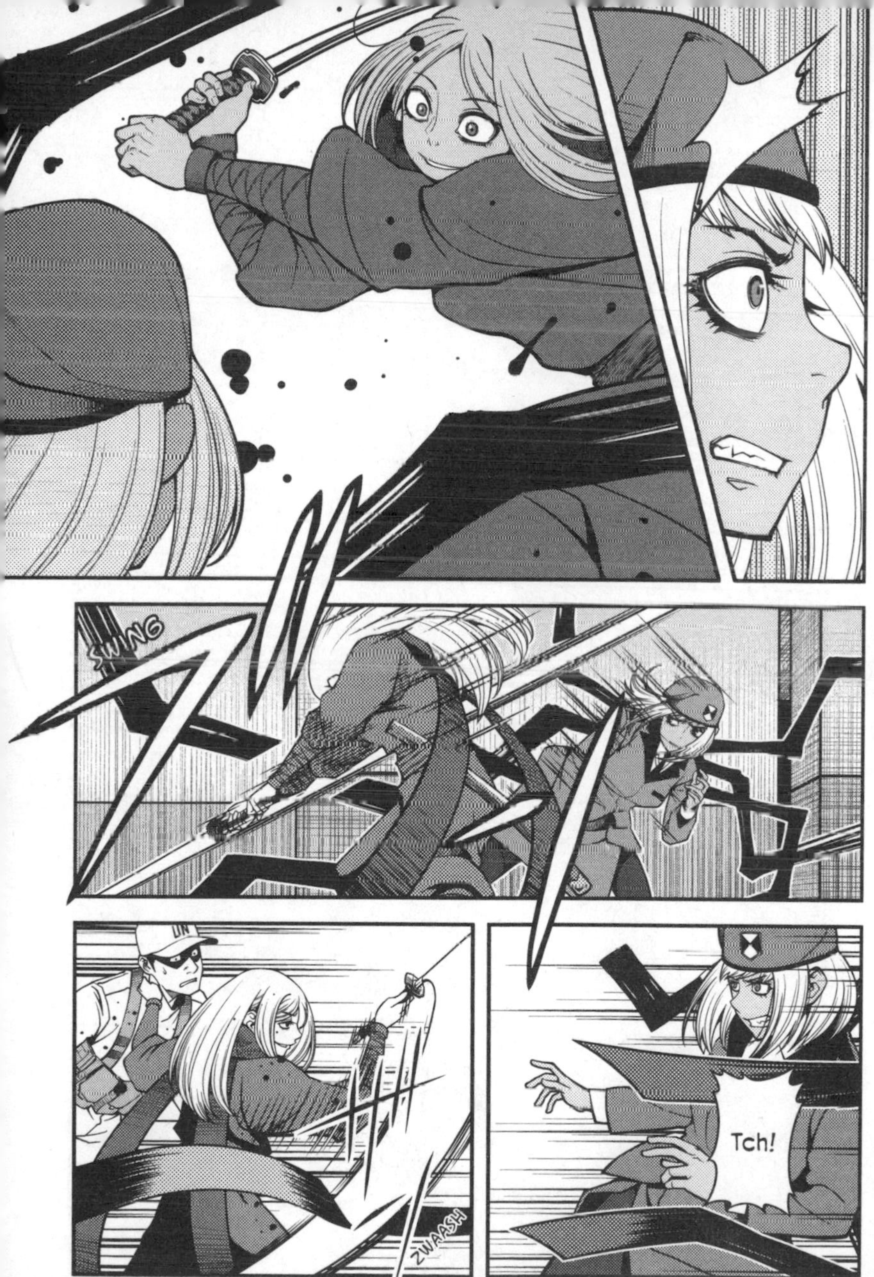
SWING
Tch!
ZWAASH

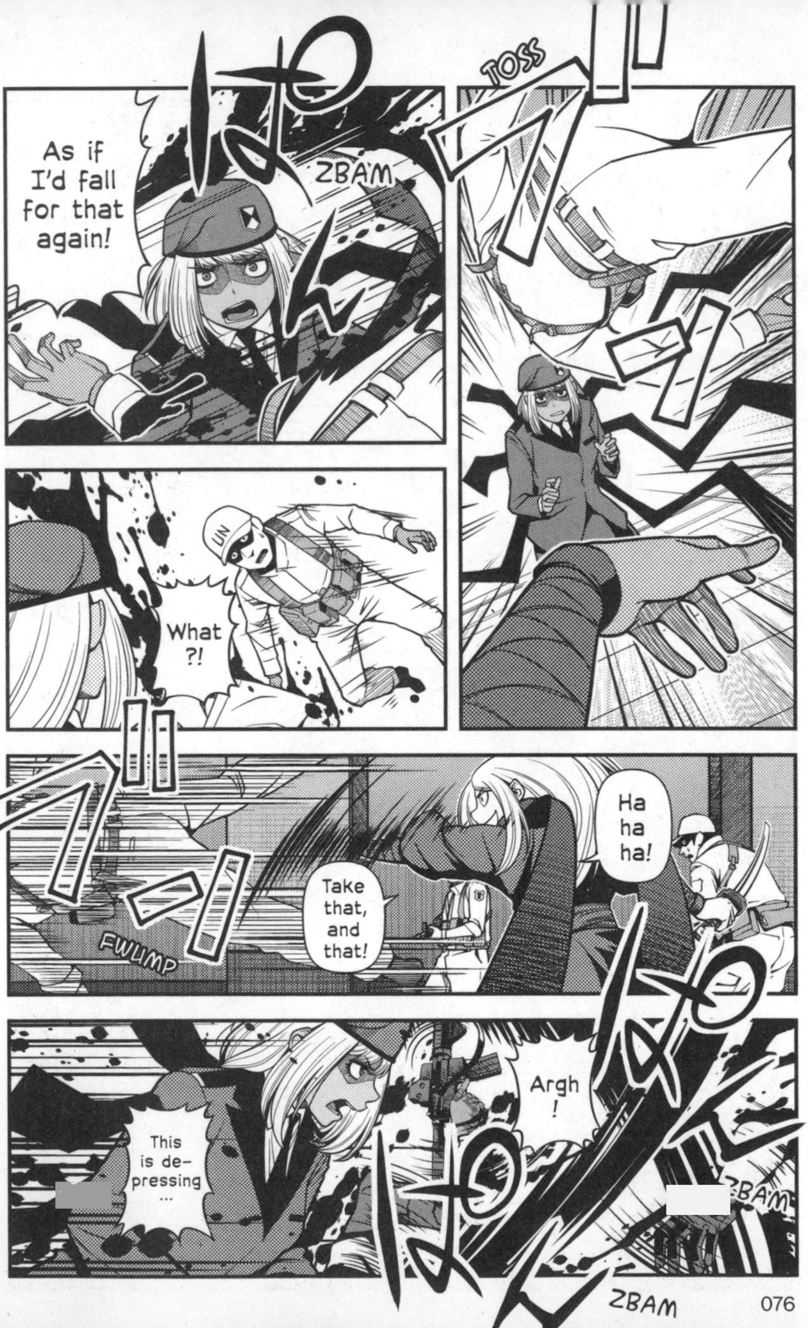
TOSS
As if I'd fall for that again!
ZBAM
What ?!
Ha ha ha!
Take that, and that!
FWUMP
Argh !
ZBAM
This is de-pressing ...
ZBAM

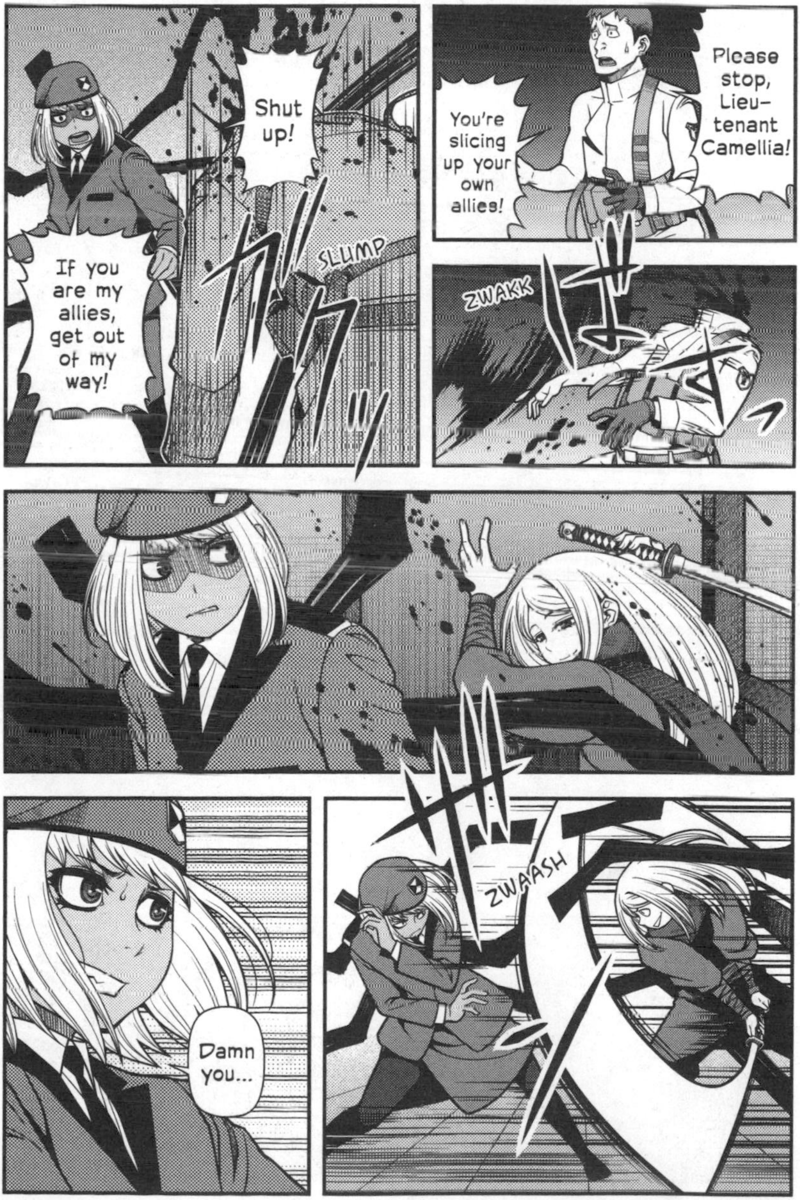

Please stop, Lieutenant Camellia!
You're slicing up your own allies!
ZWAKK
Shut up!
SLUMP
If you are my allies, get out of my way!
ZWAASH
Damn you...

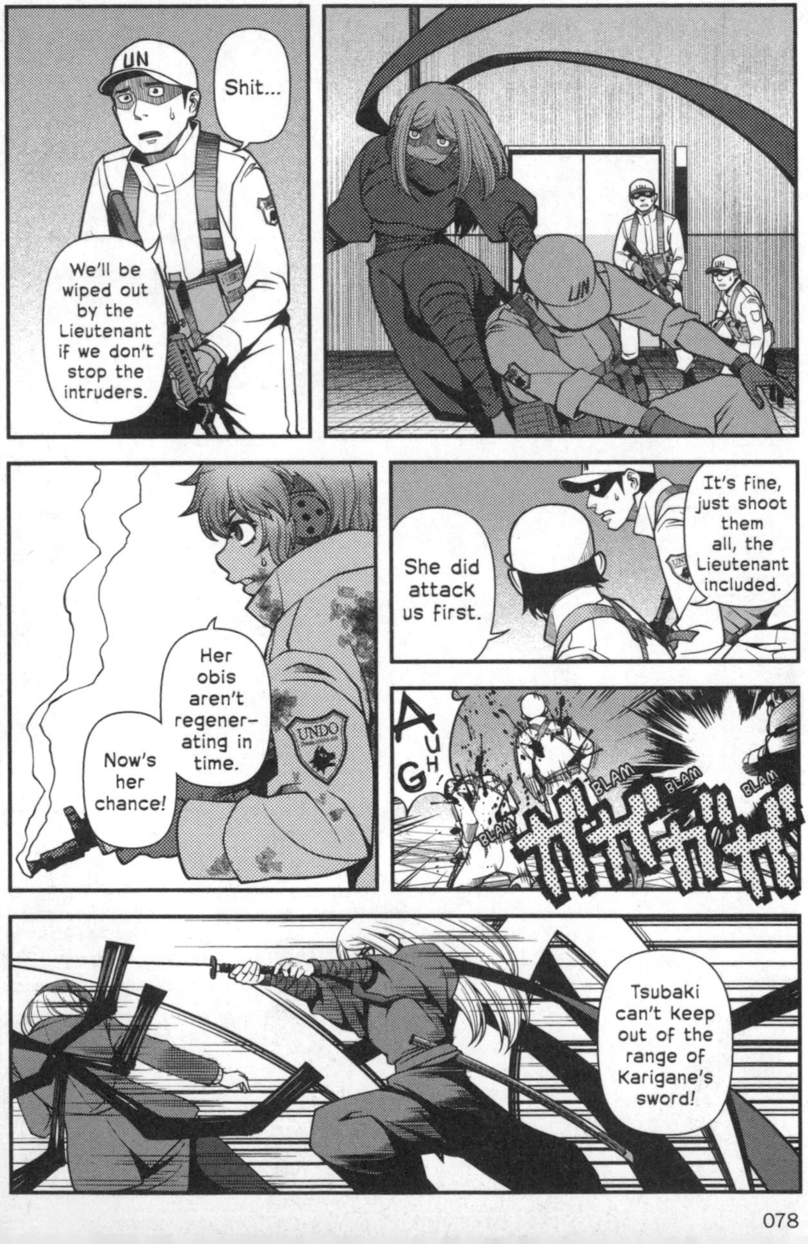
Shit...
We'll be wiped out by the Lieutenant if we don't stop the intruders.
It's fine, just shoot them all, the Lieutenant included.
She did attack us first.
AUGH!
BLAM
BLAM
BLAM
BLAM
Her obis aren't regener-ating in time.
Now's her chance!
Tsubaki can't keep out of the range of Karigane's sword!

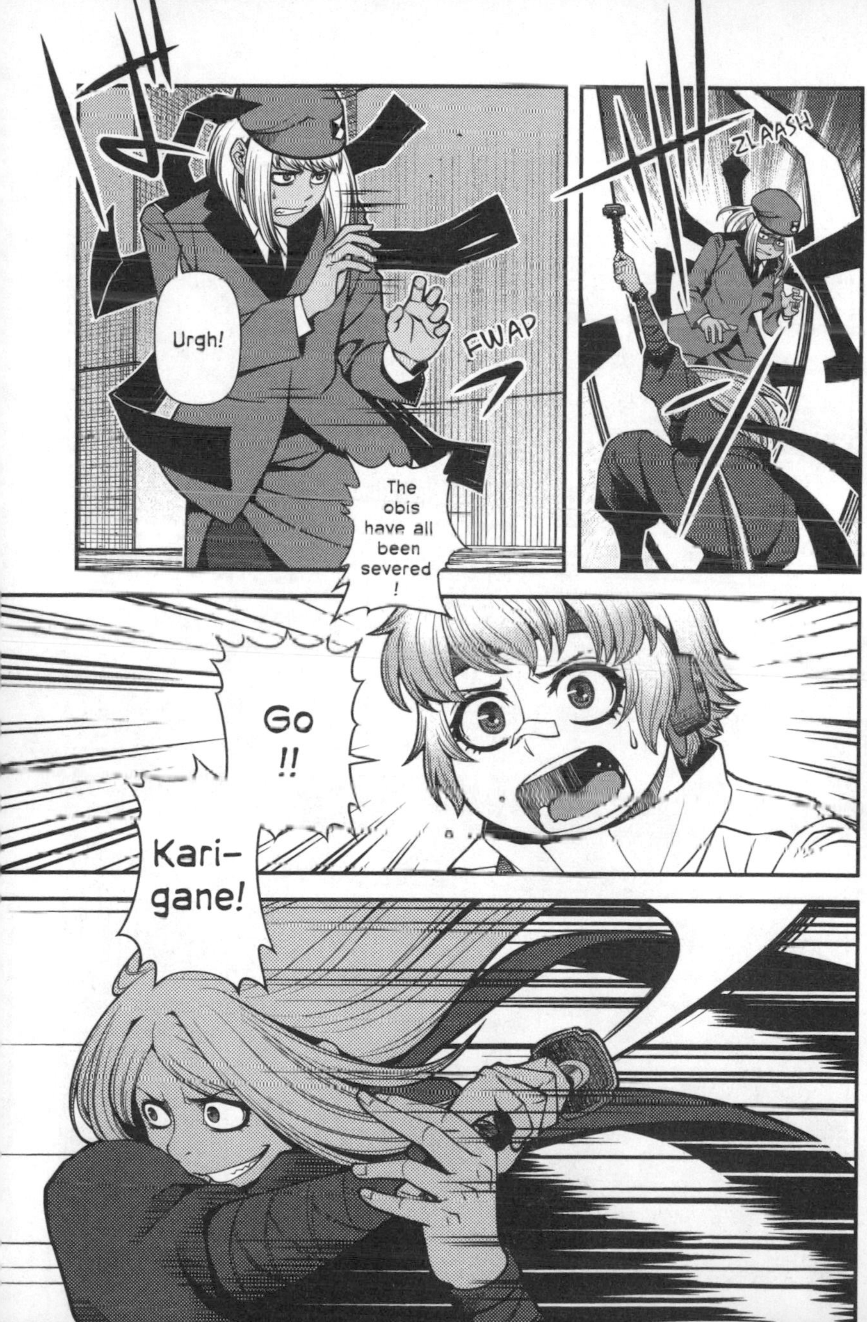
ZLAASH
Urgh!
FWAP
The obis have all been severed!
Go!!
Kari-gane!

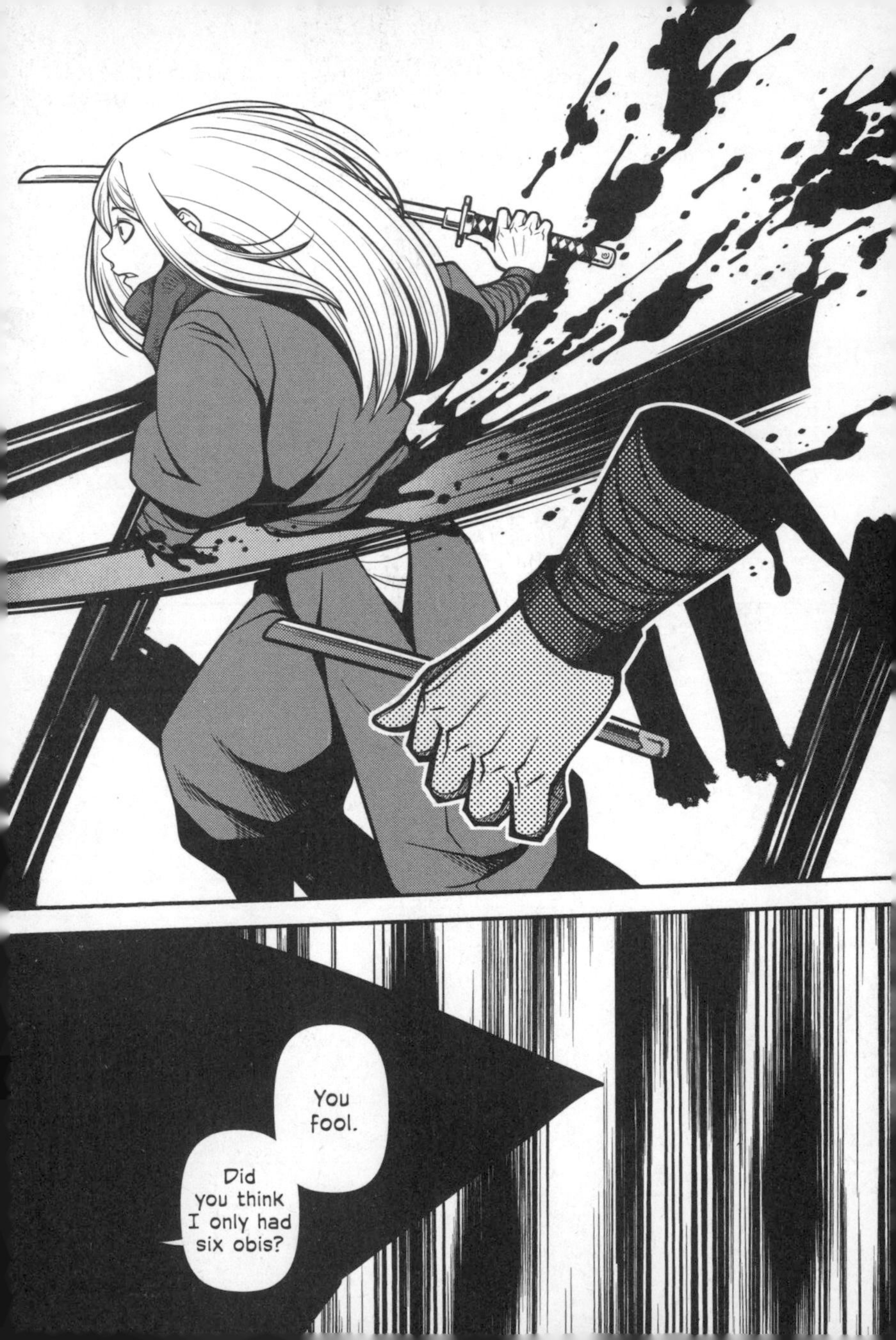
You fool.
Did you think I only had six obis?

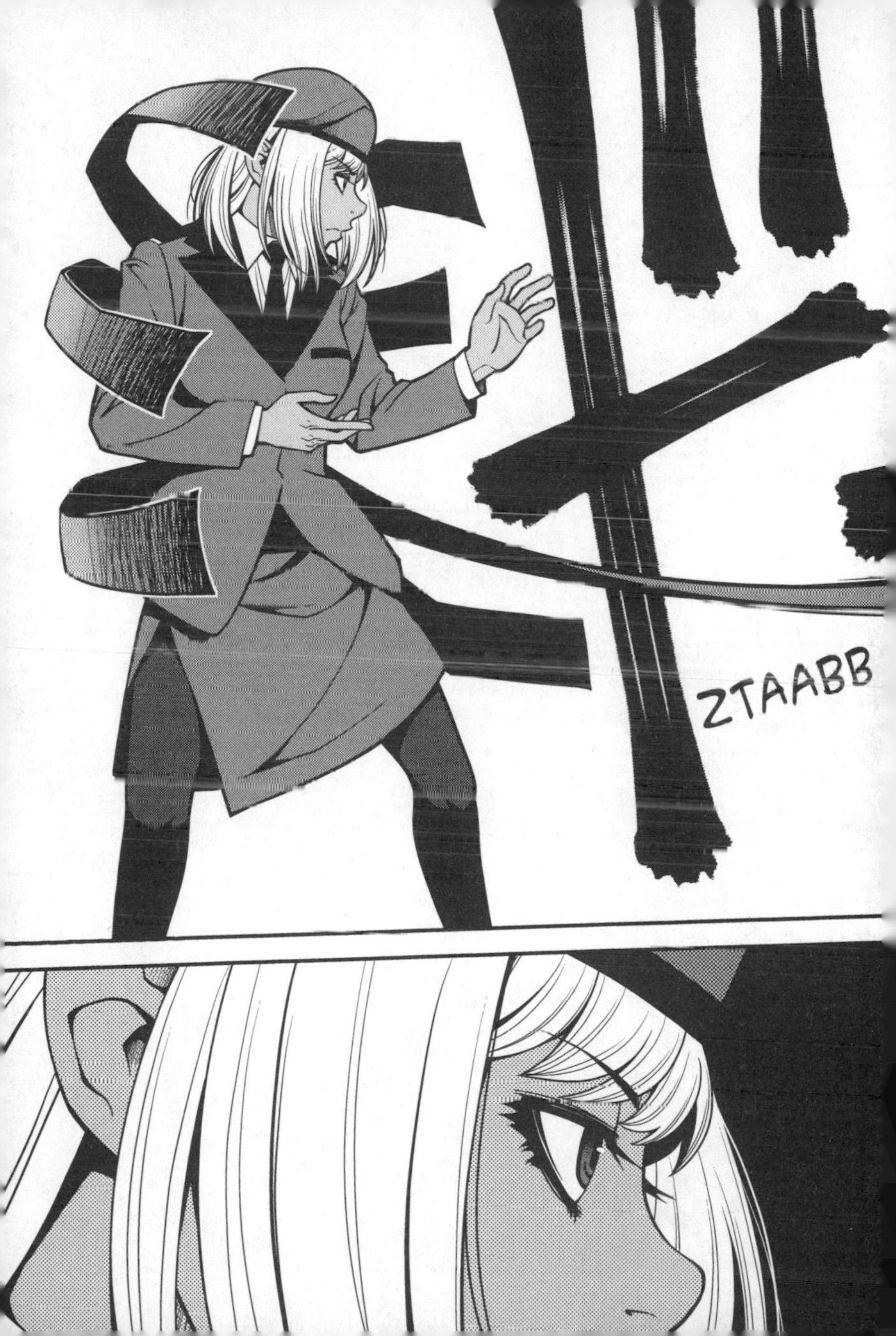
ZTAABB

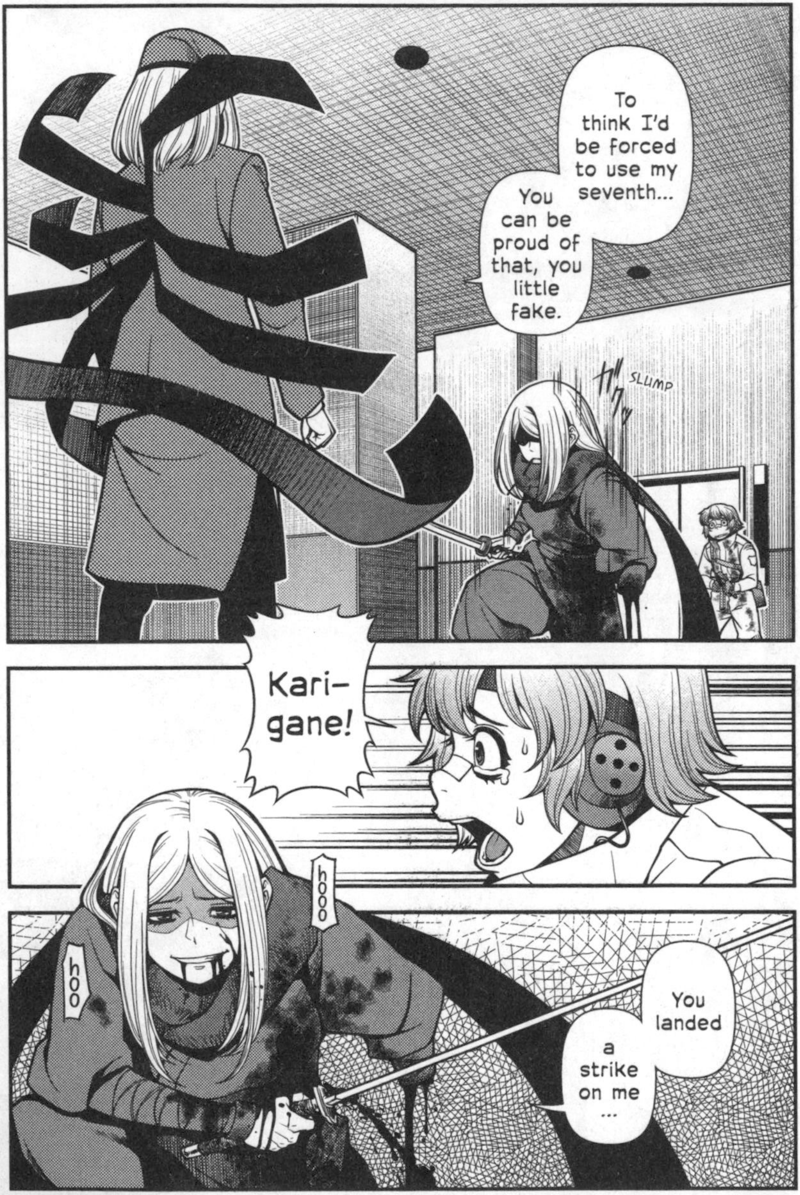
To think I'd be forced to use my seventh...
You can be proud of that, you little fake.
ガクッ SLUMP
Kari-gane!
hooo
hoo
You landed a strike on me ...

End of Chapter 36

Chapter 37

Conclusion

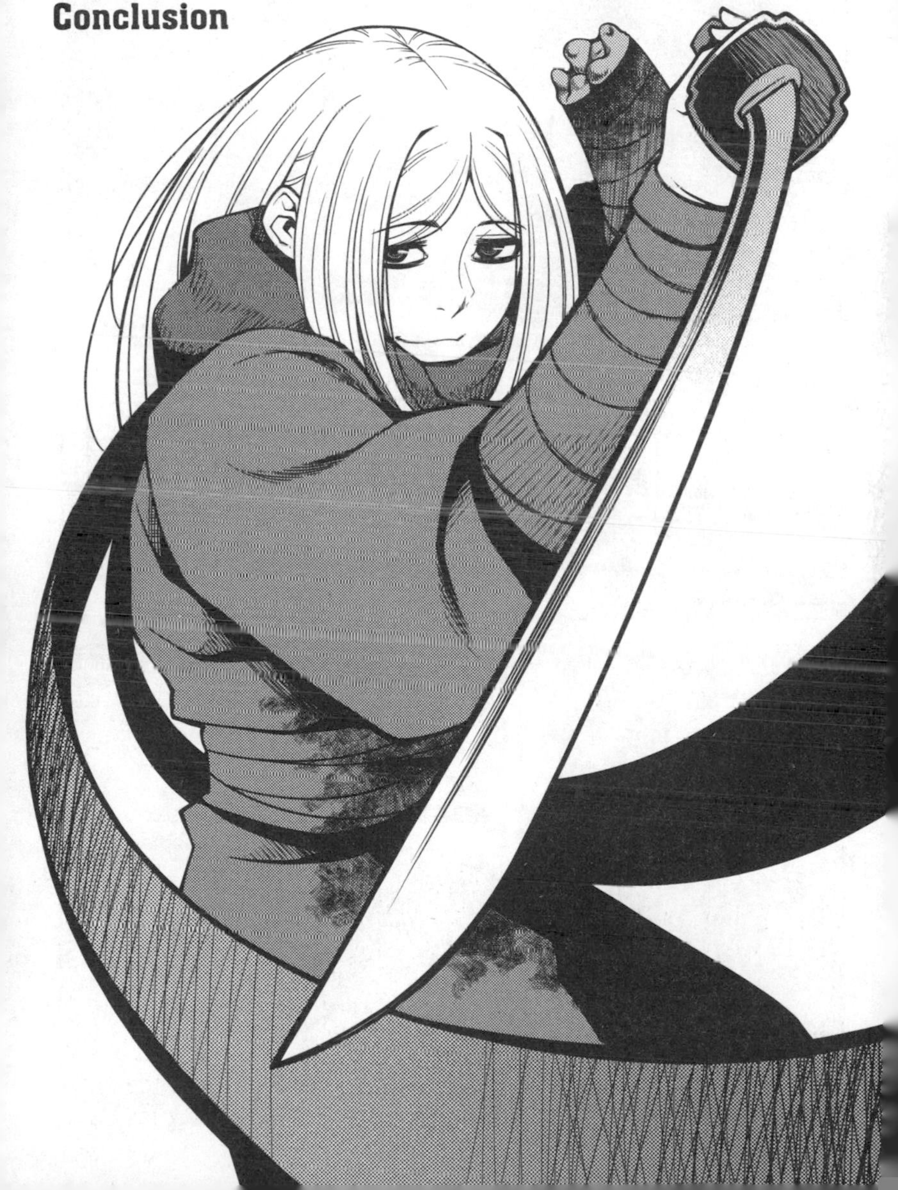

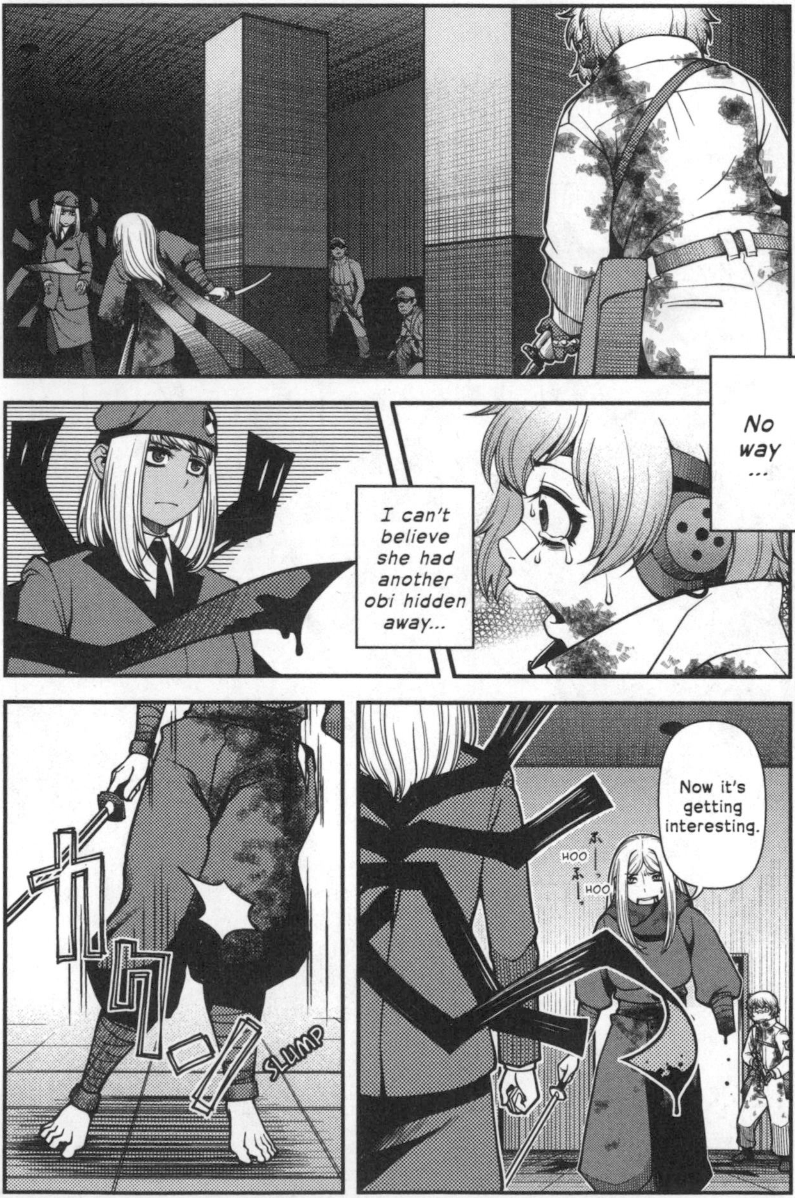
No way ...
I can't believe she had another obi hidden away...
Now it's getting interesting.
HOO
HOO
SLUMP

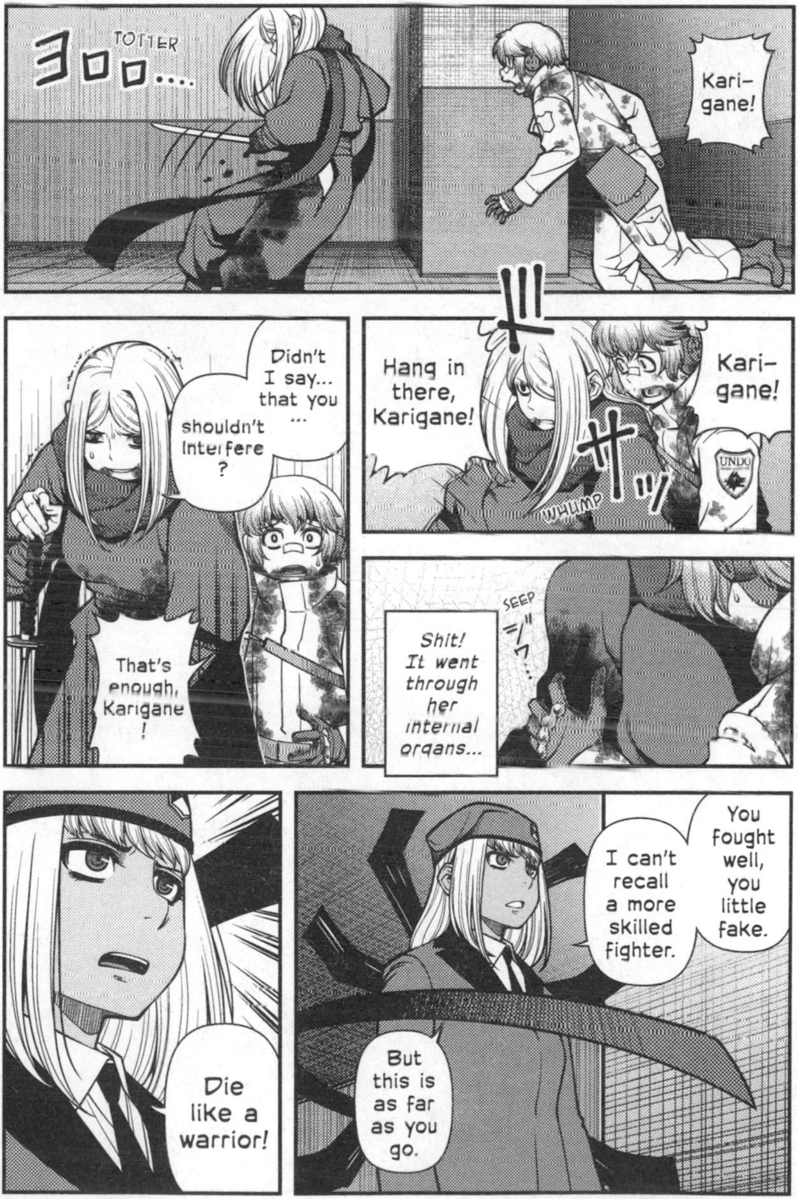
Kari-gane!
ヨロロ….
TOTTER
Kari-gane!
Hang in there, Karigane!
サッ
WHUMP
SEEP
ジワ…
Shit! It went through her internal organs...
Didn't I say... that you ... shouldn't interfere ?
That's enough, Karigane !
You fought well, you little fake.
I can't recall a more skilled fighter.
But this is as far as you go.
Die like a warrior!

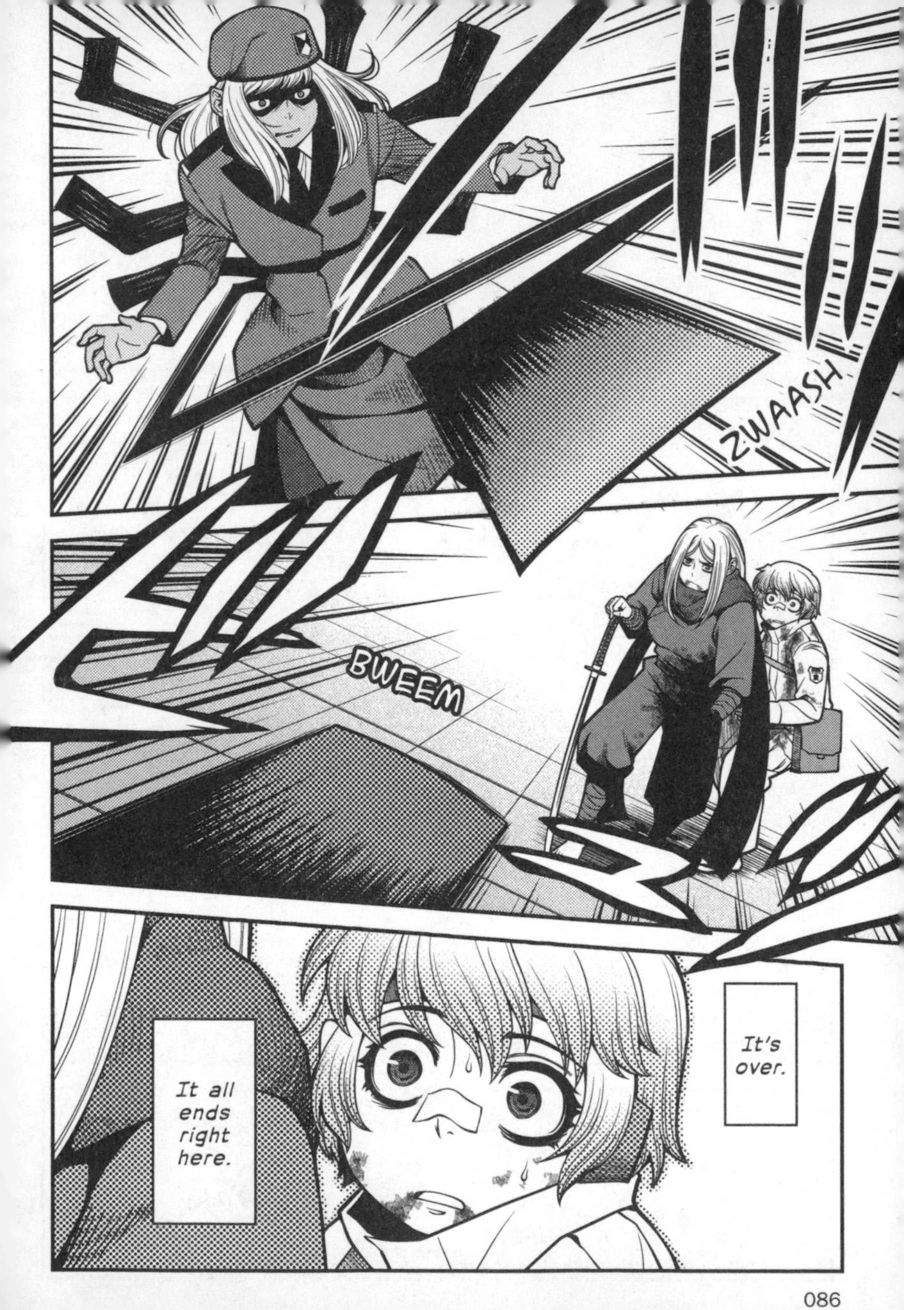
ZWAASH
BWEEM
It's over.
It all ends right here.

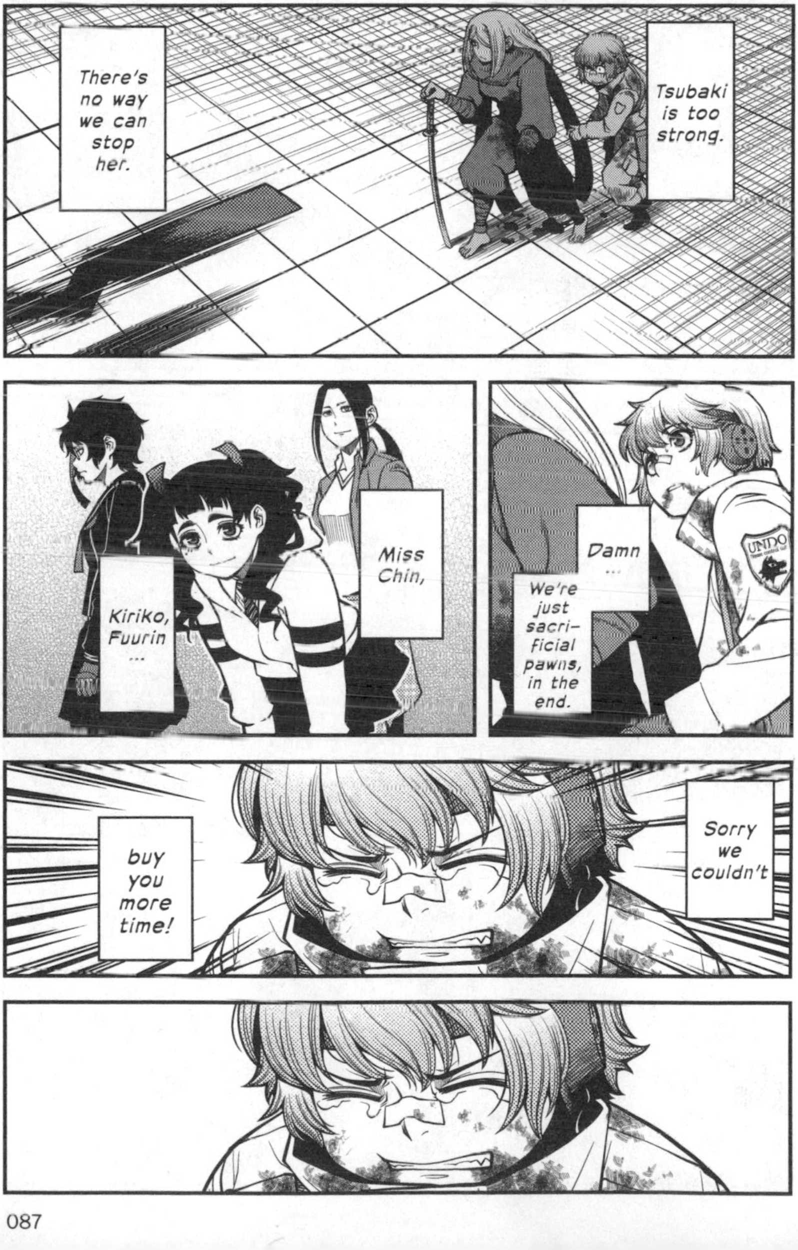
Tsubaki is too strong.
There's no way we can stop her.
Damn ...
We're just sacrificial pawns, in the end.
Miss Chin,
Kiriko, Fuurin ...
Sorry we couldn't
buy you more time!

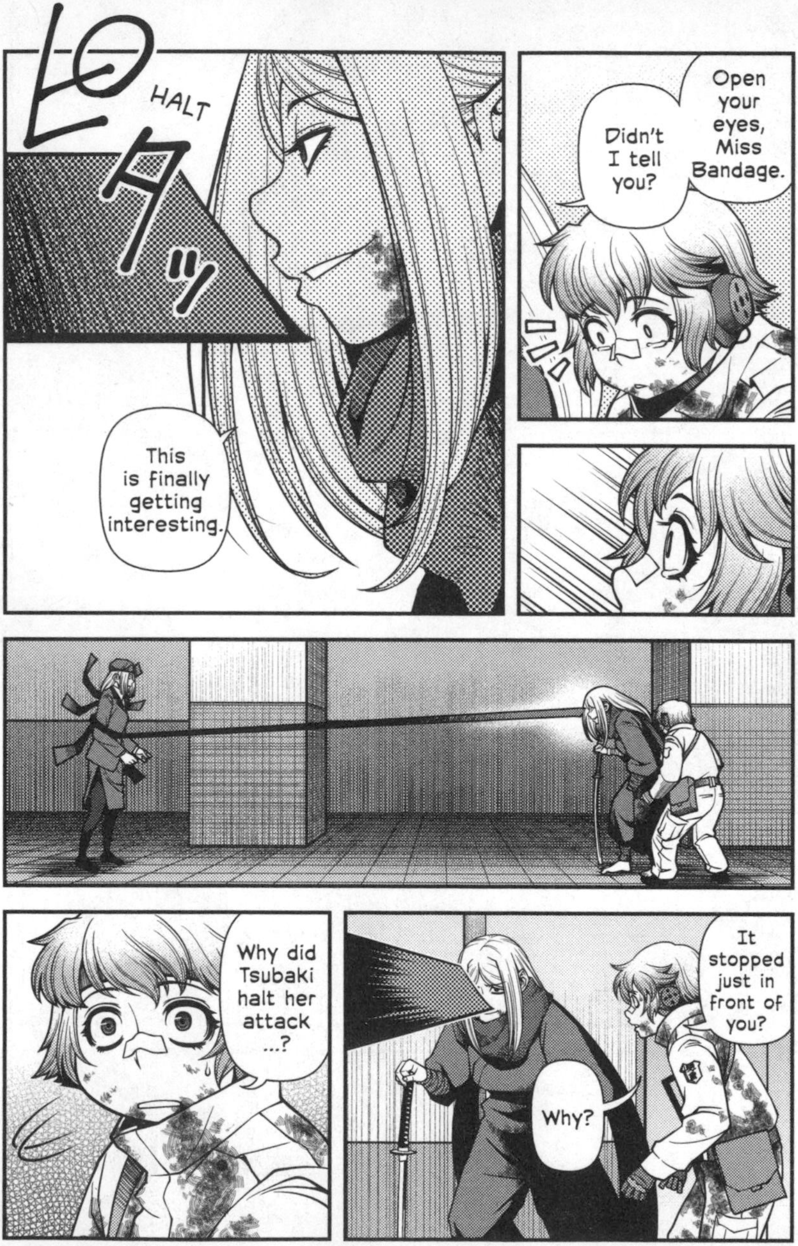
Open your eyes, Miss Bandage.
Didn't I tell you?
ピタッ
HALT
This is finally getting interesting.
It stopped just in front of you?
Why?
Why did Tsubaki halt her attack ...?

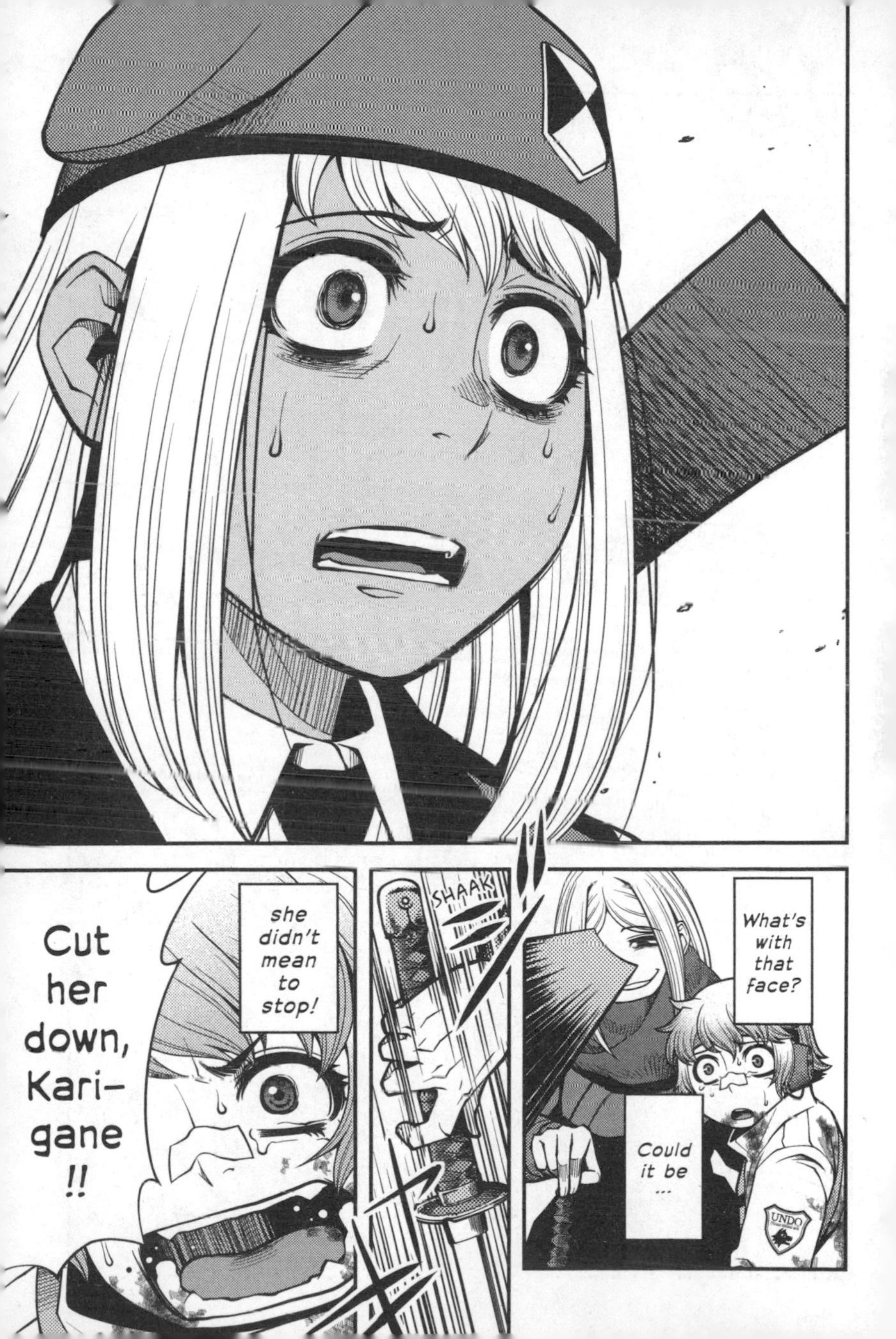
What's with that face?
Could it be ...
UNDO
SHAAK
she didn't mean to stop!
Cut her down, Kari-gane!!

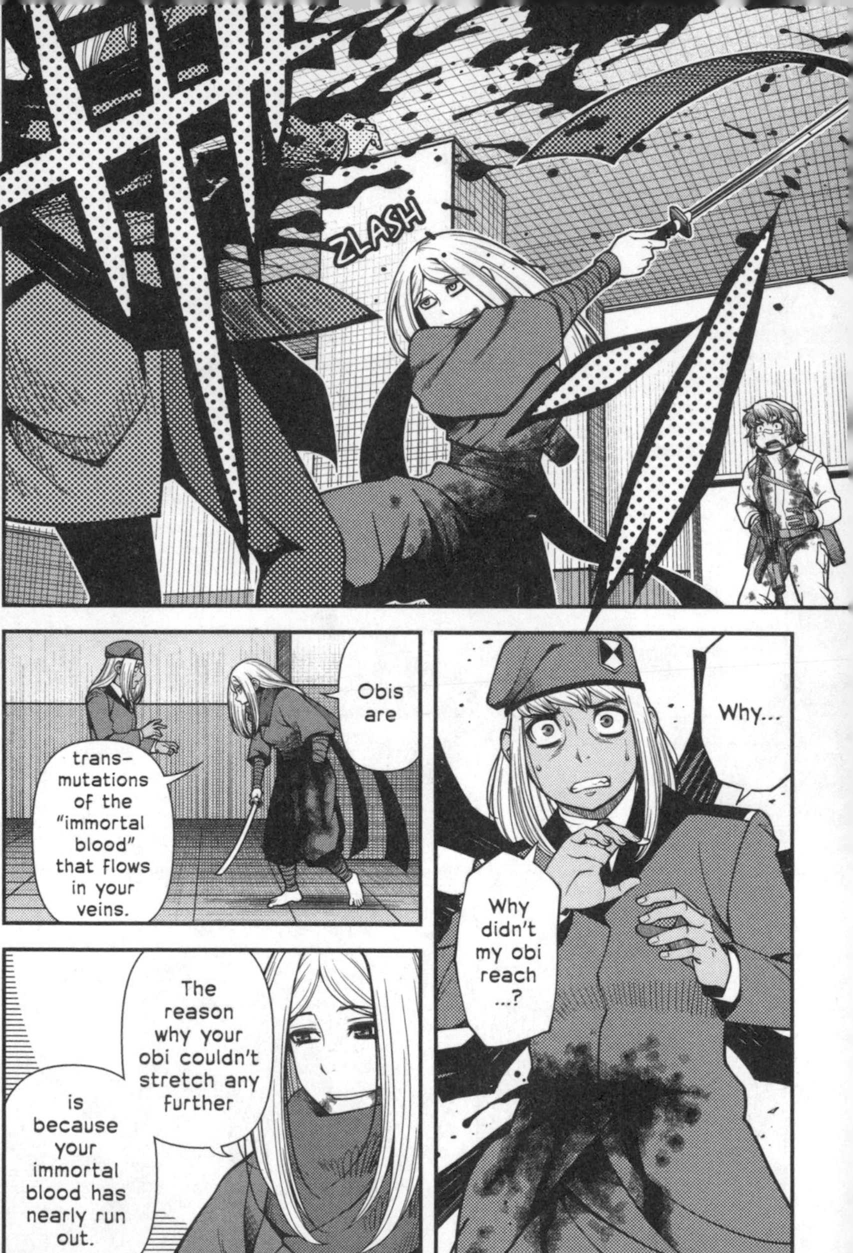
ZLASH
Why...
Why didn't my obi reach ...?
Obis are
trans-mutations of the "immortal blood" that flows in your veins.
The reason why your obi couldn't stretch any further
is because your immortal blood has nearly run out.

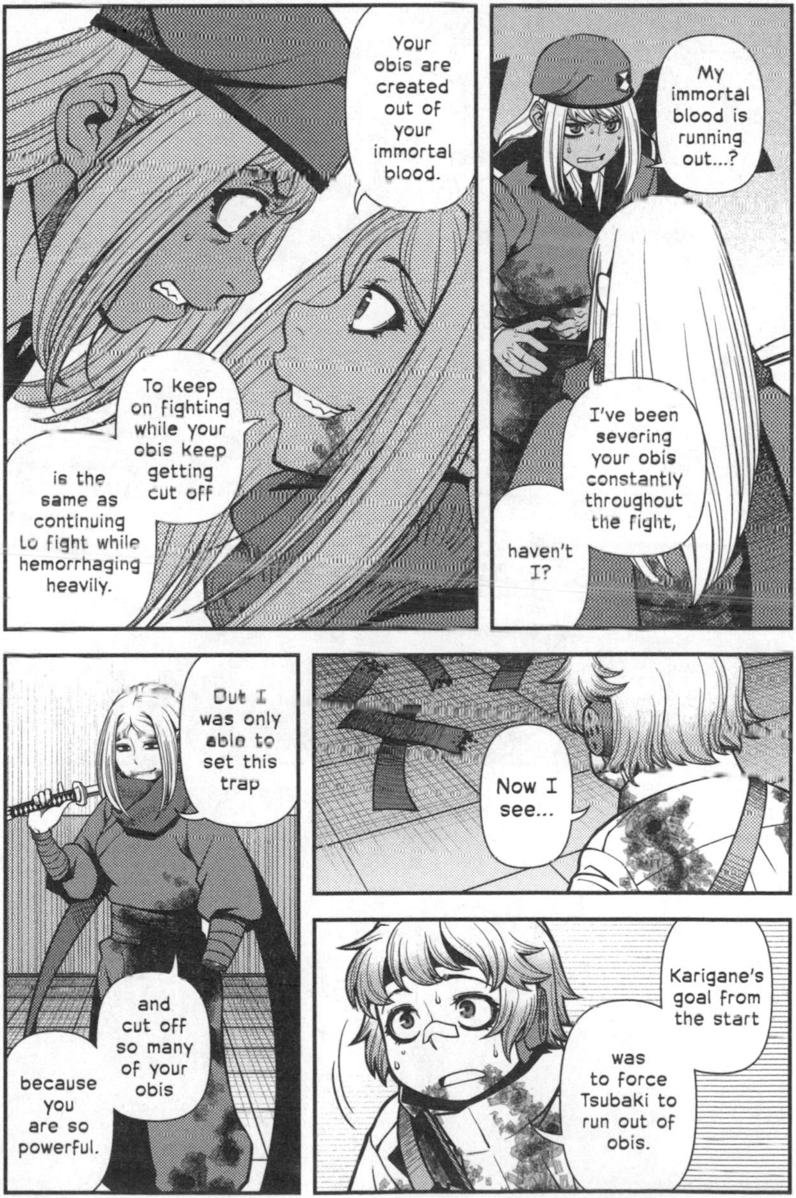
My immortal blood is running out...?
I've been severing your obis constantly throughout the fight,
haven't I?
Your obis are created out of your immortal blood.
To keep on fighting while your obis keep getting cut off
is the same as continuing to fight while hemorrhaging heavily.
Now I see...
Karigane's goal from the start
was to force Tsubaki to run out of obis.
But I was only able to set this trap
and cut off so many of your obis
because you are so powerful.

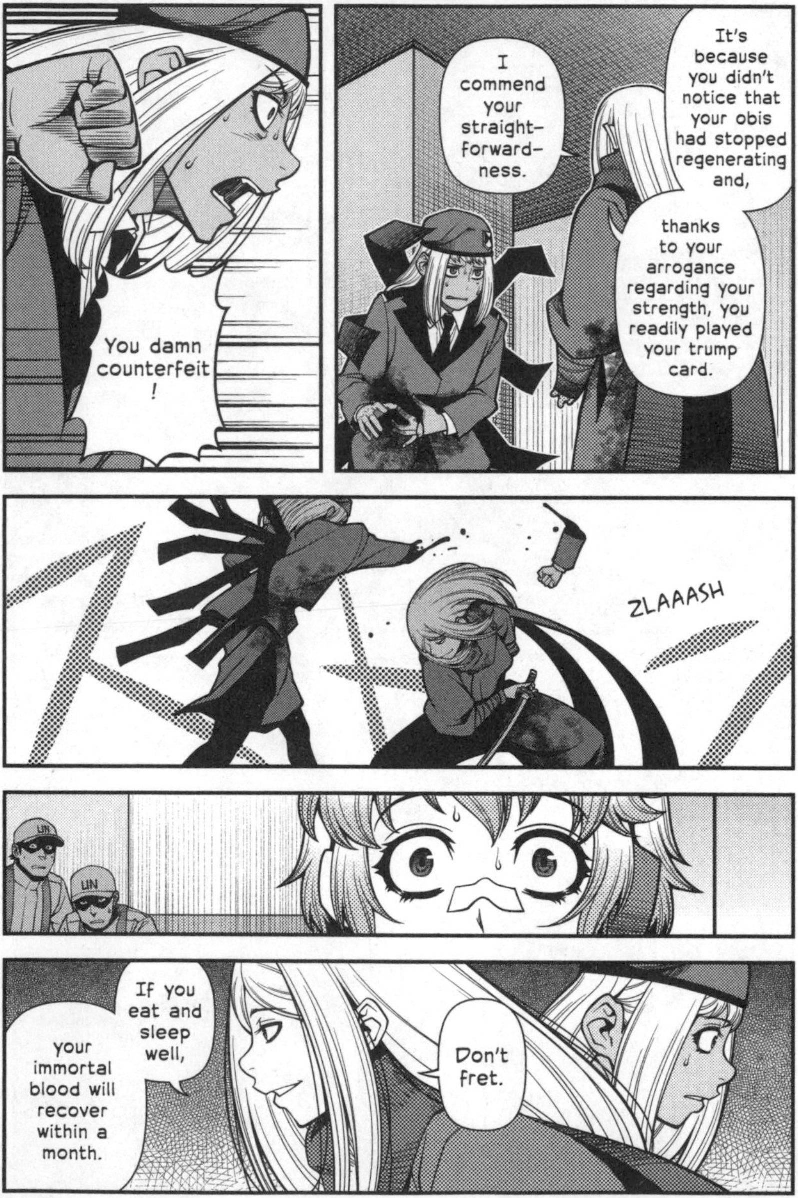

It's because you didn't notice that your obis had stopped regenerating and,
thanks to your arrogance regarding your strength, you readily played your trump card.
I commend your straight-forward-ness.
You damn counterfeit!
ZLAAASH
Don't fret.
If you eat and sleep well,
your immortal blood will recover within a month.

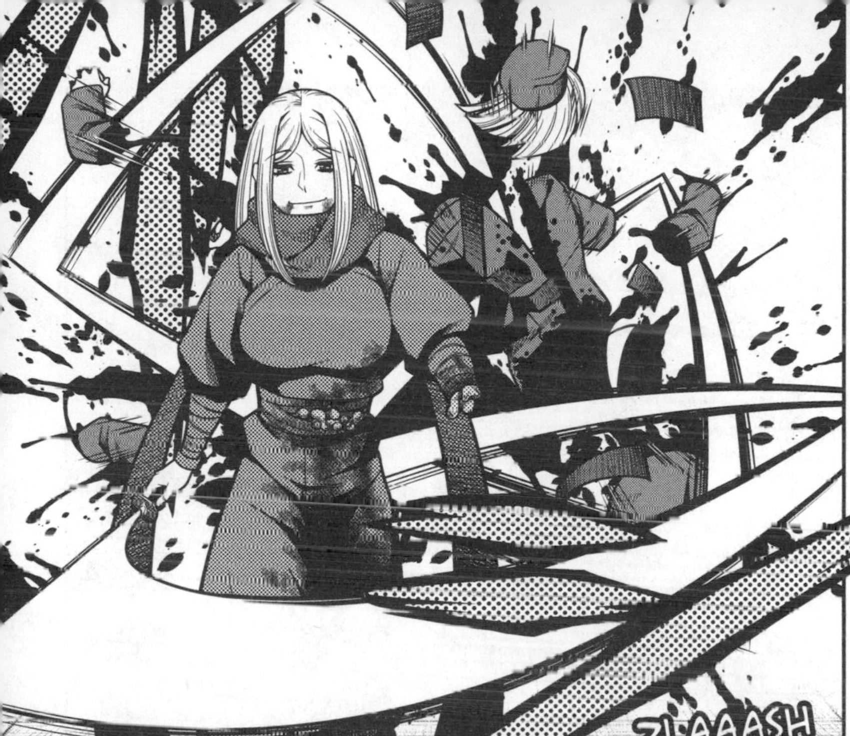
ZLAAASH

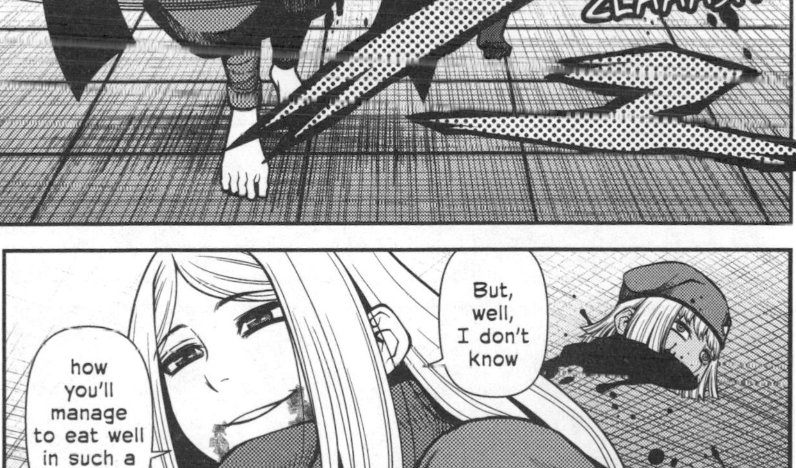
But, well, I don't know
how you'll manage to eat well in such a state.

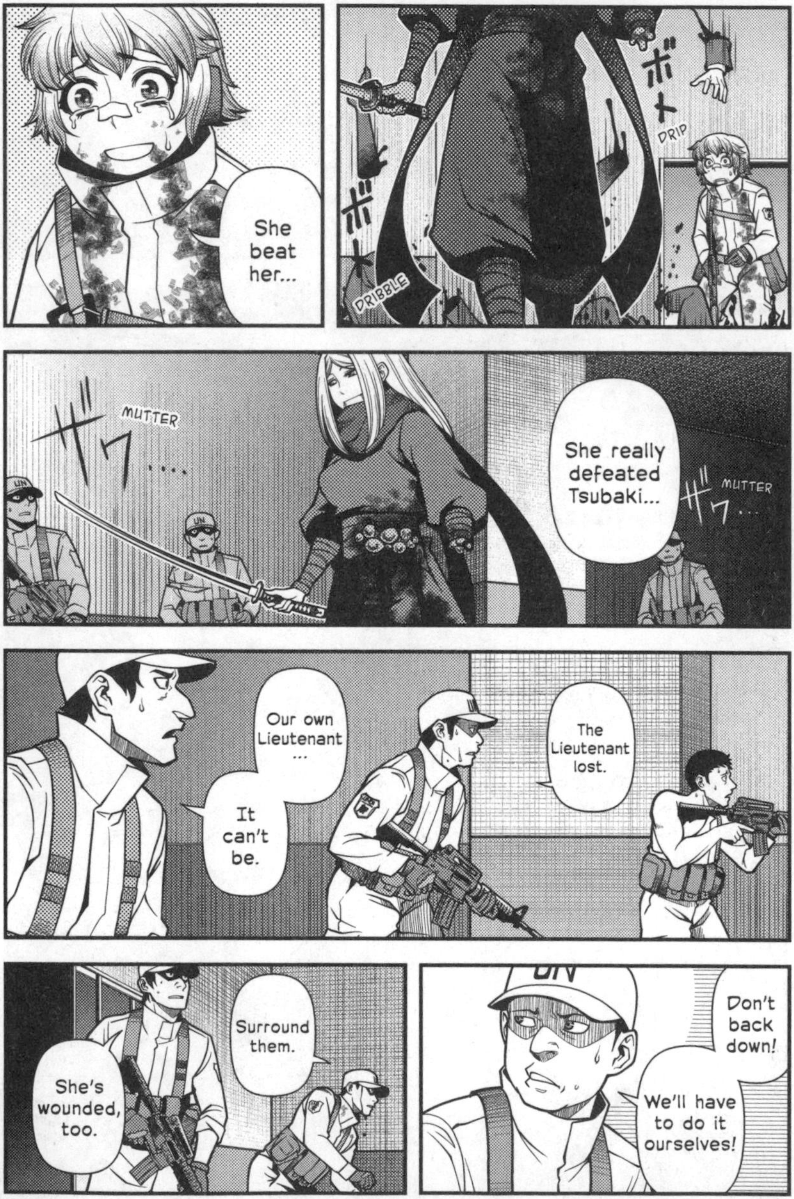
ボト
DRIP
ボ
DRIBBLE
She beat her...
ザワ...
MUTTER
She really defeated Tsubaki...
ザワ....
MUTTER
The Lieutenant lost.
Our own Lieutenant ...
It can't be.
Don't back down!
We'll have to do it ourselves!
Surround them.
She's wounded, too.

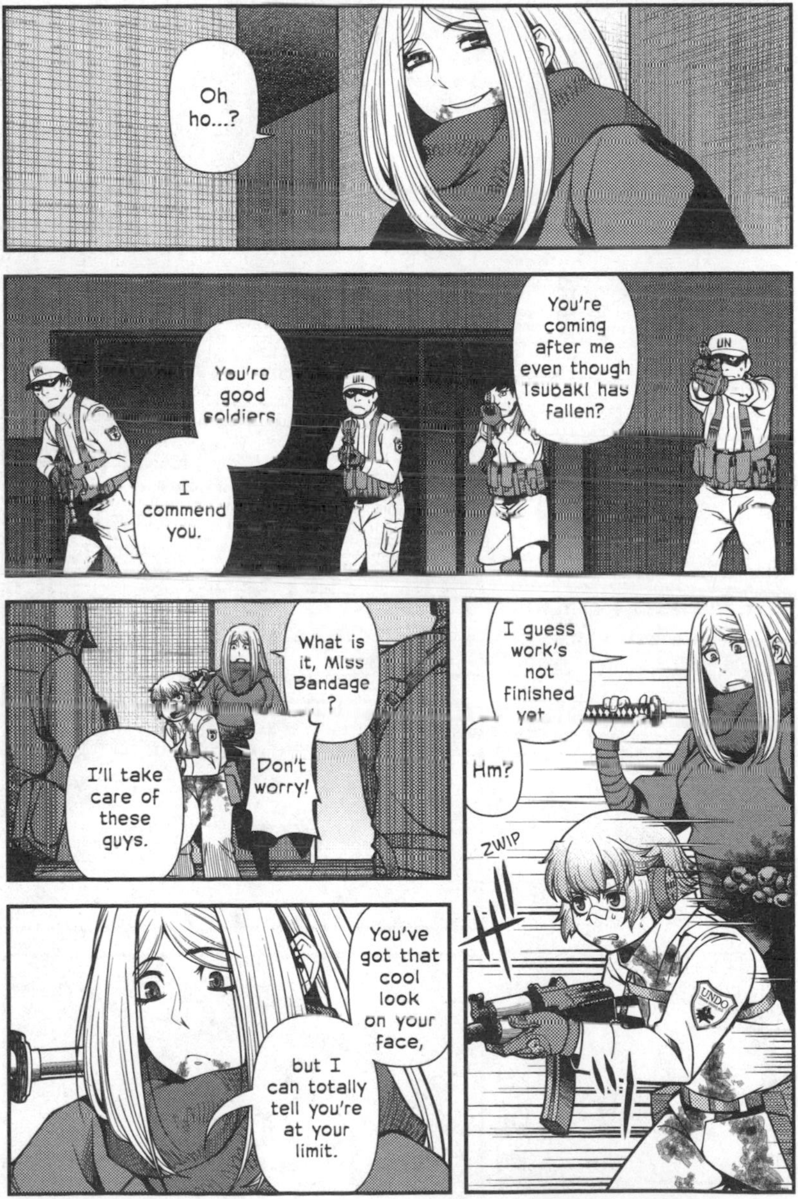
Oh ho...?
You're coming after me even though Tsubaki has fallen?
You're good soldiers
I commend you.
I guess work's not finished yet
Hm?
ZWIP
What is it, Miss Bandage?
Don't worry!
I'll take care of these guys.
You've got that cool look on your face,
but I can totally tell you're at your limit.

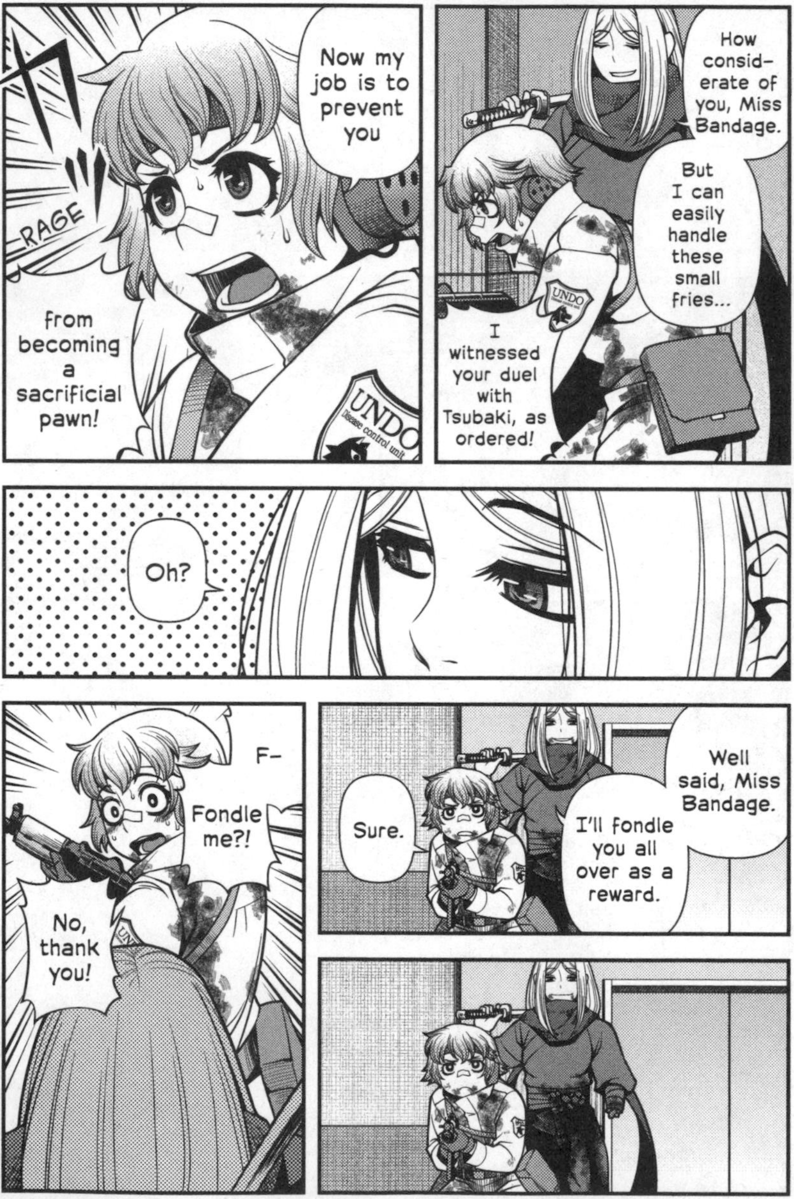
How consid-erate of you, Miss Bandage.
But I can easily handle these small fries...
UNDO
I witnessed your duel with Tsubaki, as ordered!
Now my job is to prevent you
RAGE
from becoming a sacrificial pawn!
UNDO
Oh?
Well said, Miss Bandage.
I'll fondle you all over as a reward.
Sure.
F-
Fondle me?!
No, thank you!

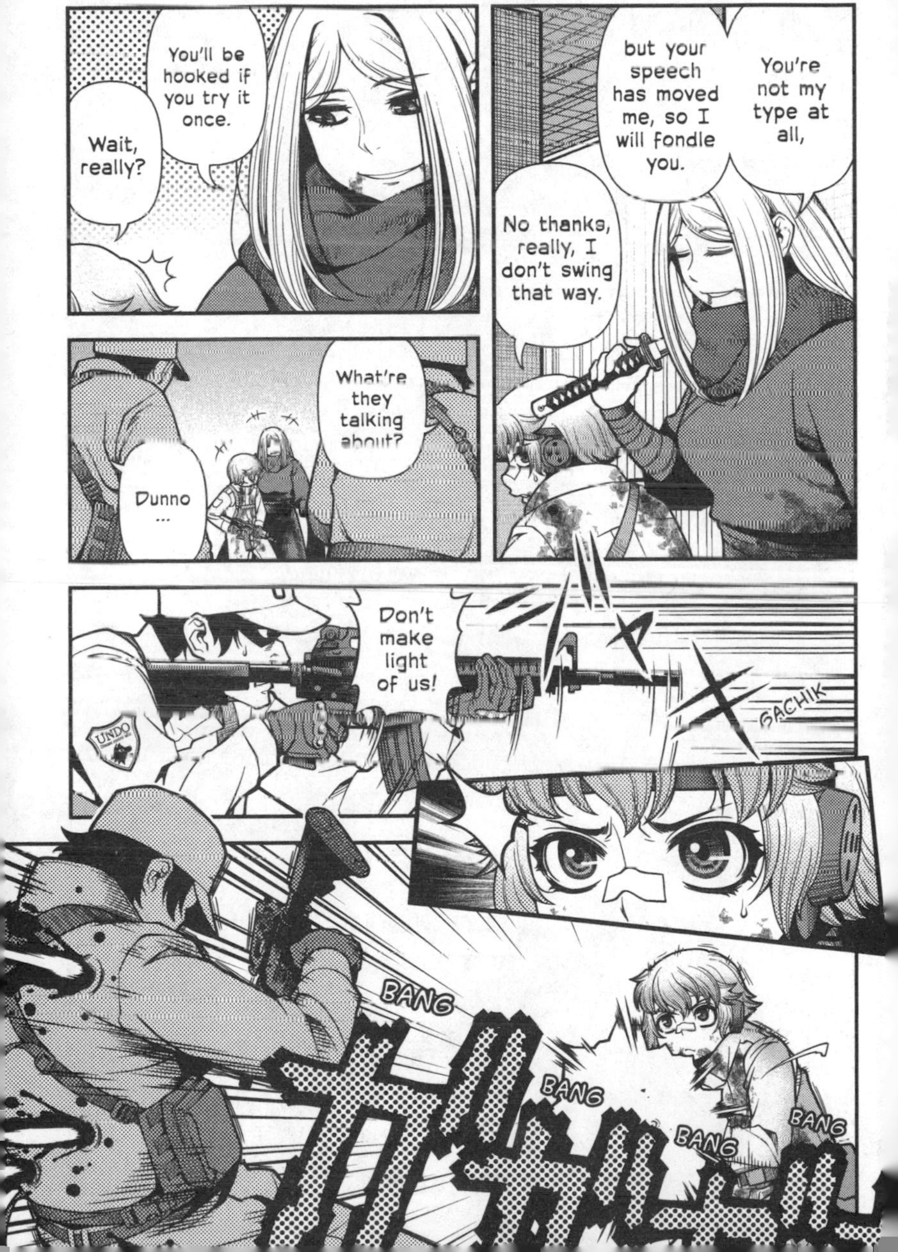
You're not my type at all,
but your speech has moved me, so I will fondle you.
No thanks, really, I don't swing that way.
You'll be hooked if you try it once.
Wait, really?
What're they talking about?
Dunno ...
GACHIK
Don't make light of us!
UNDO
BANG
BANG
BANG
BANG

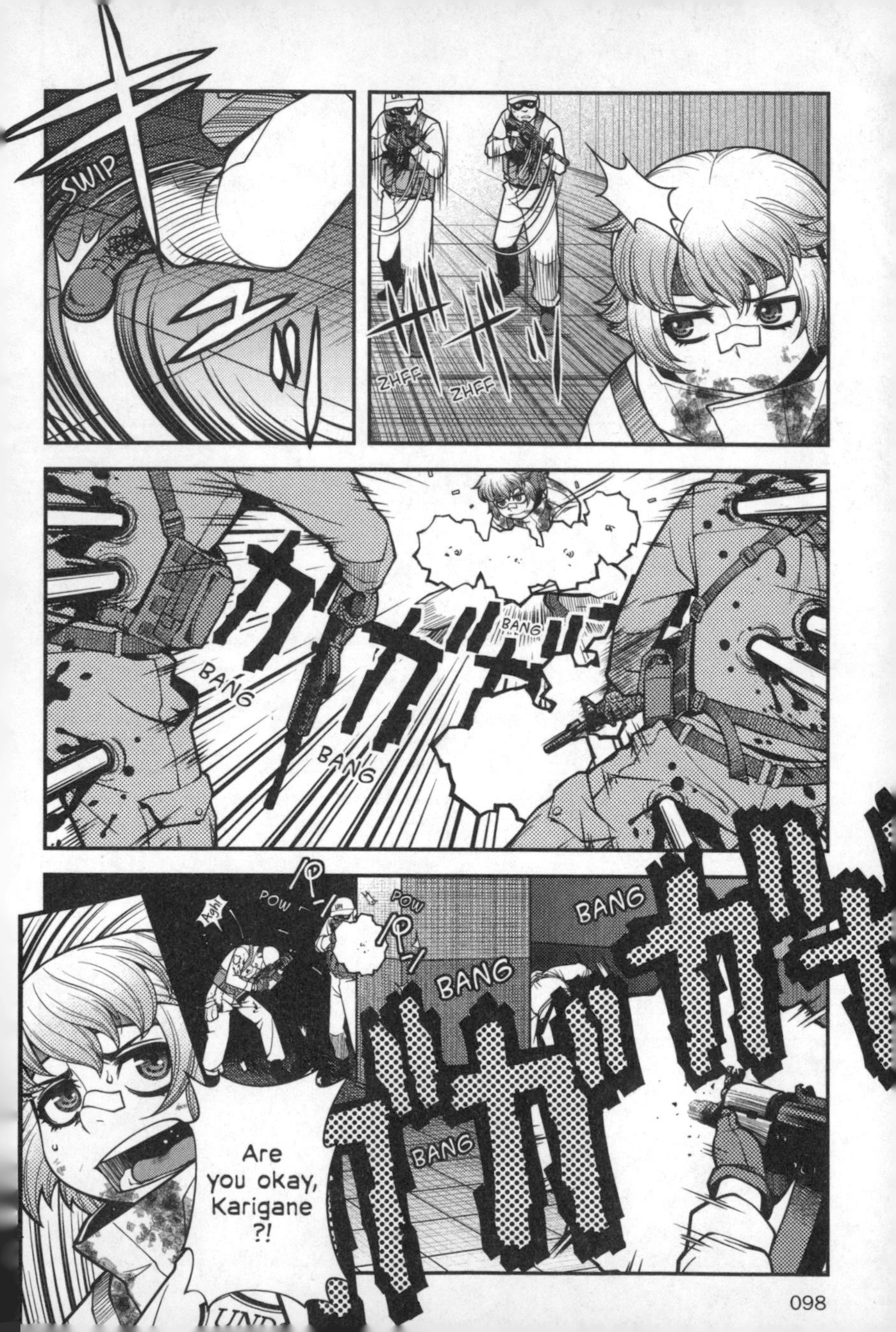
ZHFF
ZHFF
SWIP
BANG
BANG
BANG
BANG
BANG
BANG
POW
POW
Agh!
Are you okay, Karigane ?!

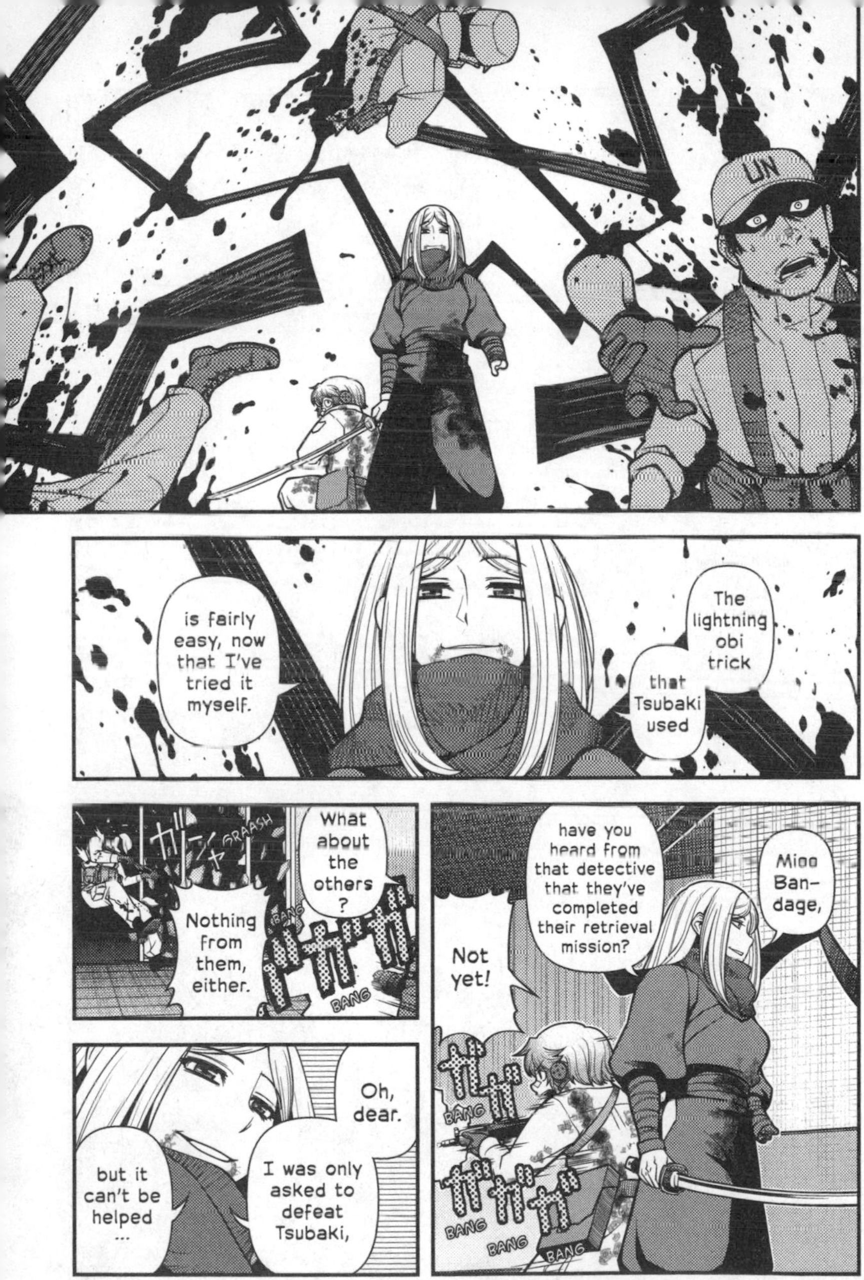

The lightning obi trick
that Tsubaki used
is fairly easy, now that I've tried it myself.
Mioo Ban-dage,
have you heard from that detective that they've completed their retrieval mission?
Not yet!
BANG
BANG
BANG
BANG
What about the others?
Nothing from them, either.
GRAASH
BANG
BANG
Oh, dear.
I was only asked to defeat Tsubaki,
but it can't be helped ...

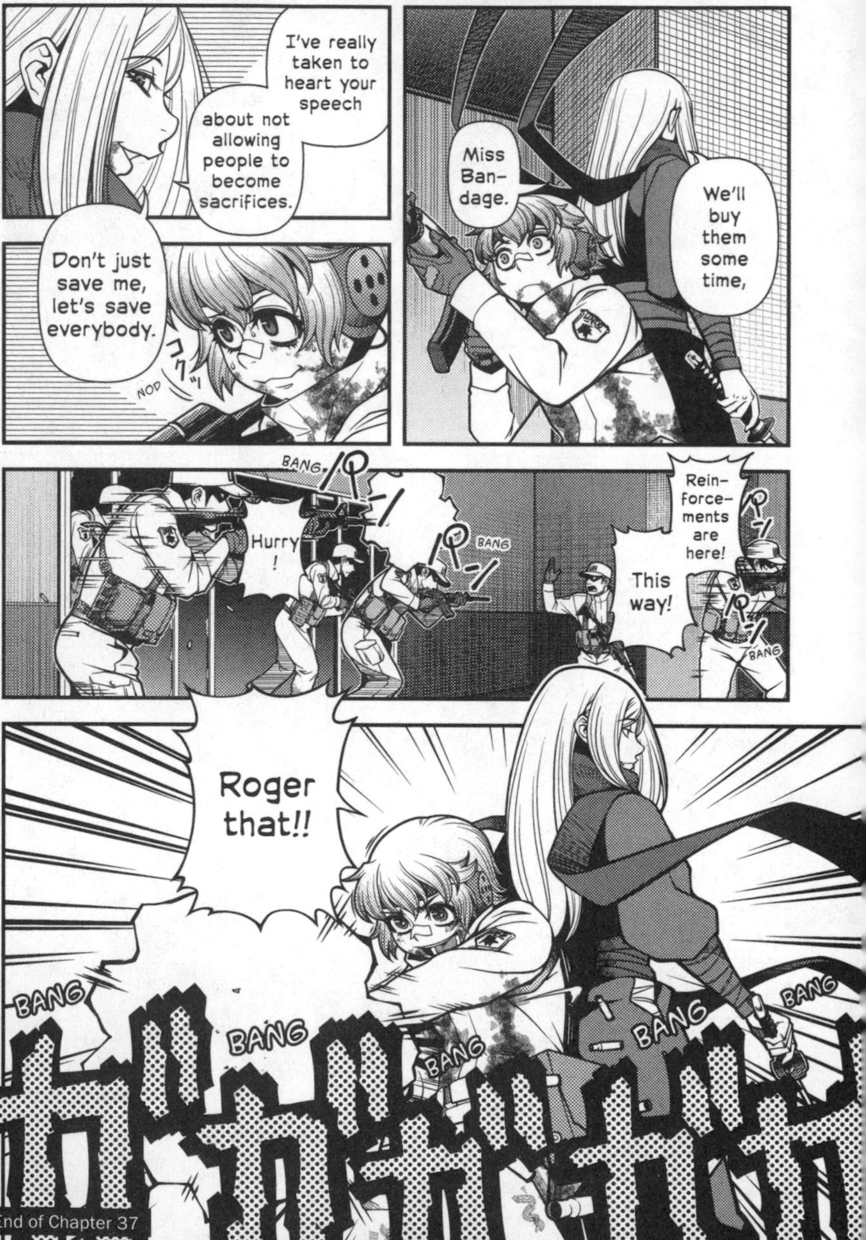
Miss Ban-dage.
We'll buy them some time,
I've really taken to heart your speech
about not allowing people to become sacrifices.
Don't just save me, let's save everybody.
NOD
BANG
Rein-force-ments are here!
This way!
BANG
BANG
Hurry!
BANG
Roger that!!
BANG
BANG
BANG
BANG
BANG
BANG

End of Chapter 37

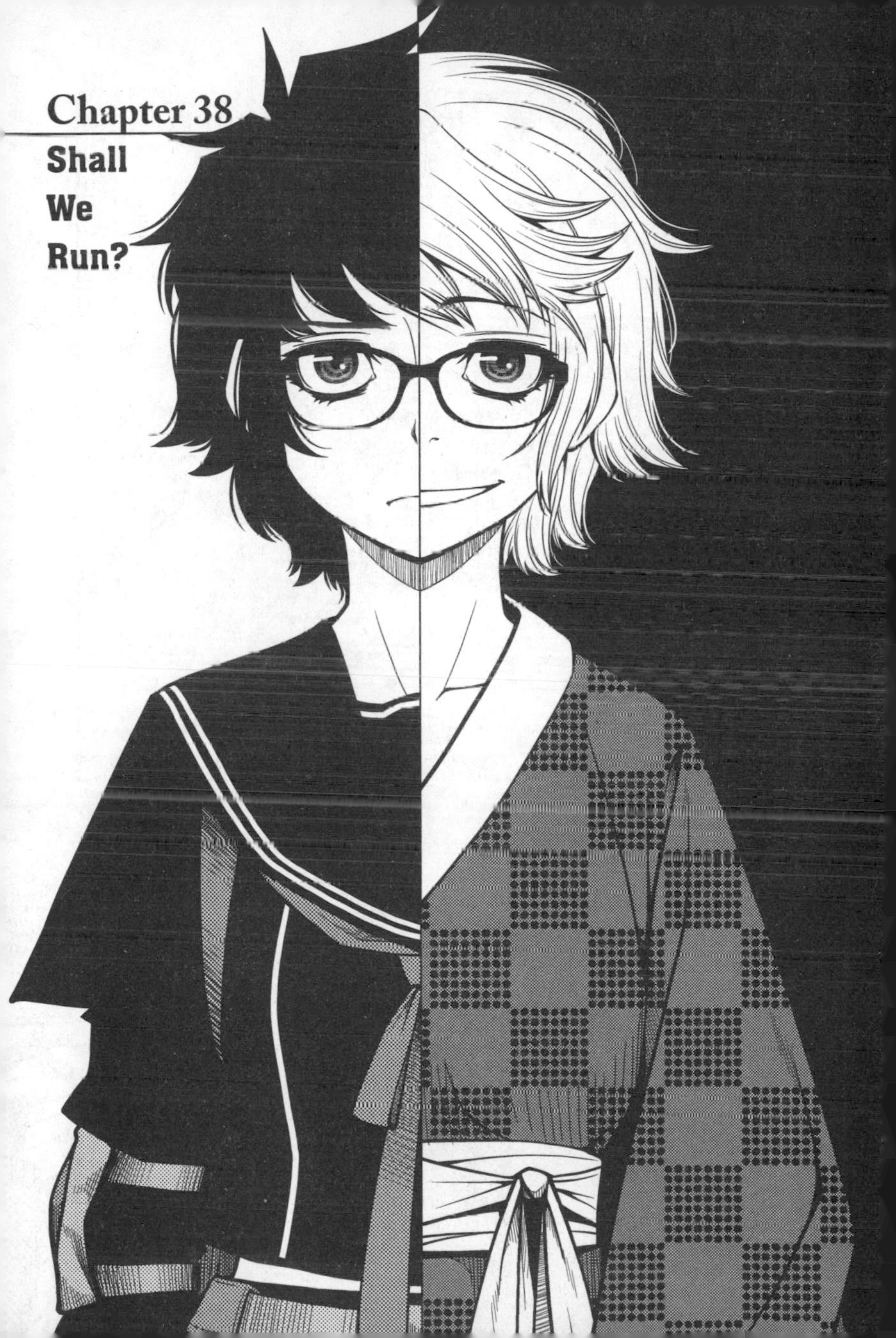
Chapter 38
Shall We Run?

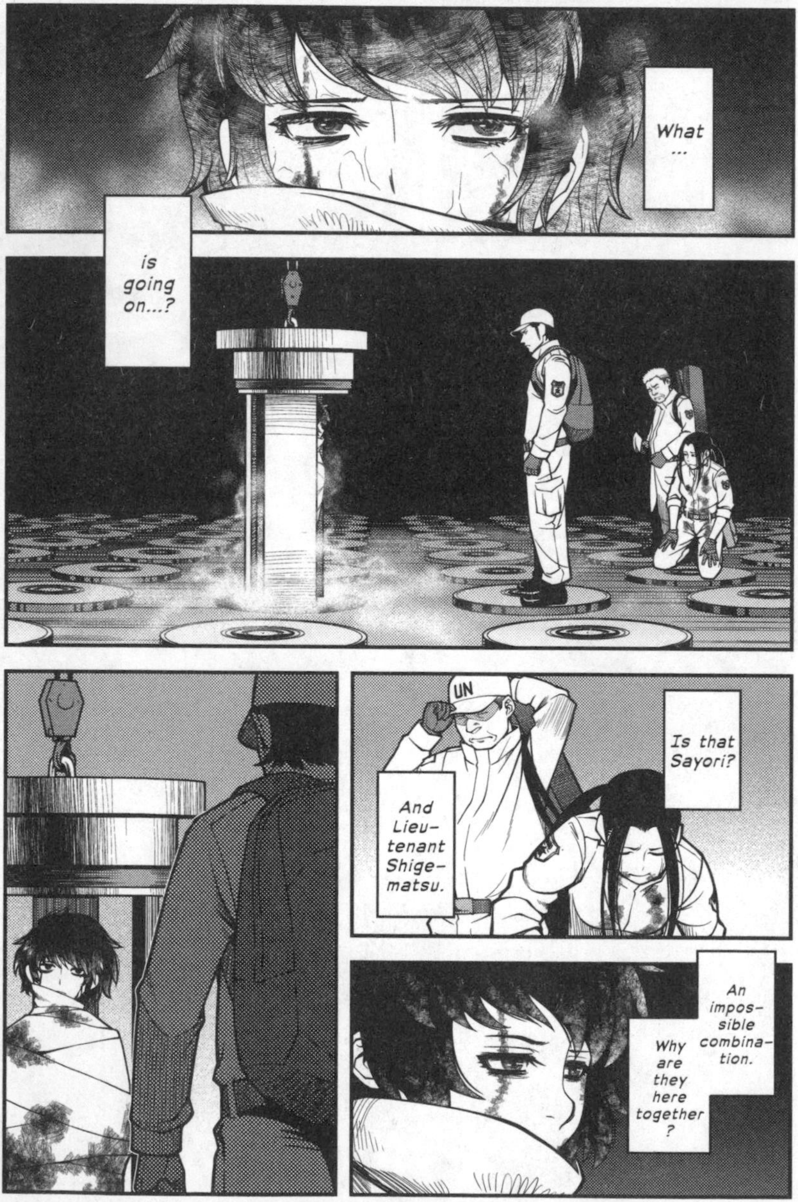
What ...
is going on...?
Is that Sayori?
And Lieutenant Shigematsu.
An impossible combination.
Why are they here together?

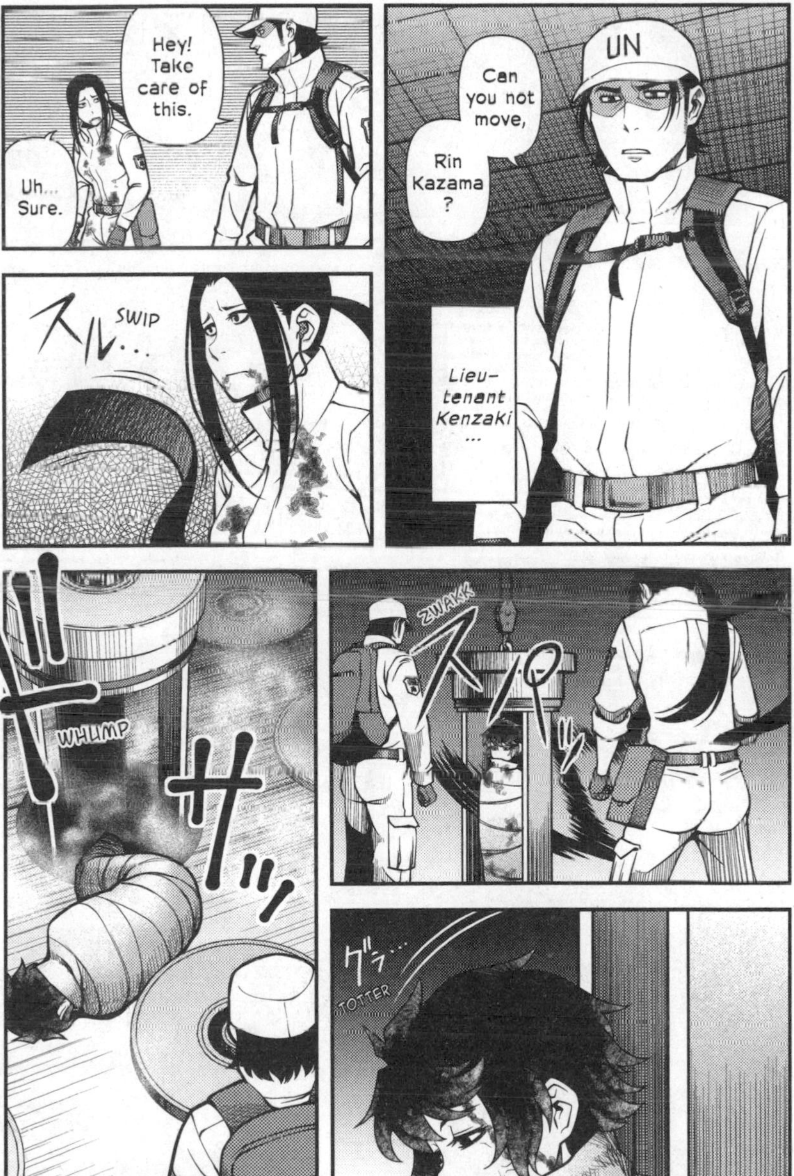
Can you not move, Rin Kazama?
Lieu-tenant Kenzaki ...
Hey! Take care of this.
Uh... Sure.
スル…
SWIP
スパッ
ZWAKK
グラ…
TOTTER
ドサッ
WHUMP

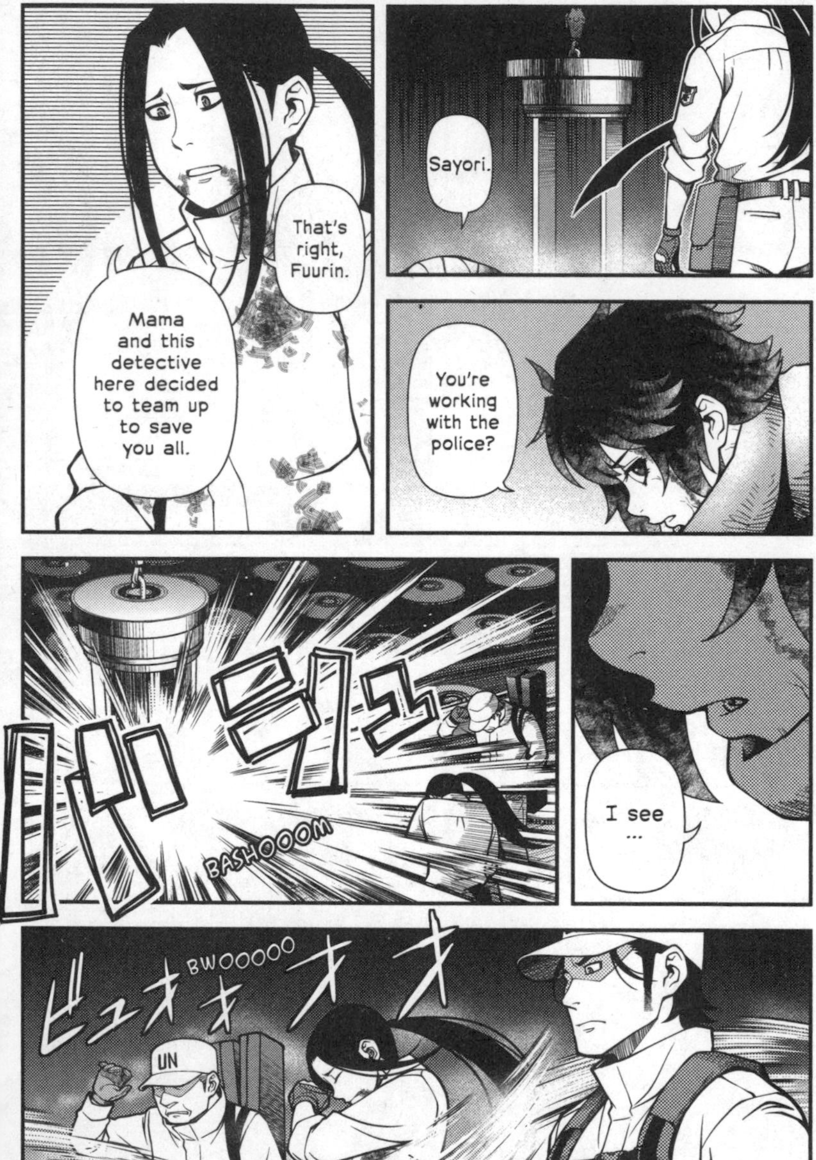

Sayori.
You're working with the police?
That's right, Fuurin.
Mama and this detective here decided to team up to save you all.
I see ...
BASHOOOM
BWOOOOO

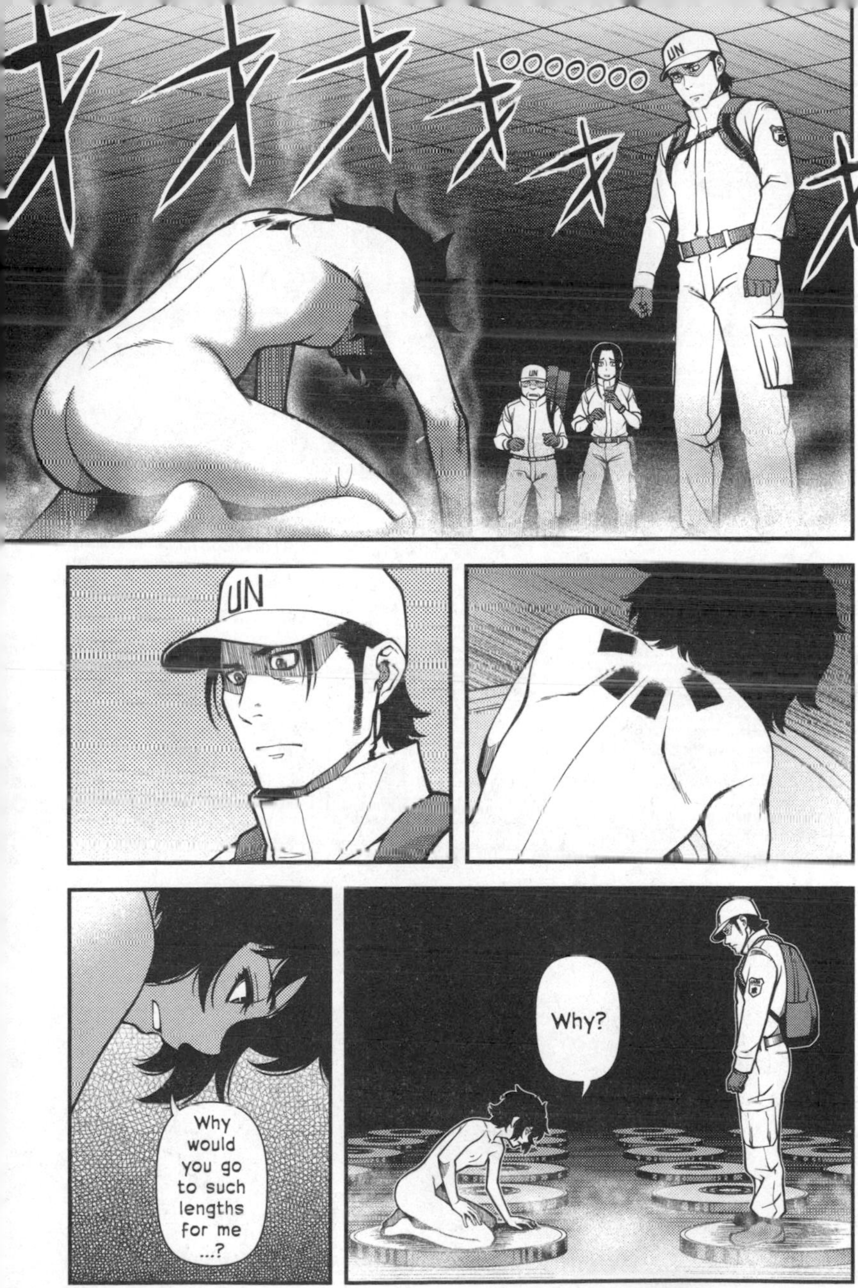
OOOOOOO
Why?
Why would you go to such lengths for me ...?

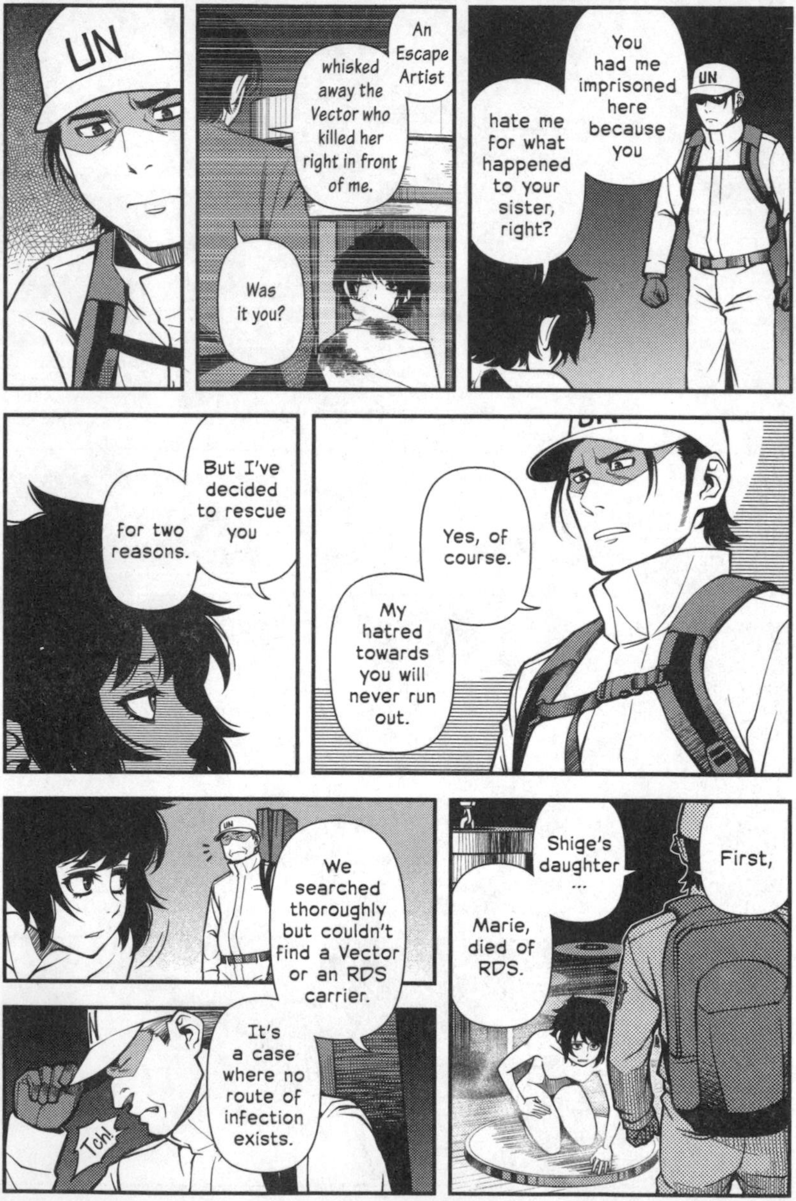
You had me imprisoned here because you
hate me for what happened to your sister, right?
An Escape Artist
whisked away the Vector who killed her right in front of me.
Was it you?
Yes, of course.
My hatred towards you will never run out.
But I've decided to rescue you
for two reasons.
First,
Shige's daughter ...
Marie, died of RDS.
We searched thoroughly but couldn't find a Vector or an RDS carrier.
It's a case where no route of infection exists.
Tch!

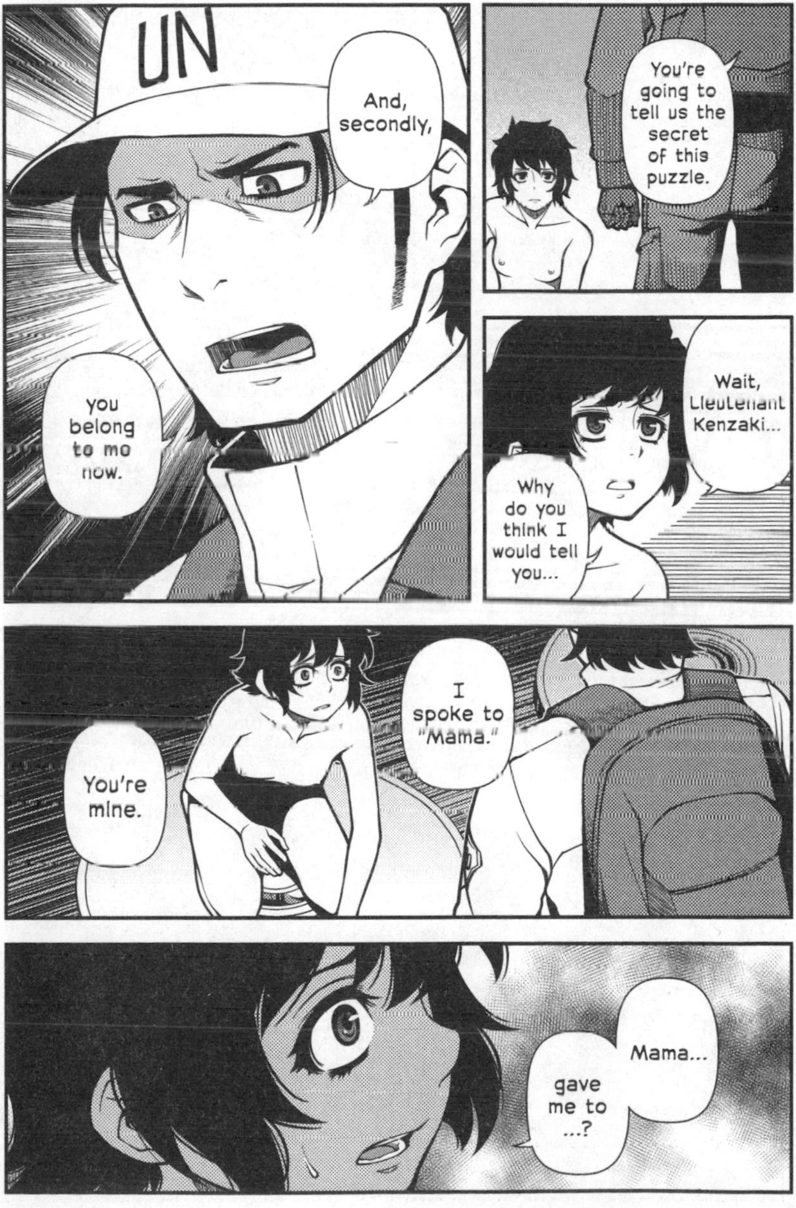

You're going to tell us the secret of this puzzle.
Wait, Lieutenant Kenzaki...
Why do you think I would tell you...
And, secondly,
you belong to me now.
I spoke to "Mama."
You're mine.
Mama...
gave me to ...?

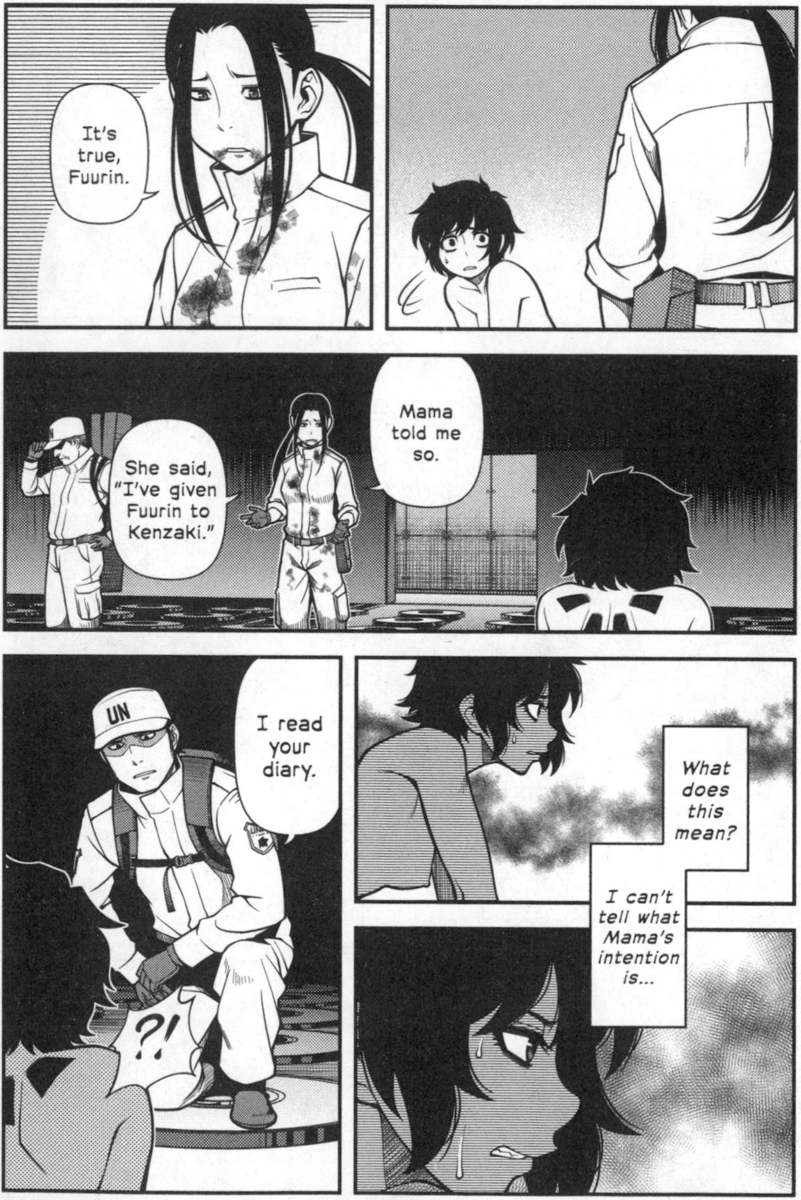
It's true, Fuurin.
Mama told me so.
She said, "I've given Fuurin to Kenzaki."
What does this mean?
I can't tell what Mama's intention is...
I read your diary.
?!

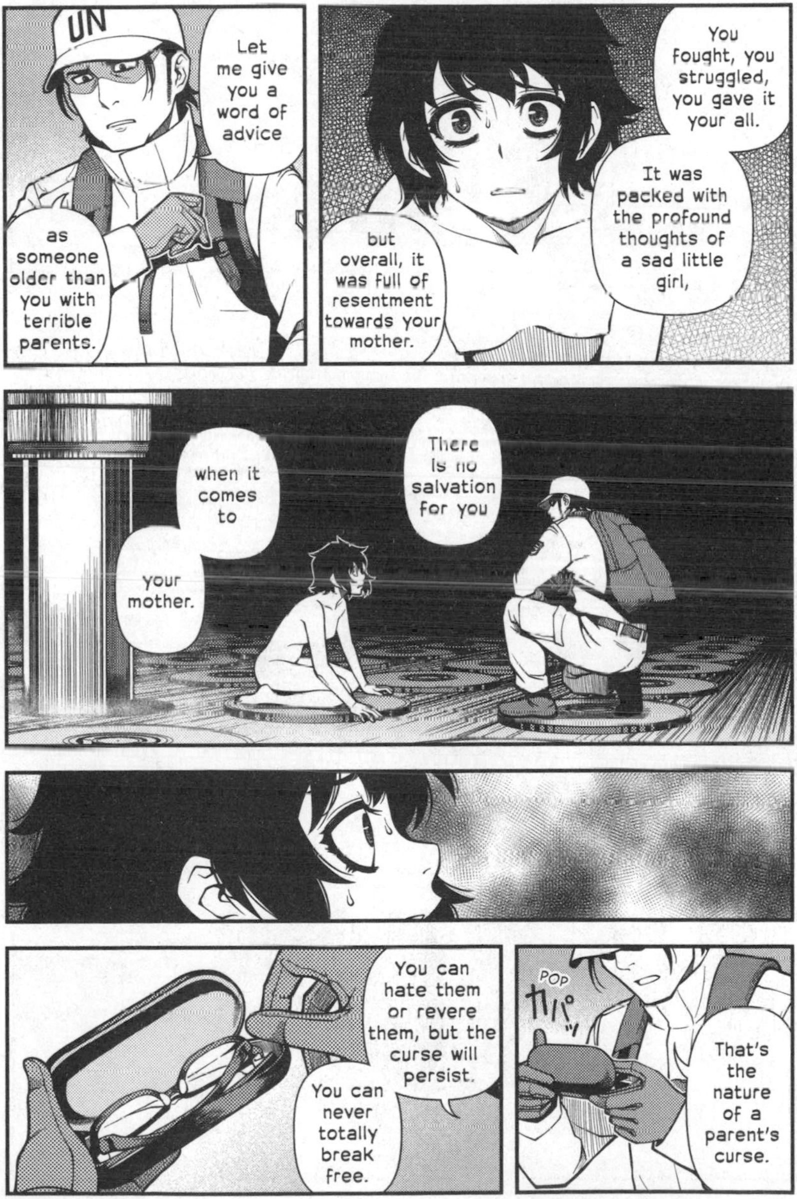
You fought, you struggled, you gave it your all.
It was packed with the profound thoughts of a sad little girl,
but overall, it was full of resentment towards your mother.
Let me give you a word of advice
as someone older than you with terrible parents.
There is no salvation for you
when it comes to
your mother.
POP
カパッ
That's the nature of a parent's curse.
You can hate them or revere them, but the curse will persist.
You can never totally break free.

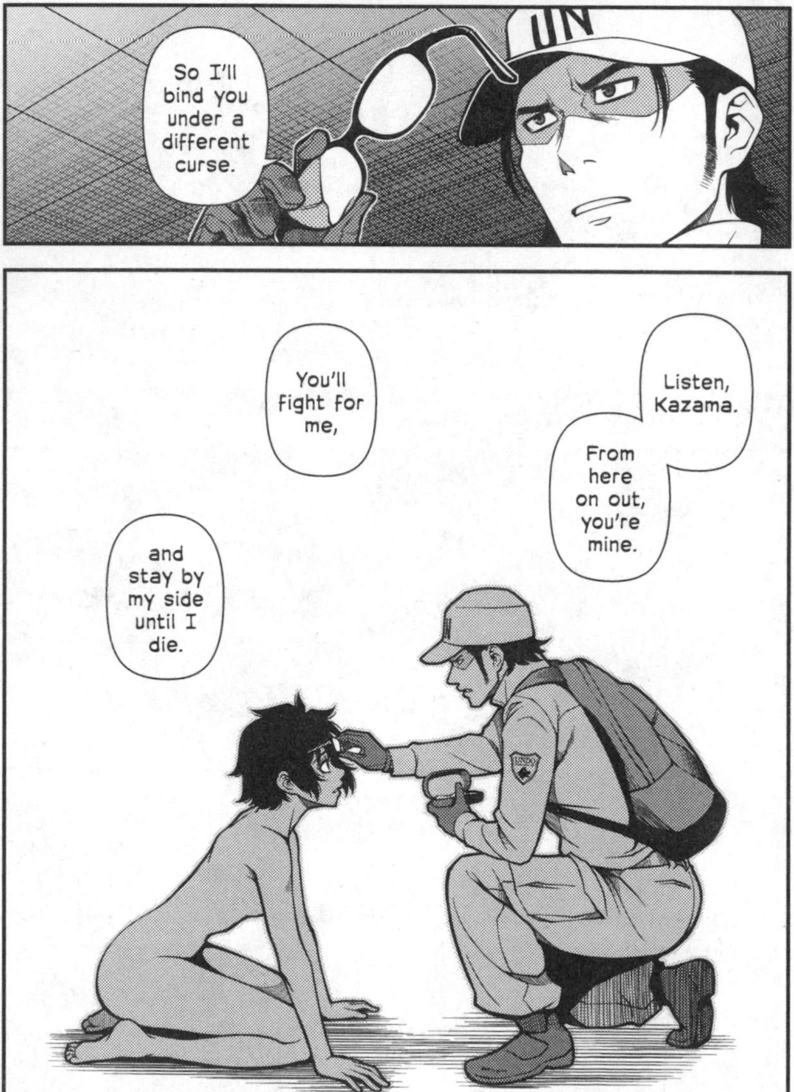
So I'll bind you under a different curse.
Listen, Kazama.
From here on out, you're mine.
You'll fight for me,
and stay by my side until I die.

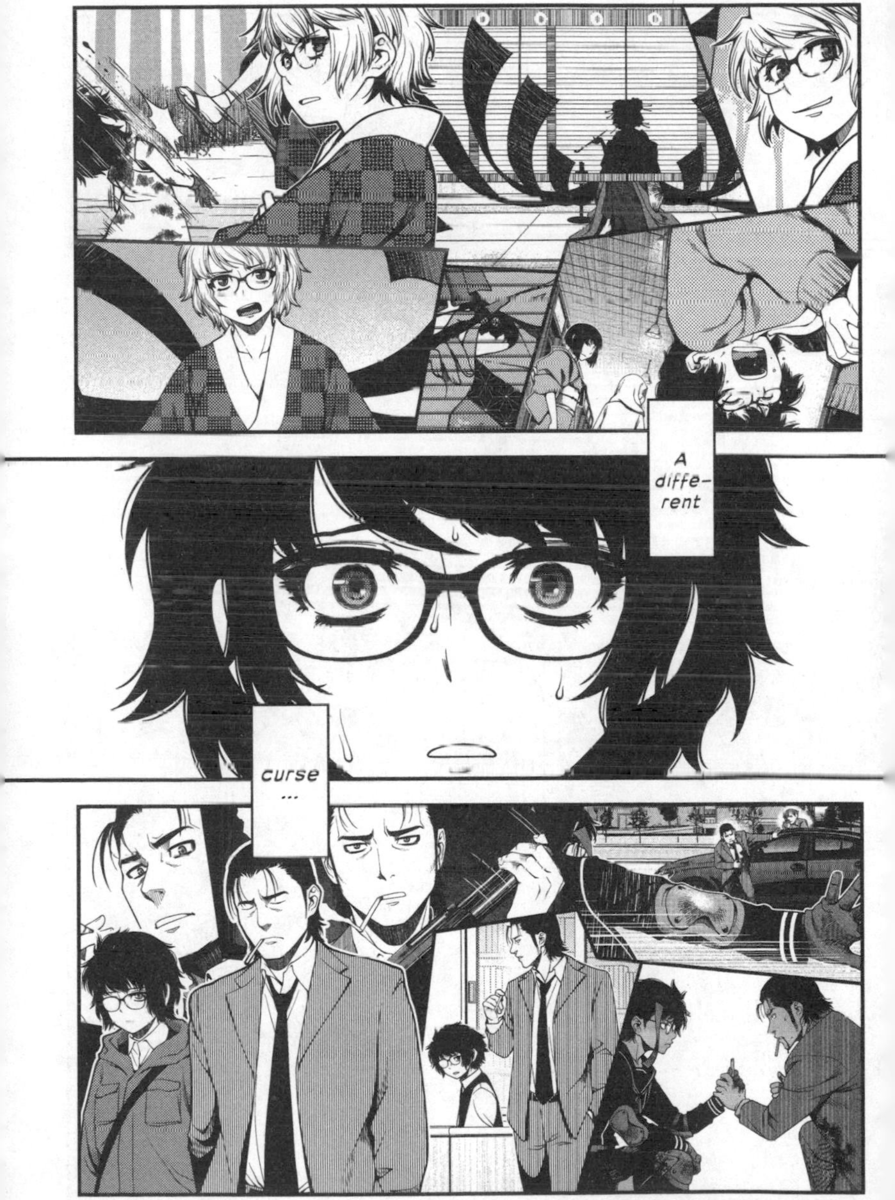
A diffe-rent
curse ...

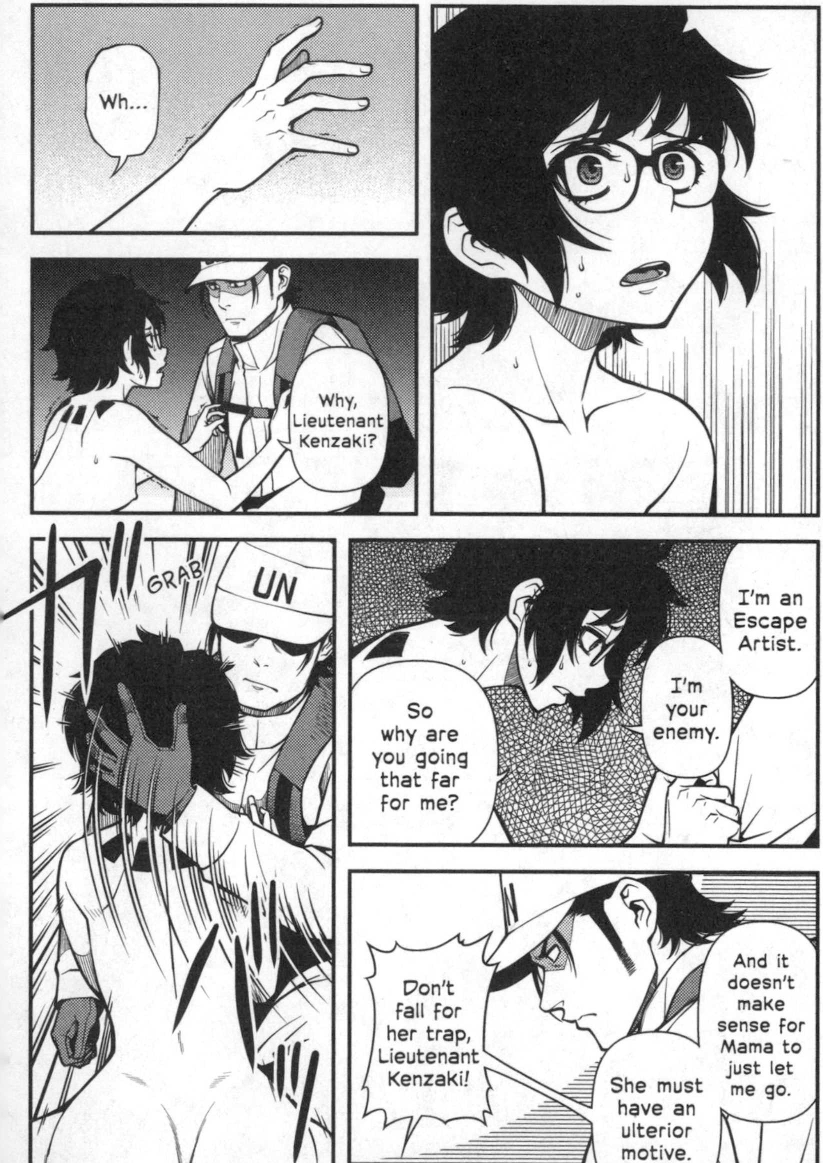
Wh...
Why, Lieutenant Kenzaki?
I'm an Escape Artist.
I'm your enemy.
So why are you going that far for me?
And it doesn't make sense for Mama to just let me go.
She must have an ulterior motive.
Don't fall for her trap, Lieutenant Kenzaki!
GRAB
UN

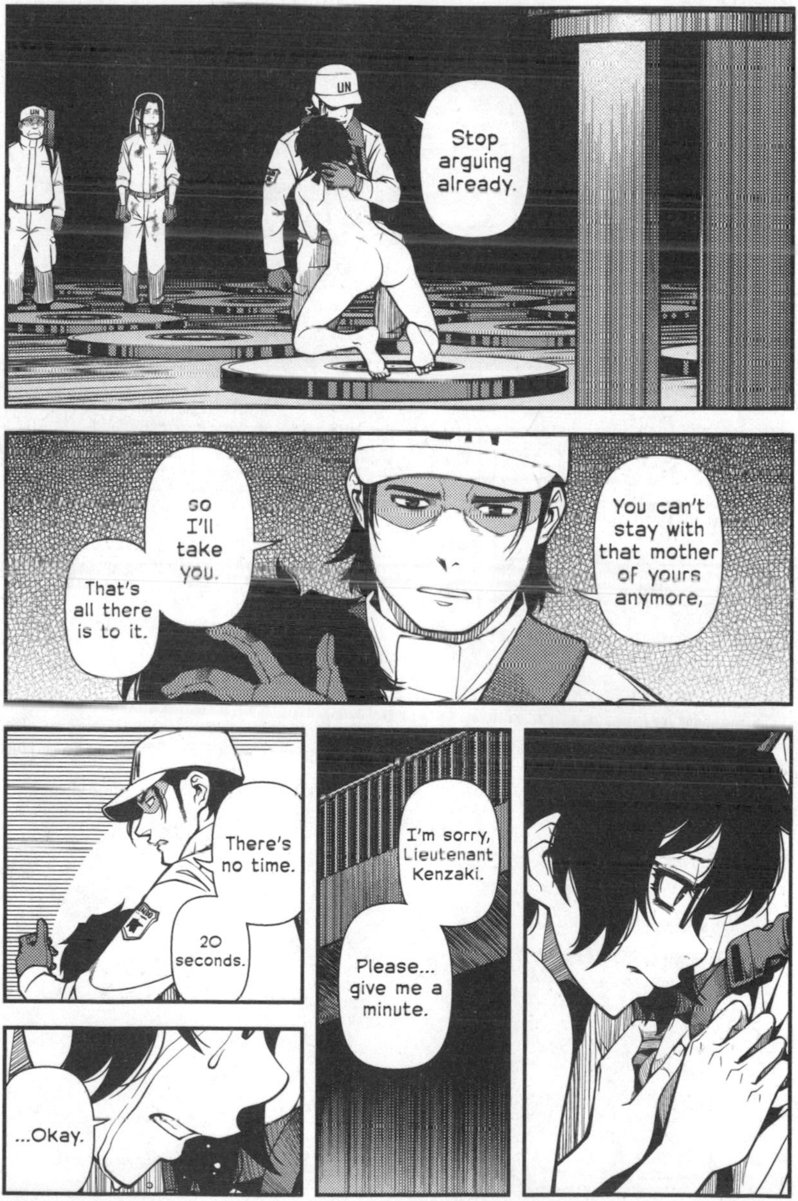
Stop arguing already.
You can't stay with that mother of yours anymore,
so I'll take you.
That's all there is to it.
I'm sorry, Lieutenant Kenzaki.
Please... give me a minute.
There's no time.
20 seconds.
...Okay.

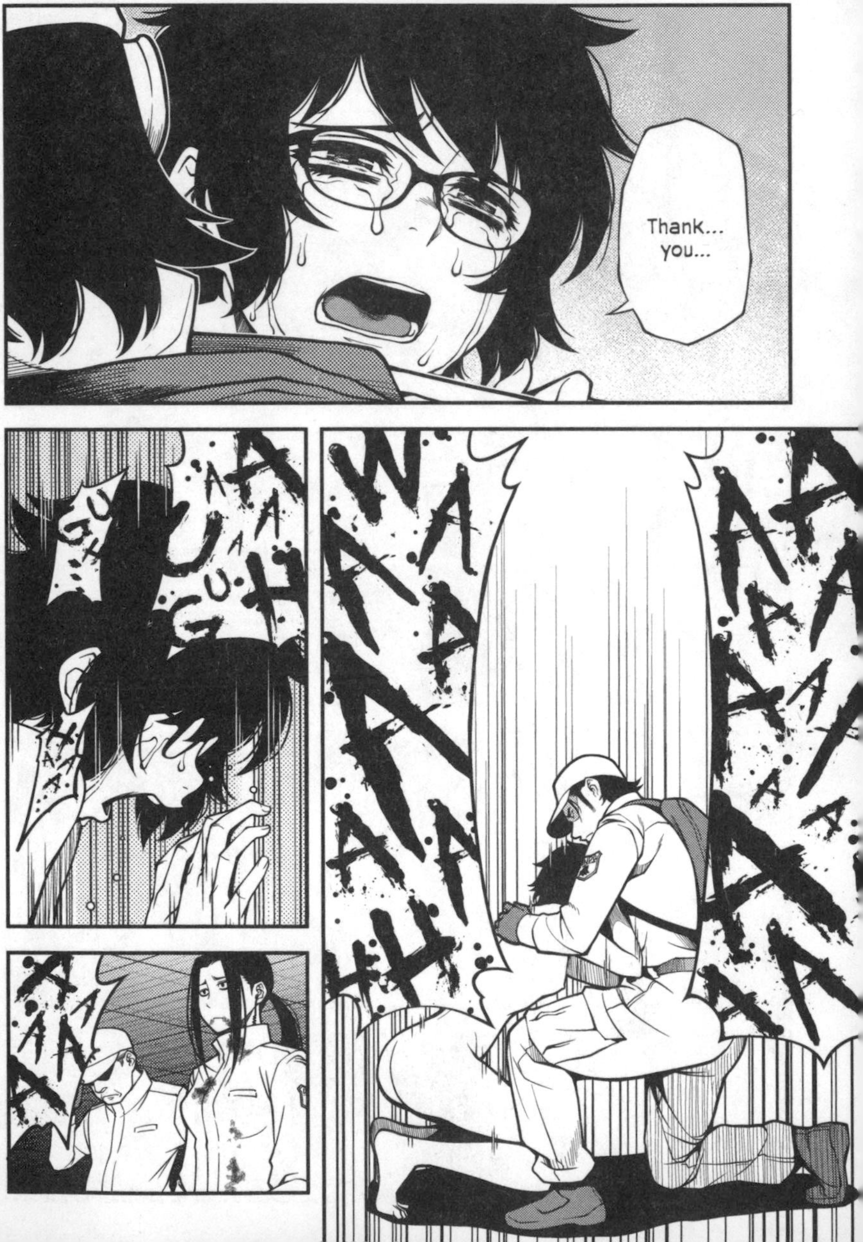
Thank... you...

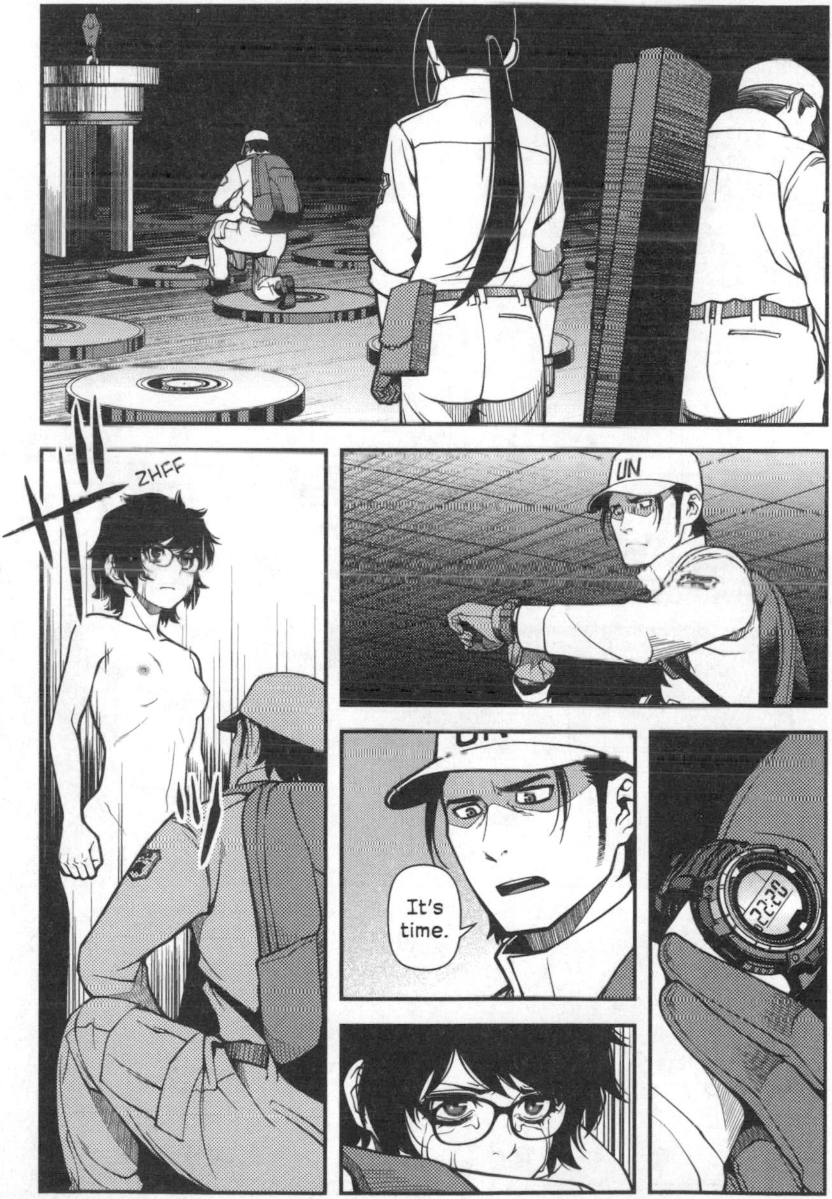
It's time.
ZHFF

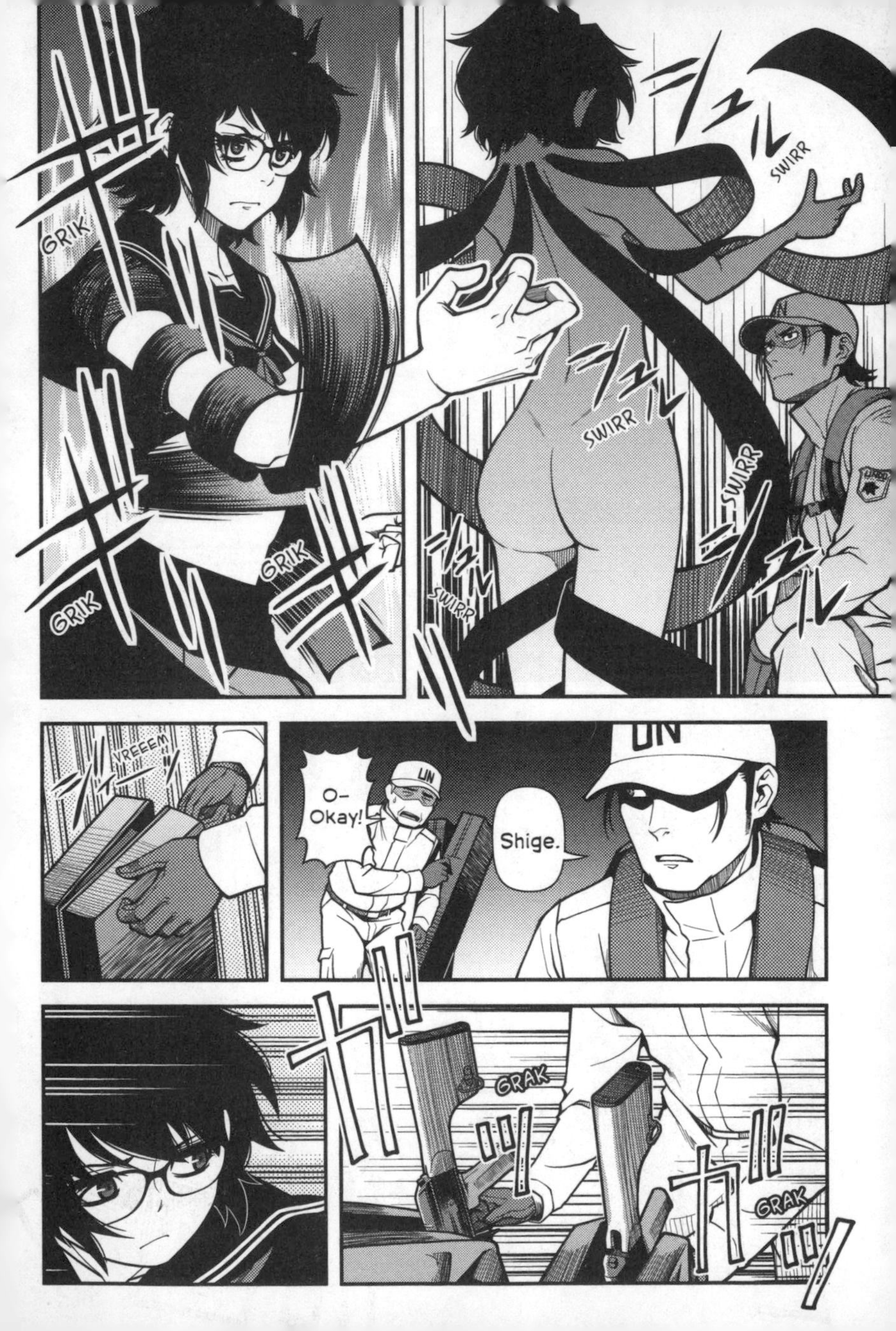
SWIRR
SWIRR
SWIRR
SWIRR
GRIK
GRIK
GRIK
Shige.
O-Okay!
VREEEM
GRAK
GRAK

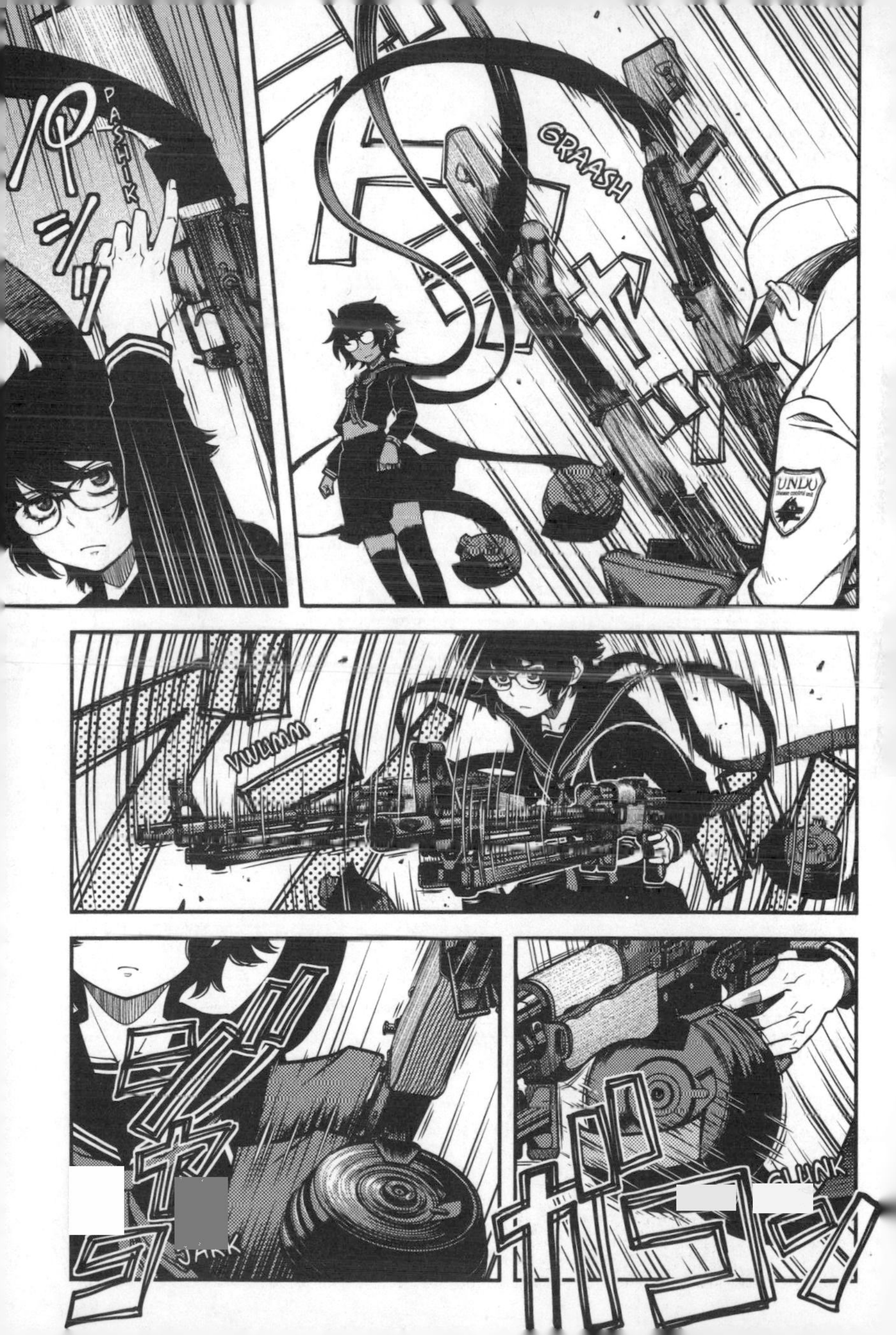
GRAASH
PASHIK
VWUMM
CLUNK

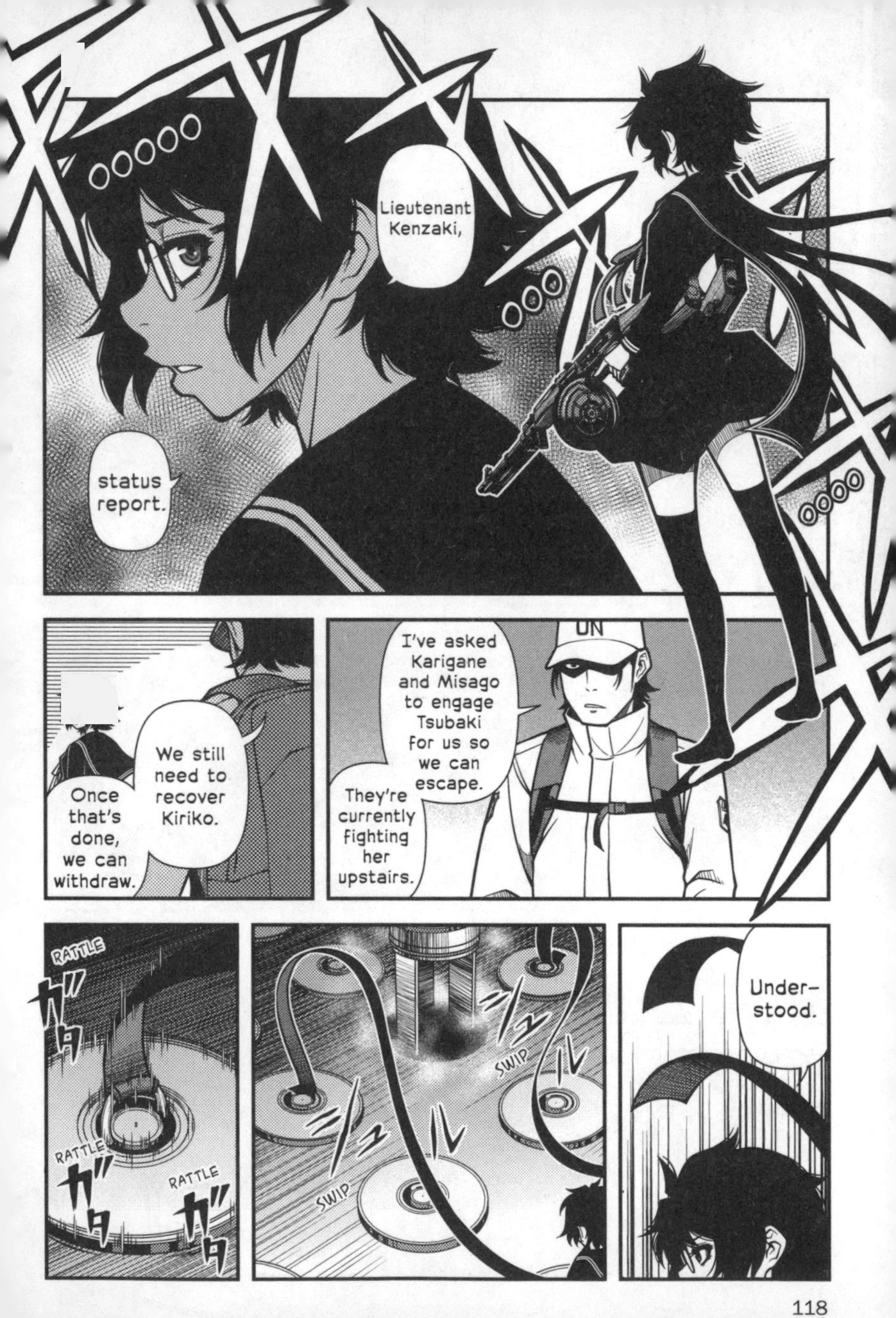

Lieutenant Kenzaki,
status report.
I've asked Karigane and Misago to engage Tsubaki for us so we can escape.
They're currently fighting her upstairs.
We still need to recover Kiriko.
Once that's done, we can withdraw.
Under-stood.
シュル
SWIP
シュル
SWIP
RATTLE
ガタ
RATTLE
ガタ
RATTLE
ガタ

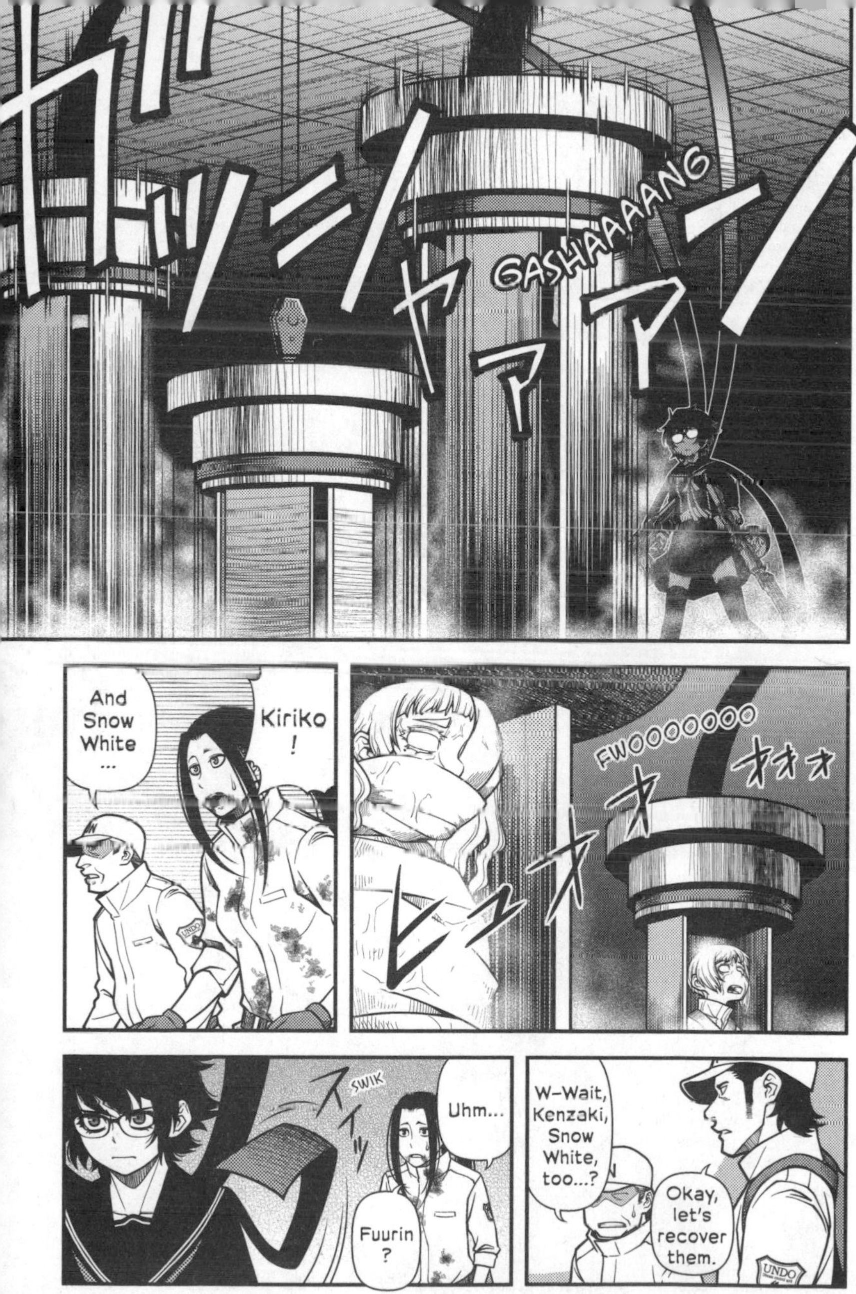
GASHAAAANG
FWOOOOOOO
Kiriko!
And Snow White...
W-Wait, Kenzaki, Snow White, too...?
Okay, let's recover them.
SWIK
Uhm...
Fuurin?

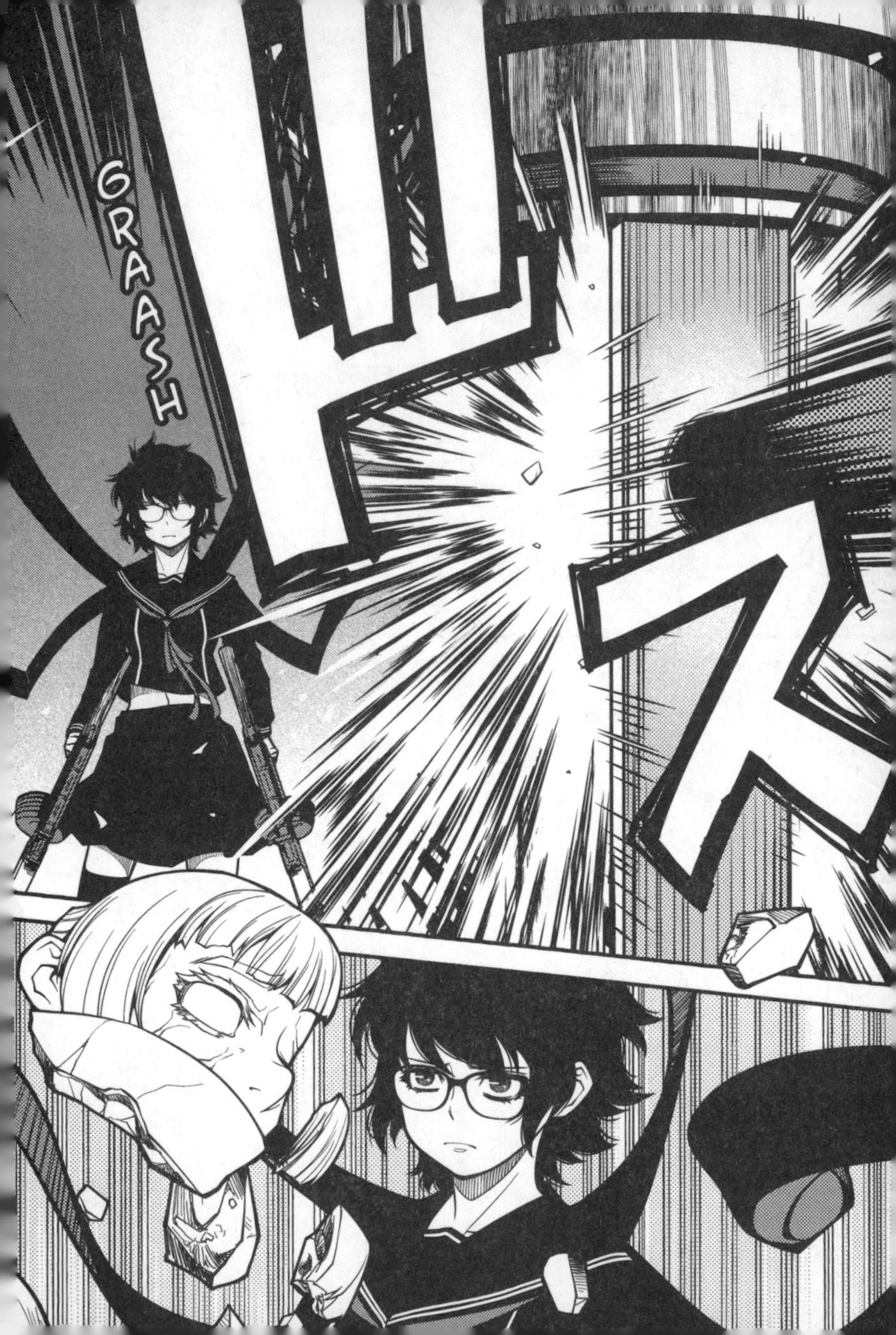
GRAASH

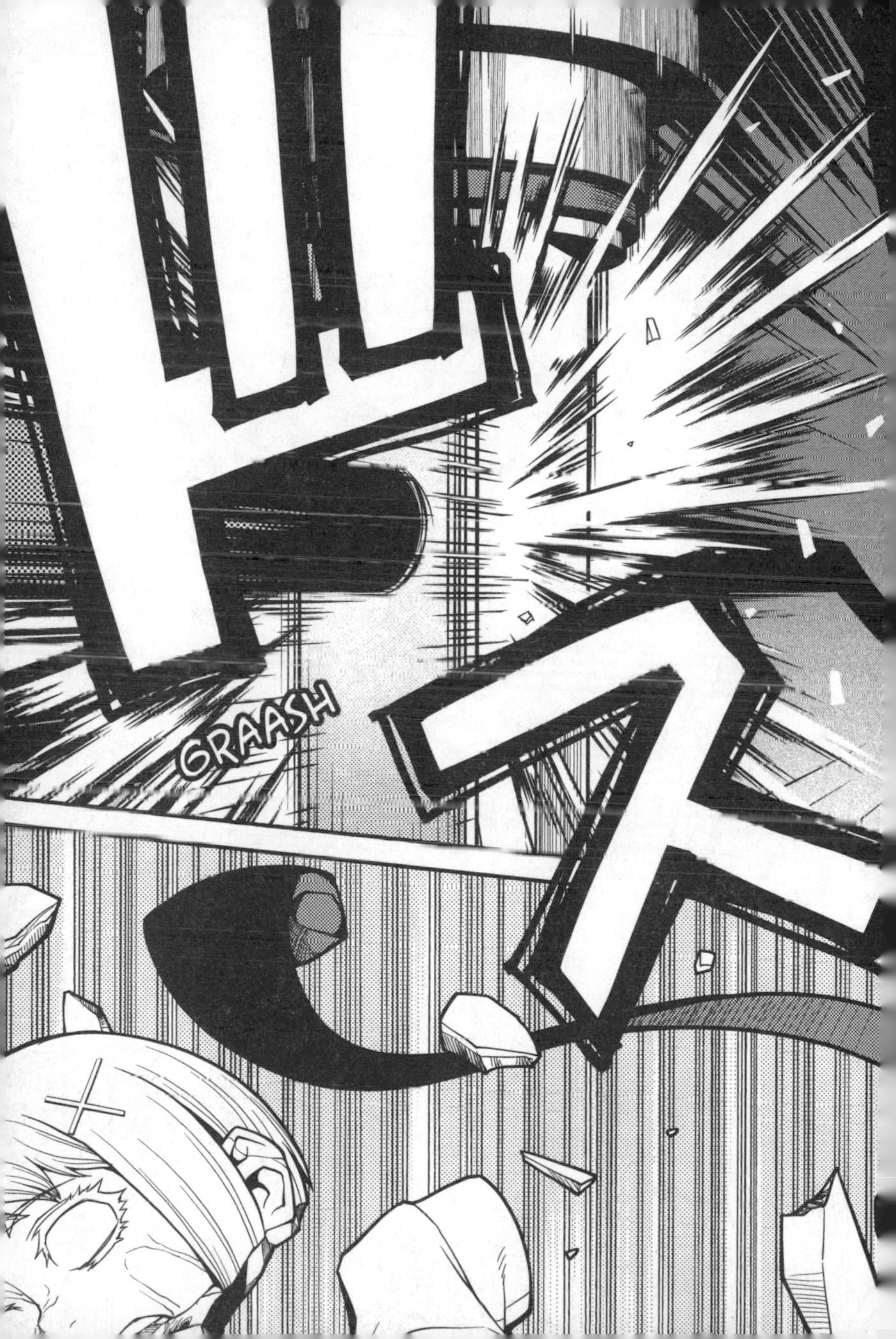
GRAASH

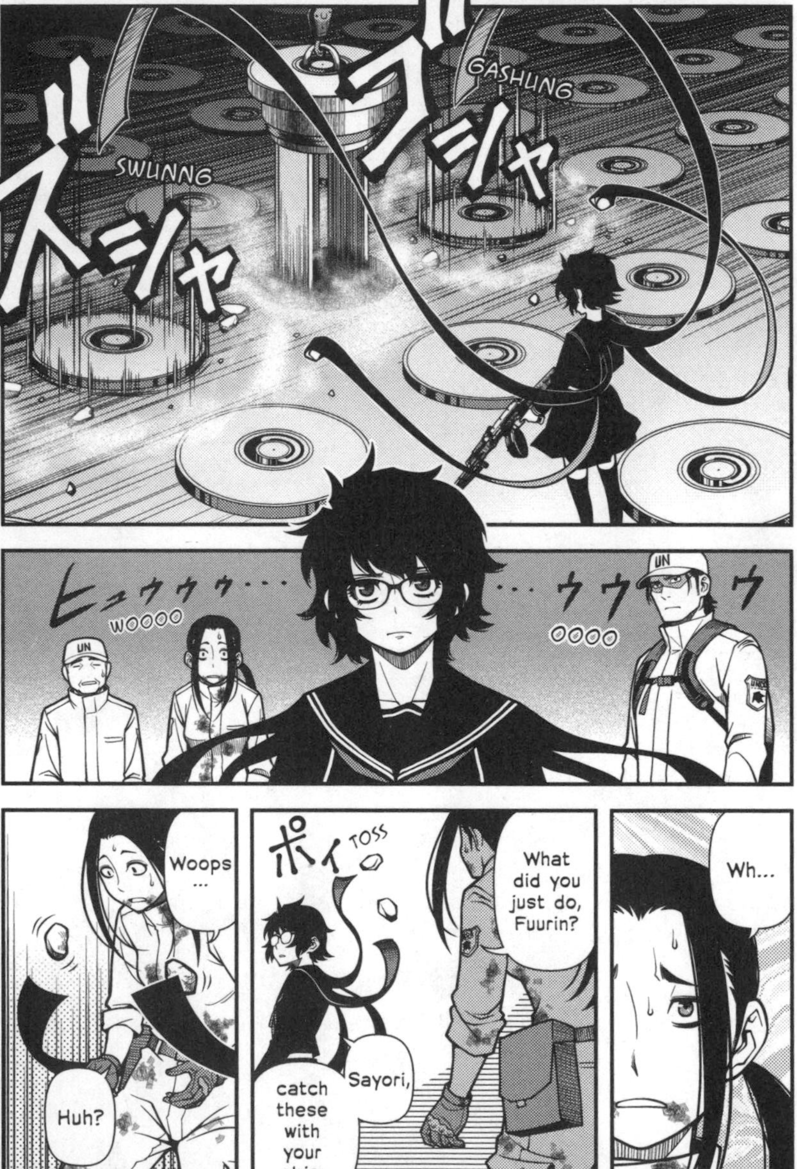

ゴシャ
GASHUNG
ズシャ
SWUNNG
ヒュウウウ…
WOOOO
…ウウウ
OOOO
Wh...
What did you just do, Fuurin?
ポイ
TOSS
Sayori,
catch these with your obis.
Woops ...
Huh?

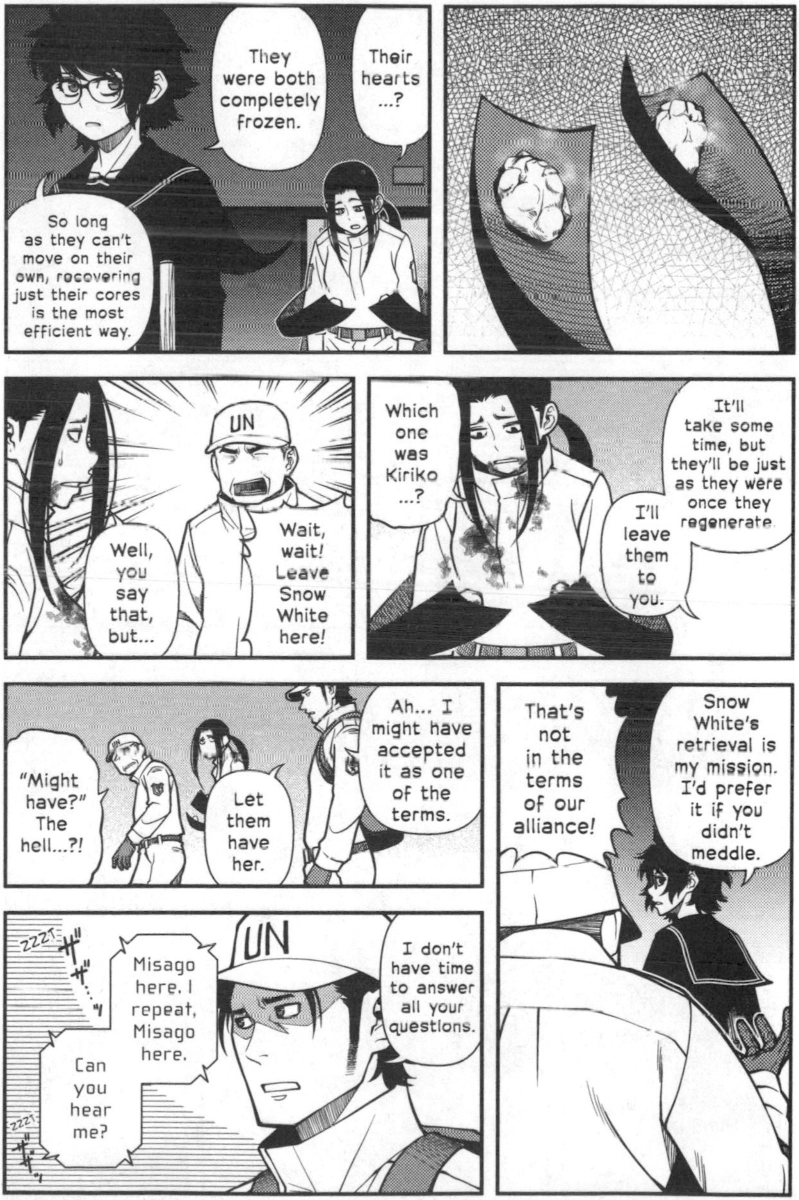
Their hearts ...?
They were both completely frozen.
So long as they can't move on their own, recovering just their cores is the most efficient way.
It'll take some time, but they'll be just as they were once they regenerate.
Which one was Kiriko ...?
I'll leave them to you.
Wait, wait! Leave Snow White here!
Well, you say that, but...
Snow White's retrieval is my mission. I'd prefer it if you didn't meddle.
That's not in the terms of our alliance!
Ah... I might have accepted it as one of the terms.
Let them have her.
"Might have?" The hell...?!
I don't have time to answer all your questions.
Misago here. I repeat, Misago here.
Can you hear me?
ZZZT
ZZZT

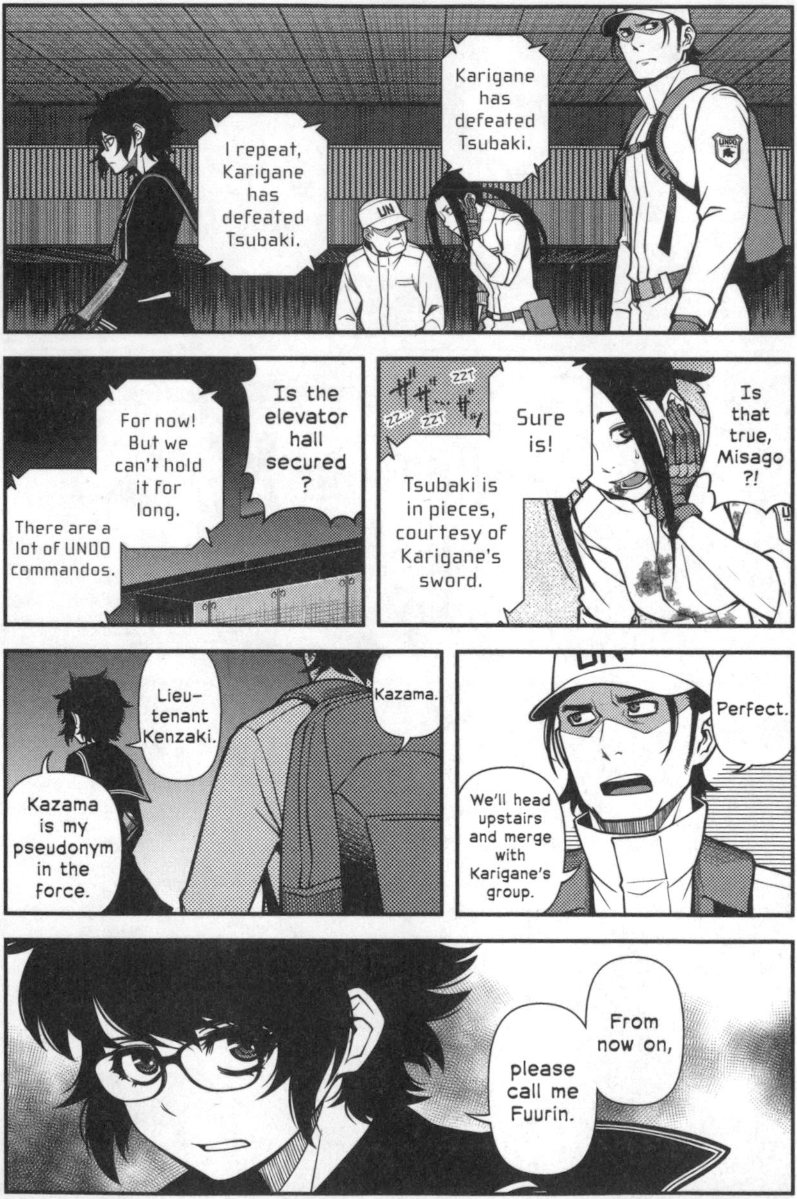
Karigane has defeated Tsubaki.
I repeat, Karigane has defeated Tsubaki.
Is that true, Misago ?!
ZZT
ZZT
ZZ...
Sure is!
Tsubaki is in pieces, courtesy of Karigane's sword.
Is the elevator hall secured ?
For now! But we can't hold it for long.
There are a lot of UNDO commandos.
Perfect.
We'll head upstairs and merge with Karigane's group.
Kazama.
Lieu-tenant Kenzaki.
Kazama is my pseudonym in the force.
From now on,
please call me Fuurin.

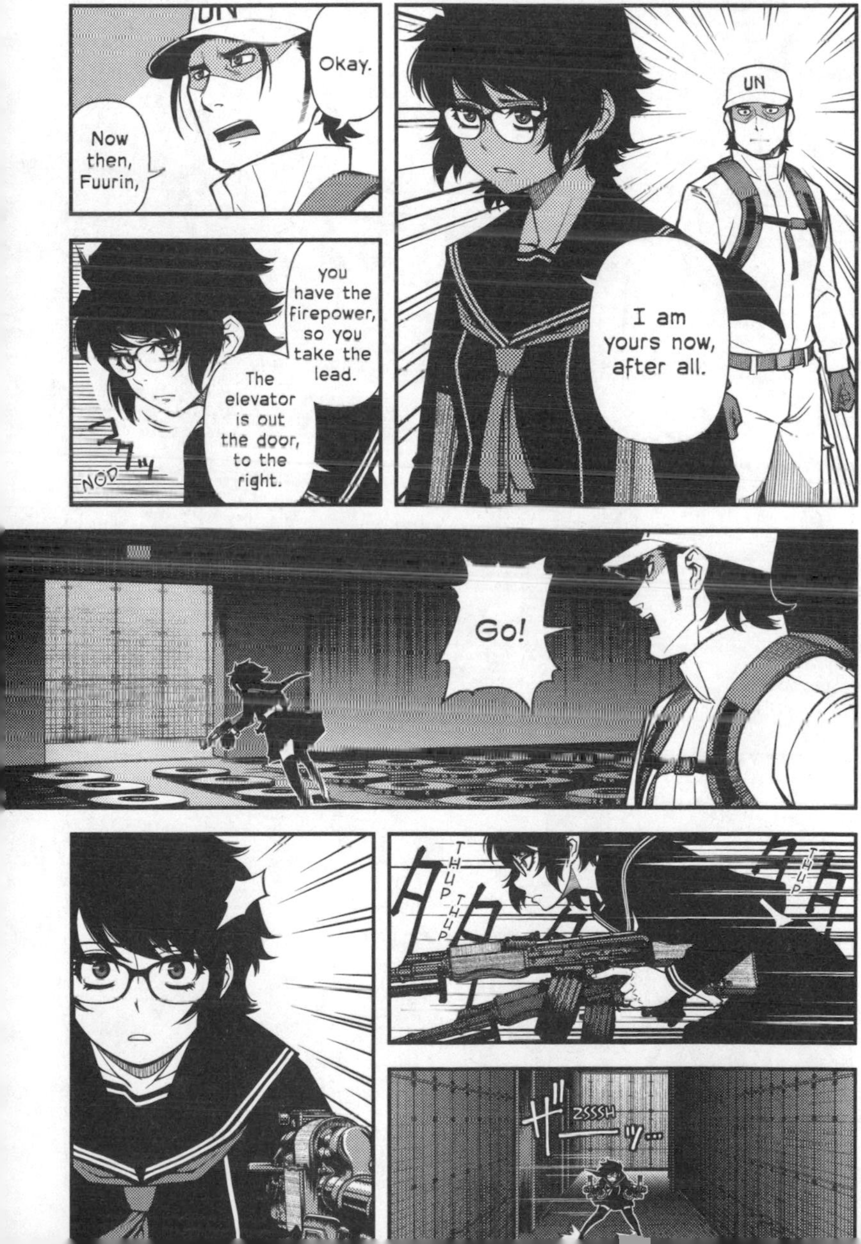
I am yours now, after all.
Okay.
Now then, Fuurin,
you have the firepower, so you take the lead.
The elevator is out the door, to the right.
NOD
Go!
THUP
THUP
THUP
ZSSSH

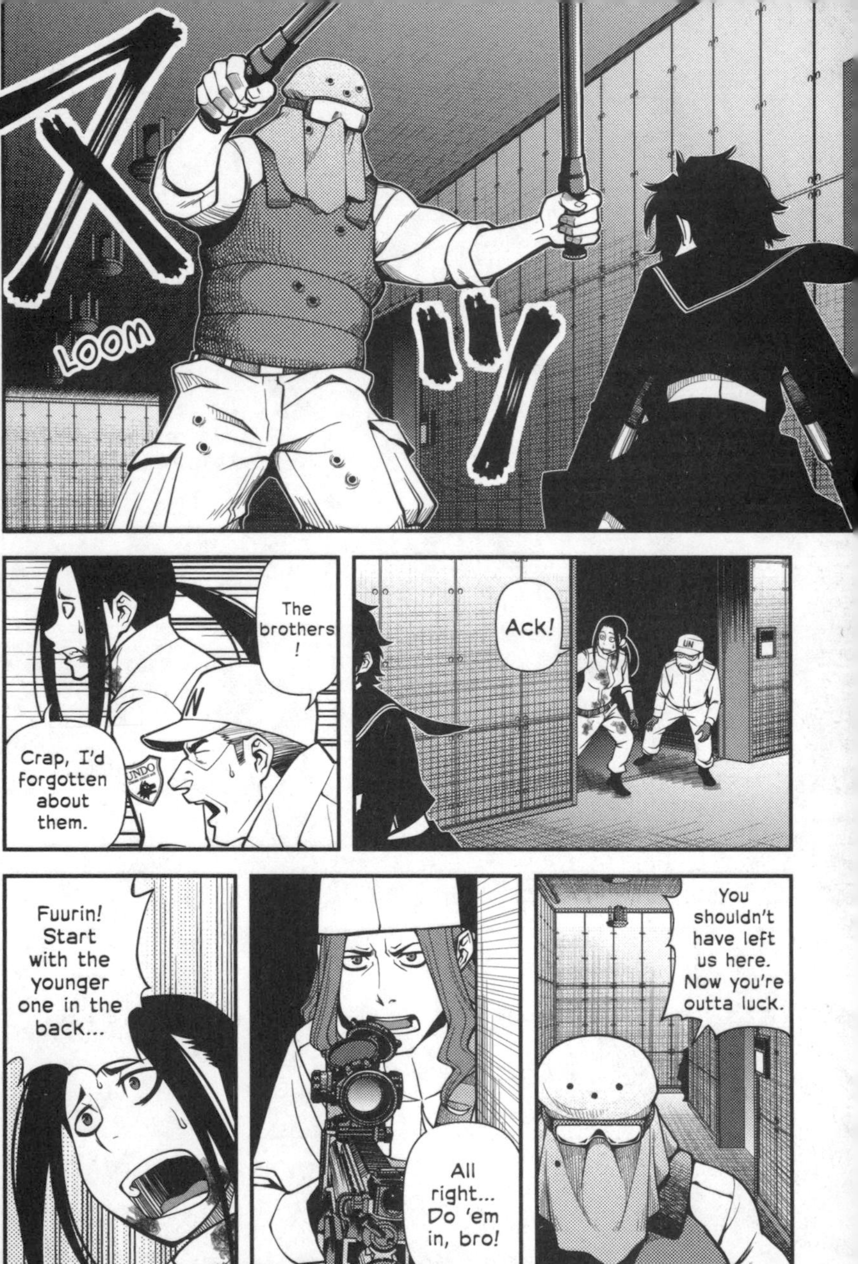
LOOM
Ack!
The brothers!
Crap, I'd forgotten about them.
You shouldn't have left us here. Now you're outta luck.
All right... Do 'em in, bro!
Fuurin! Start with the younger one in the back...

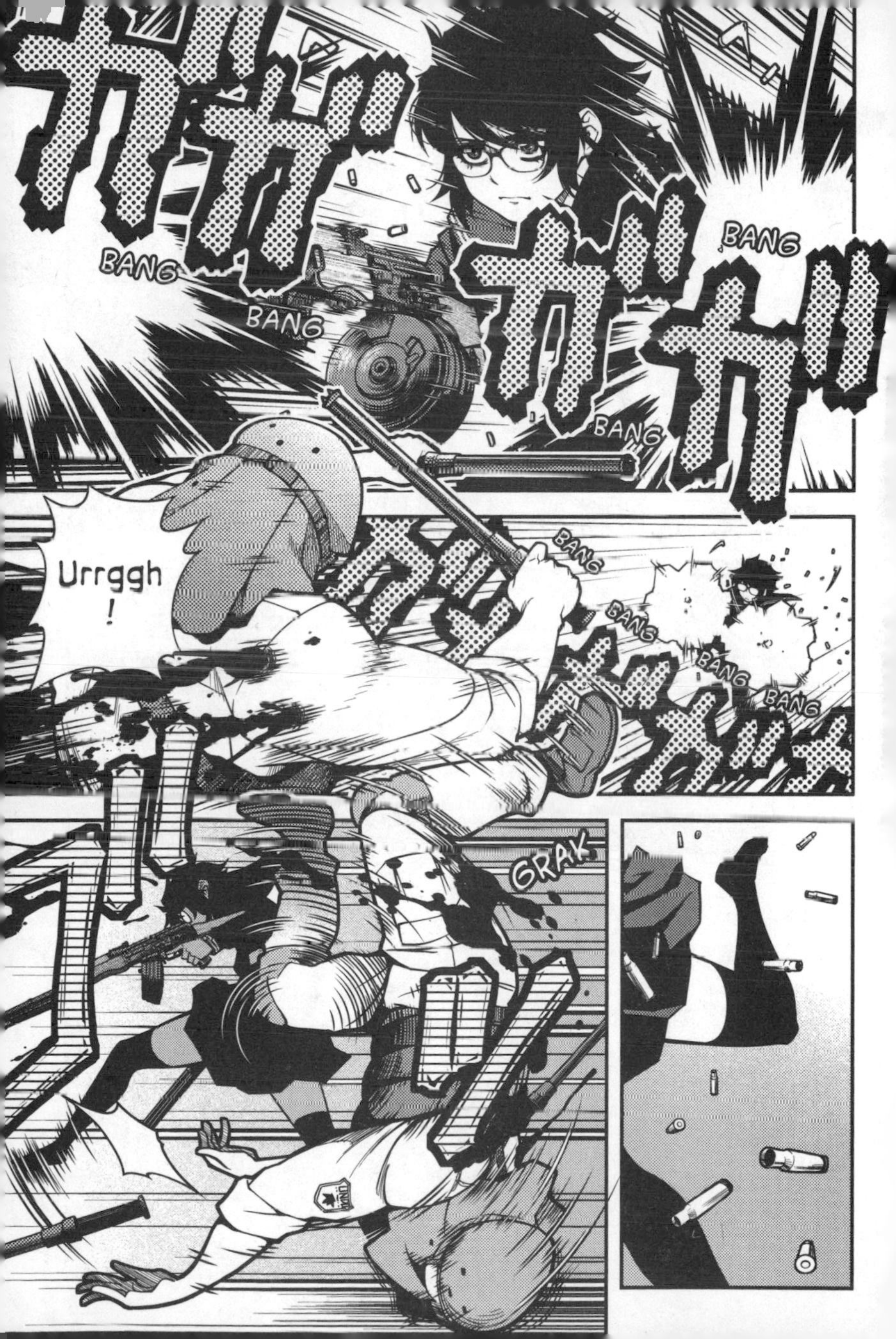
BANG
BANG
BANG
BANG
BANG
BANG
BANG
BANG
Urrggh!
GRAK

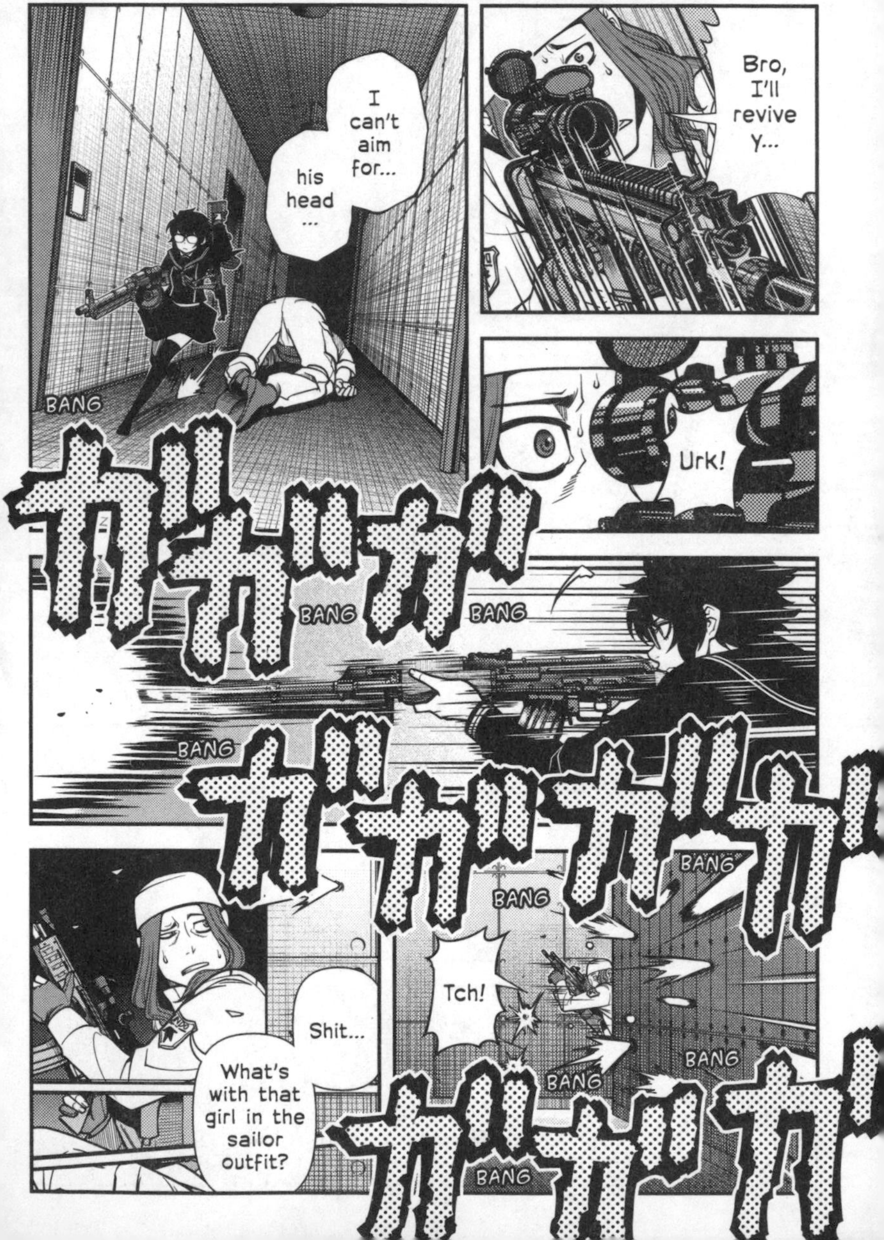
Bro, I'll revive y...
Urk!
I can't aim for... his head ...
BANG
BANG
BANG
BANG
BANG
BANG
Tch!
BANG
BANG
BANG
Shit...
What's with that girl in the sailor outfit?

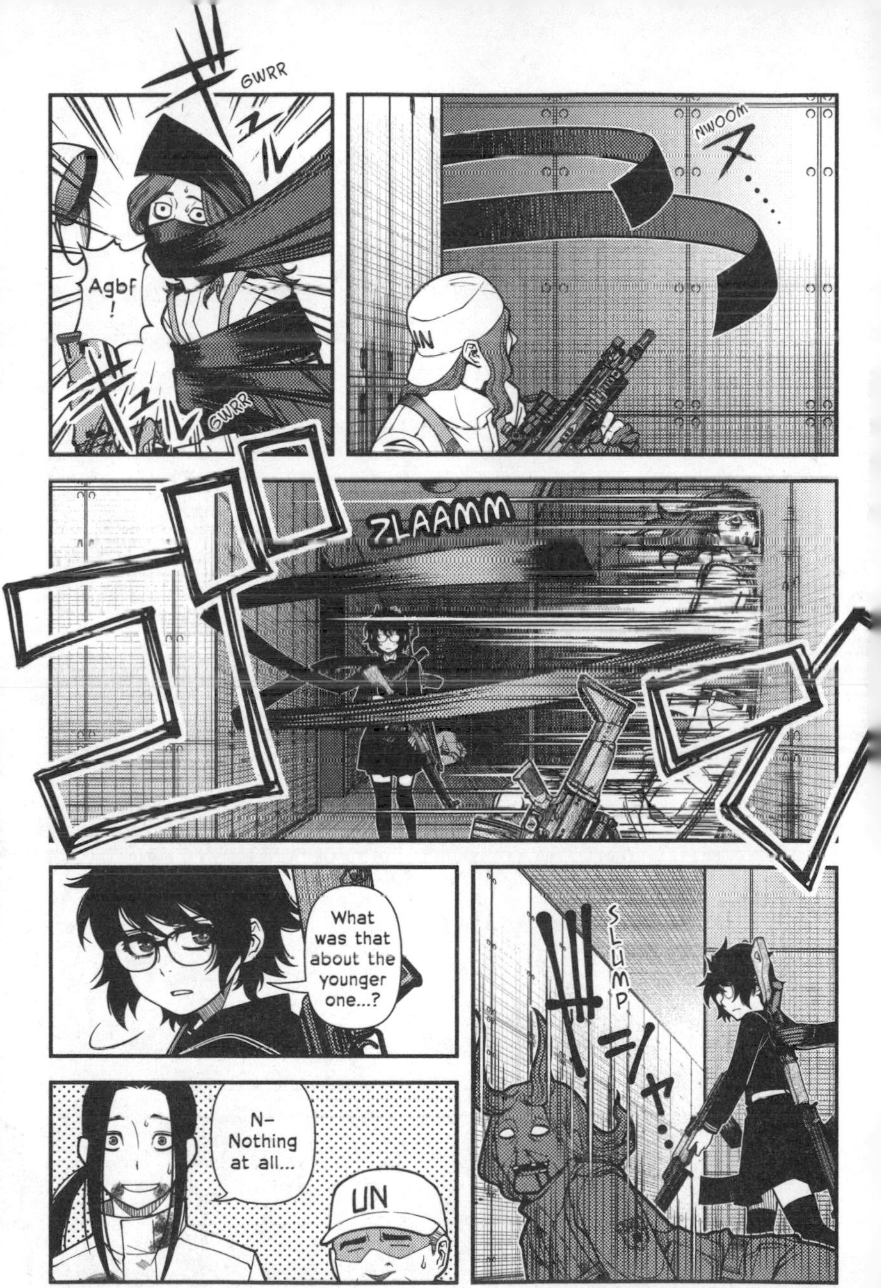
NWOOM
UN
GWRR
Agbf!
GWRR
ZLAAMM
SLUMP
What was that about the younger one...?
N– Nothing at all...
UN

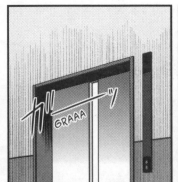GRAAA

First
Floor
Elevator
Hall

ギ—ィ... DING

?!

ZHFF

ZHFF

Yeah.

What a
thorough
job...

130

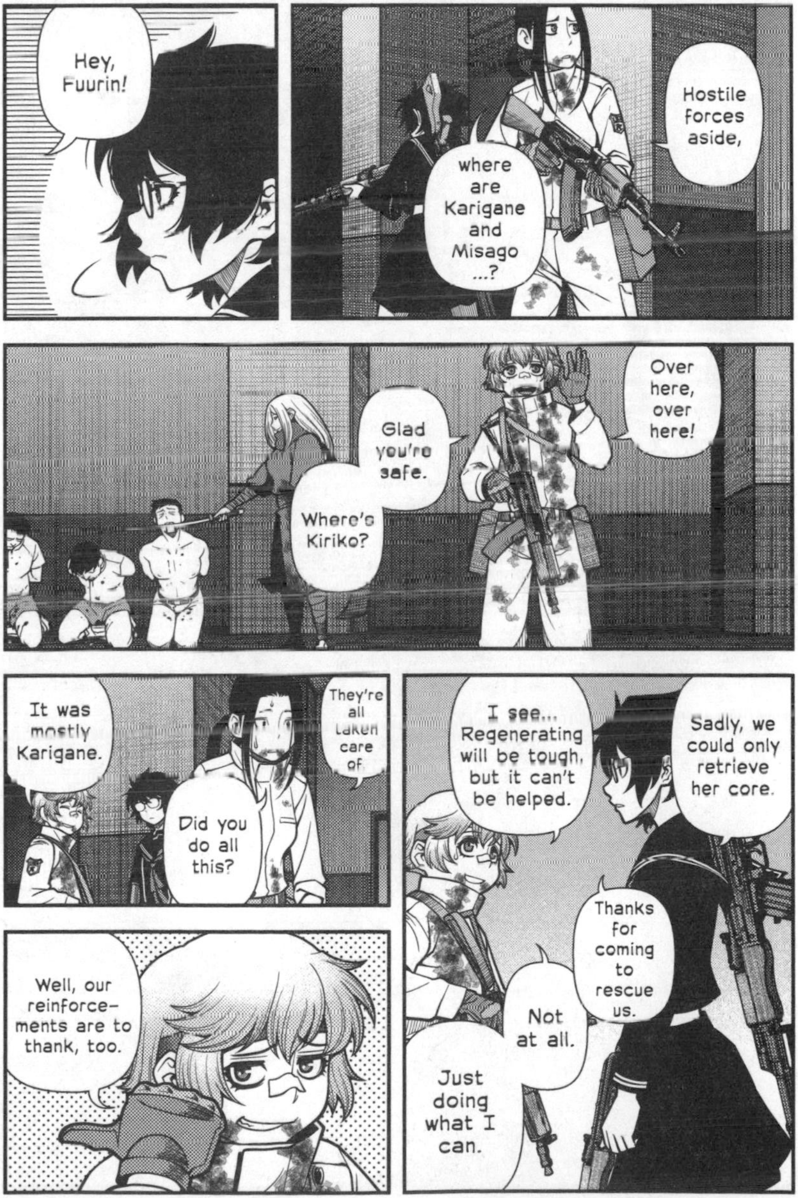
Hostile forces aside,
where are Karigane and Misago ...?
Hey, Fuurin!
Over here, over here!
Glad you're safe.
Where's Kiriko?
Sadly, we could only retrieve her core.
I see... Regenerating will be tough, but it can't be helped.
Thanks for coming to rescue us.
Not at all.
Just doing what I can.
They're all taken care of.
Did you do all this?
It was mostly Karigane.
Well, our reinforcements are to thank, too.

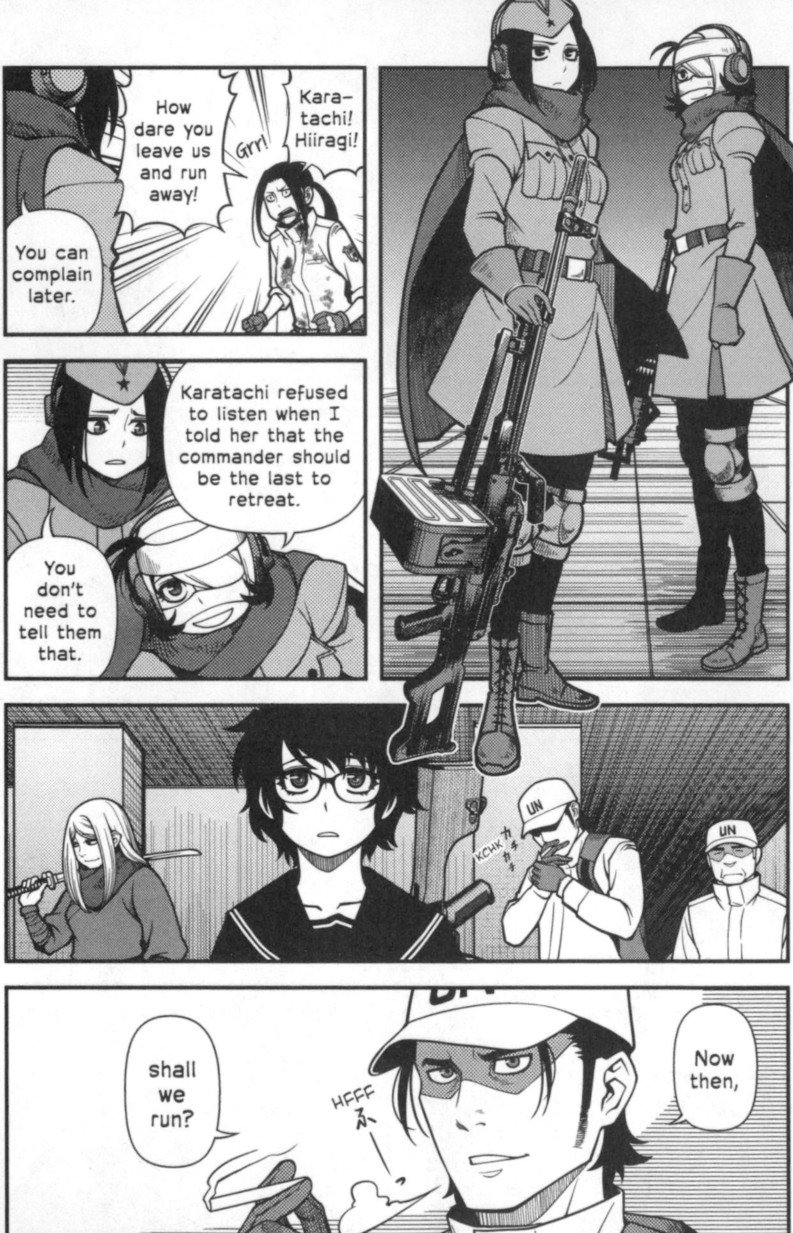
Kara-tachi! Hiiragi!
Grr!
How dare you leave us and run away!
You can complain later.
Karatachi refused to listen when I told her that the commander should be the last to retreat.
You don't need to tell them that.
KCHK
Now then,
HFFF
shall we run?

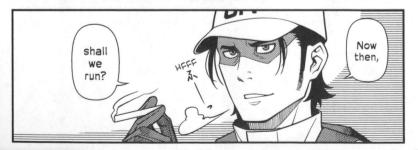

Chapter 39
Truth

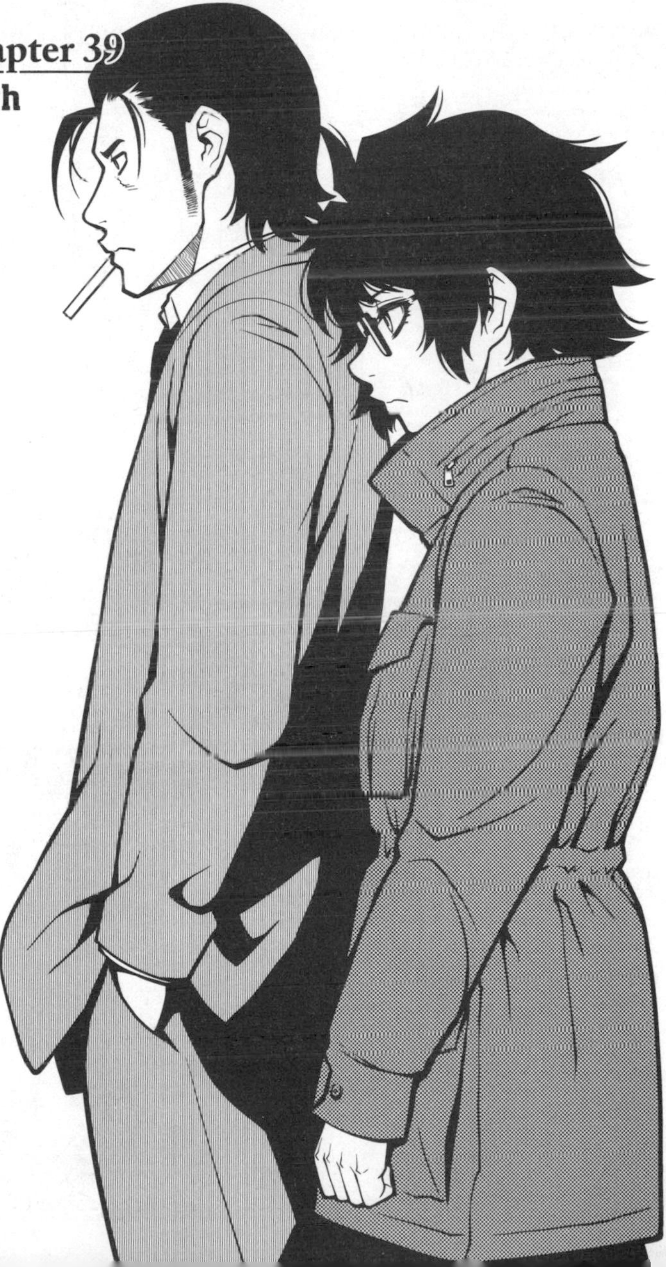

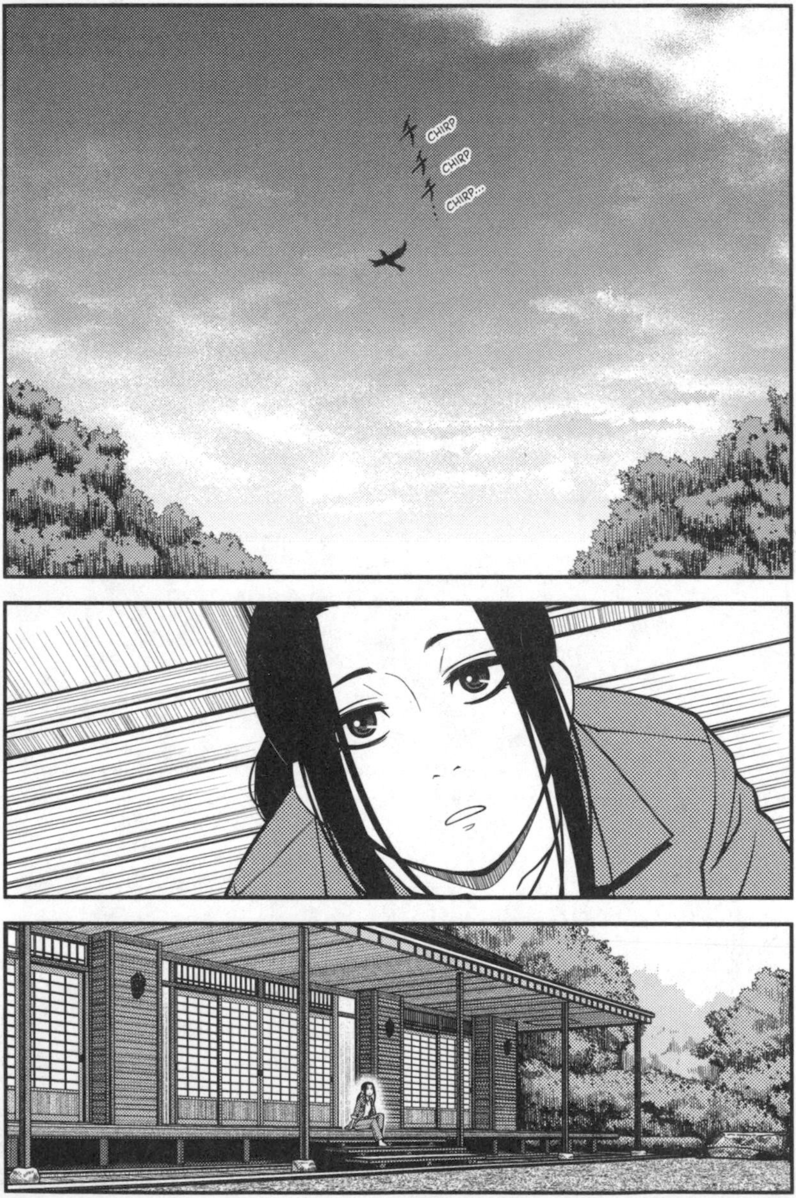
チチチ…
CHIRP
CHIRP
CHIRP...

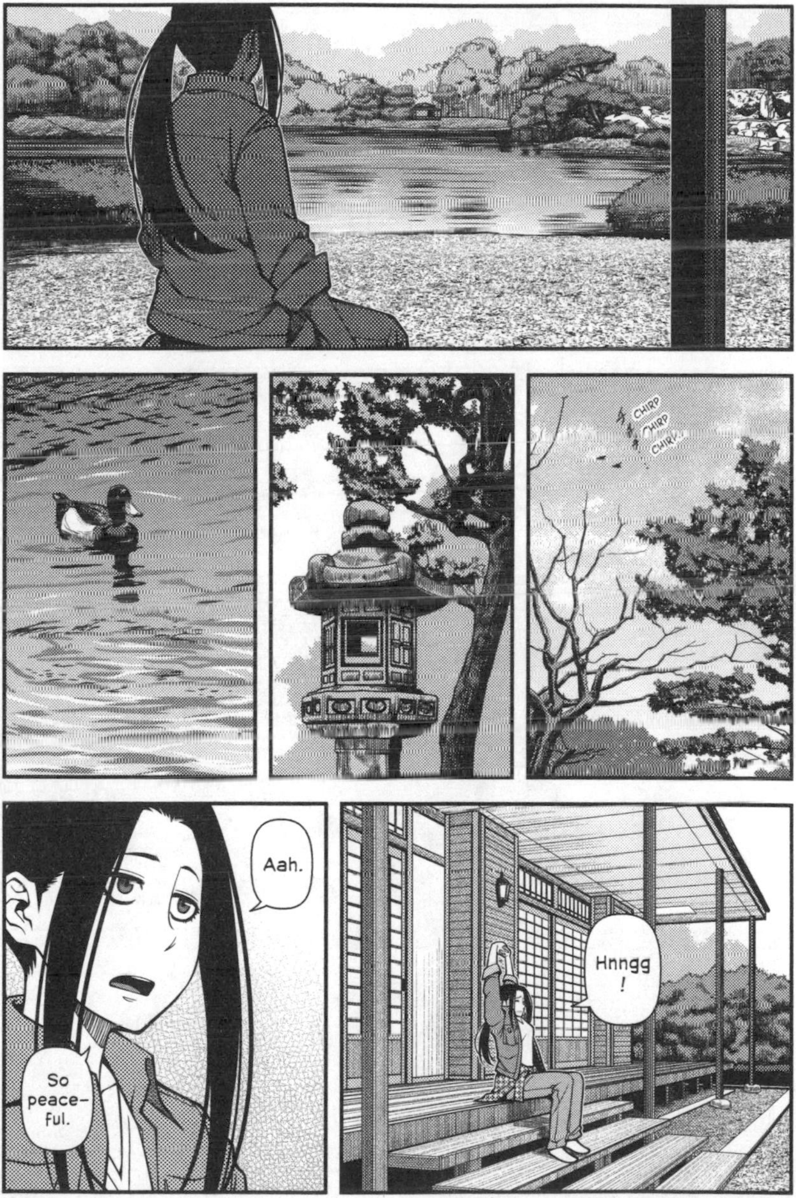
CHIRP
CHIRP
Hnngg!
Aah.
So peace-ful.

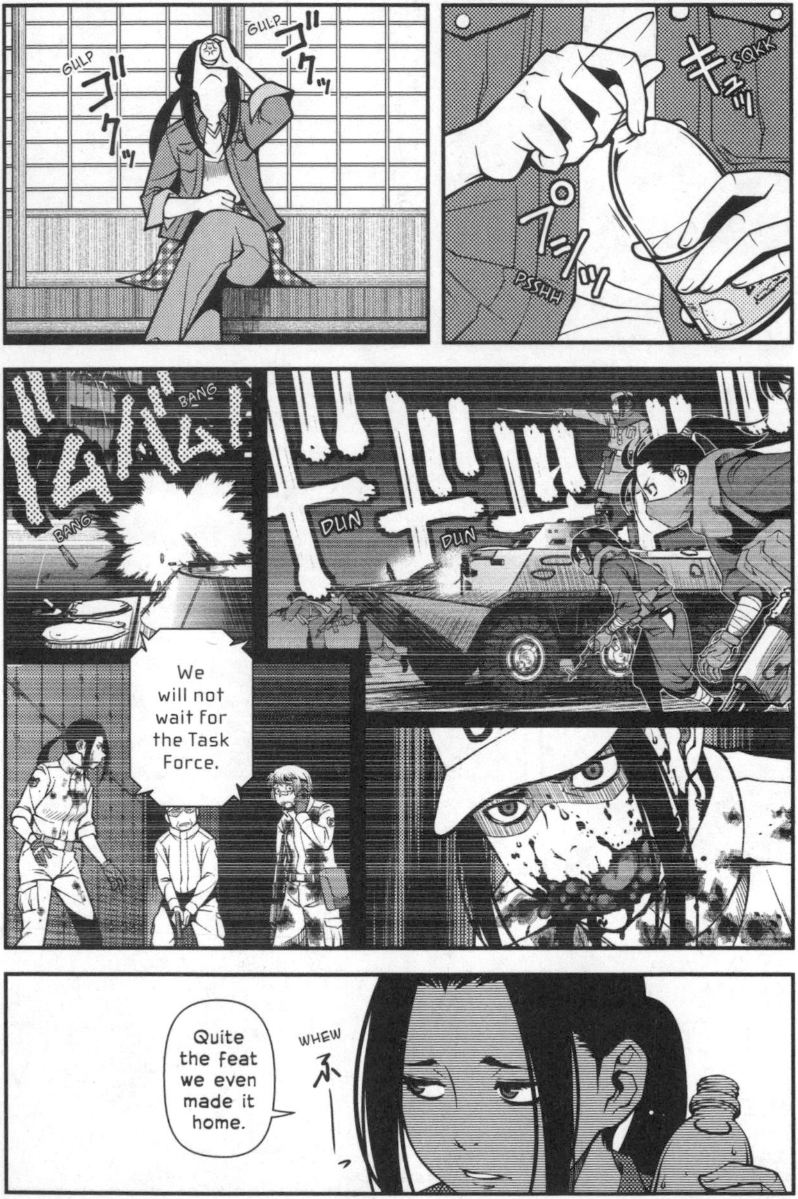
SQKK
PSSHH
GULP
GULP
DUN
DUN
BANG
BANG
We will not wait for the Task Force.
WHEW
Quite the feat we even made it home.

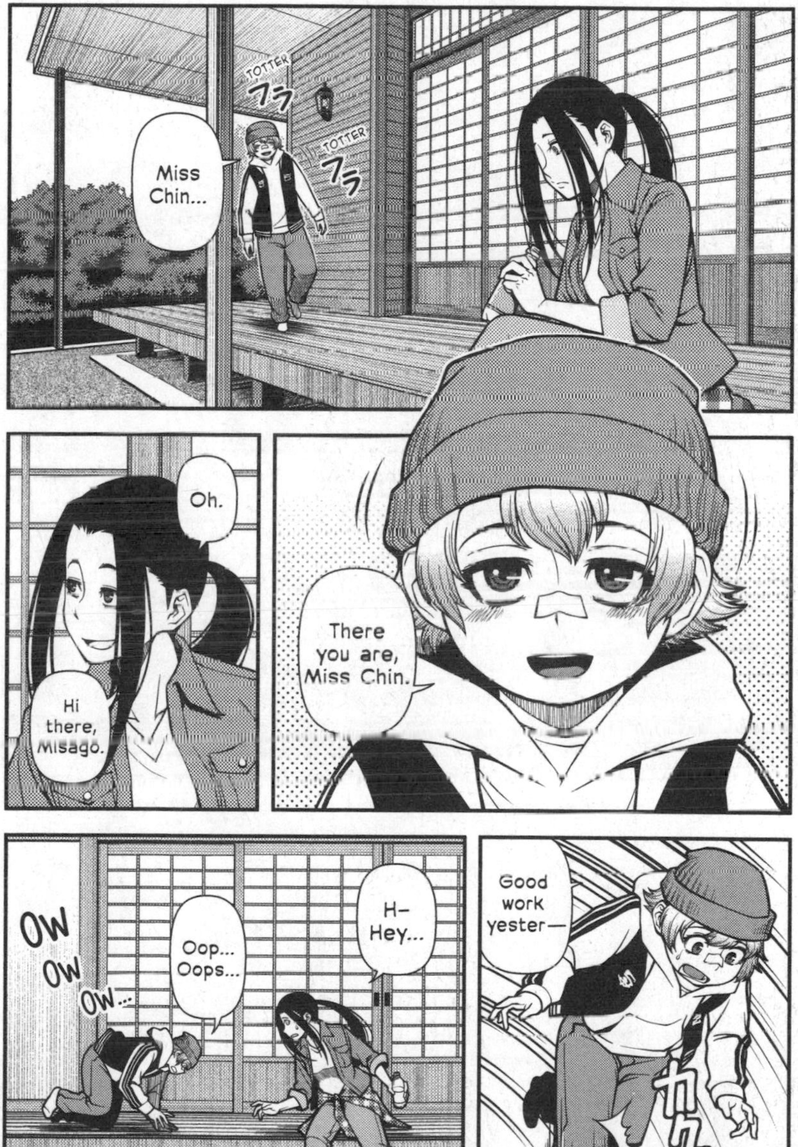
TOTTER
フラ
TOTTER
フラ
Miss Chin...
There you are, Miss Chin.
Oh.
Hi there, Misago.
Good work yester—
カクッ
KRIK
H- Hey...
Oop... Oops...
OW OW OW...

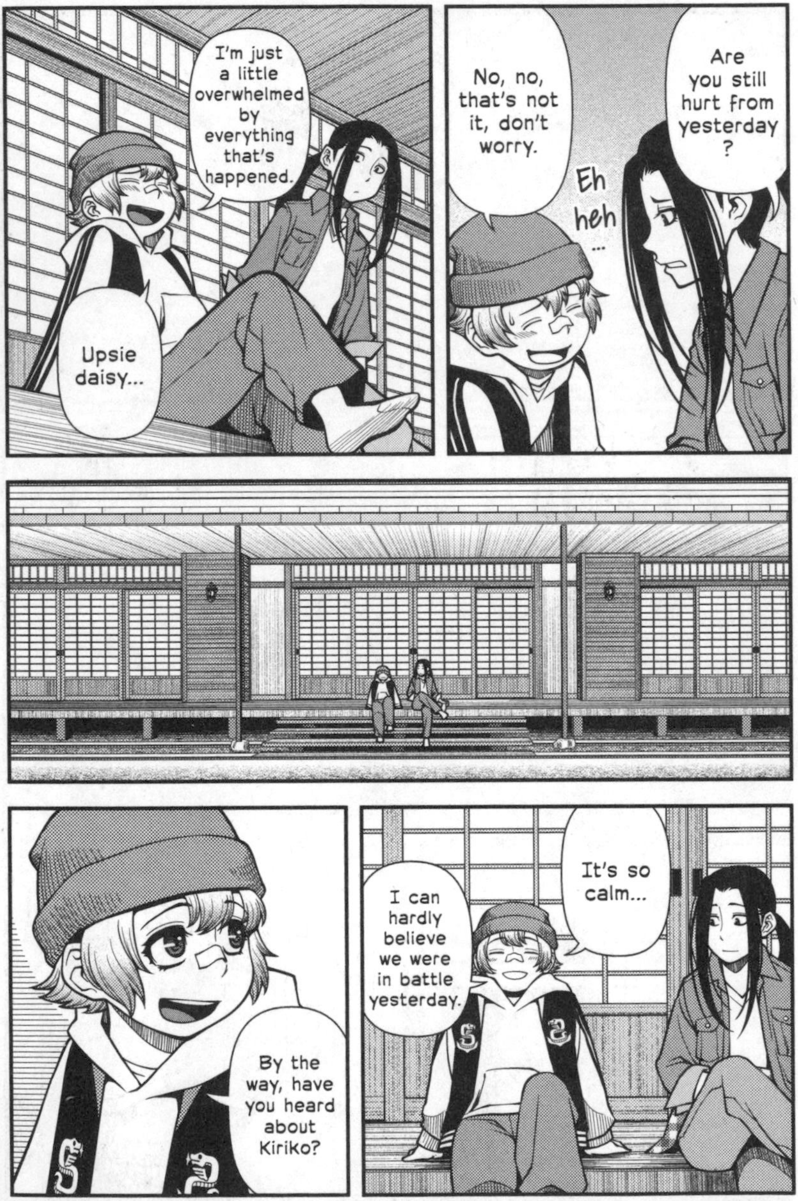
Are you still hurt from yesterday?
Eh heh...
No, no, that's not it, don't worry.
I'm just a little overwhelmed by everything that's happened.
Upsie daisy...
It's so calm...
I can hardly believe we were in battle yesterday.
By the way, have you heard about Kiriko?

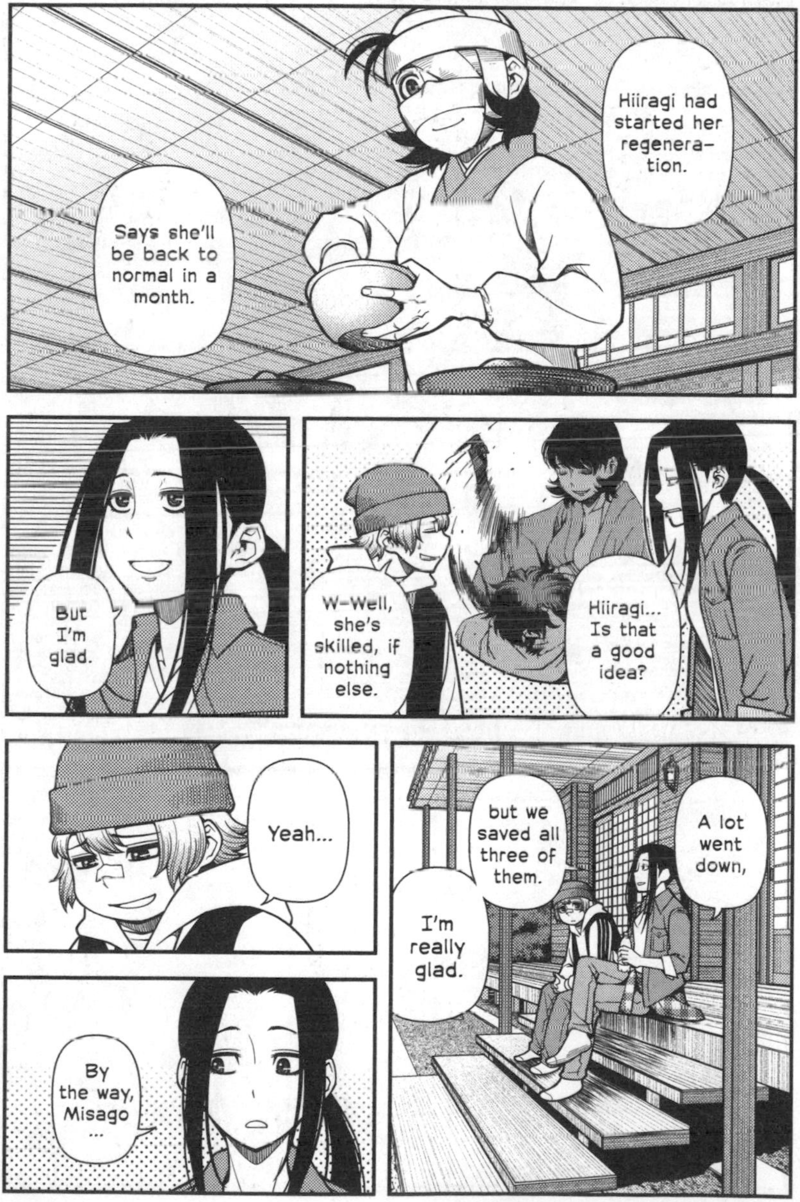
Hiiragi had started her regenera-tion.
Says she'll be back to normal in a month.
Hiiragi... Is that a good idea?
W-Well, she's skilled, if nothing else.
But I'm glad.
A lot went down,
but we saved all three of them.
I'm really glad.
Yeah...
By the way, Misago ...

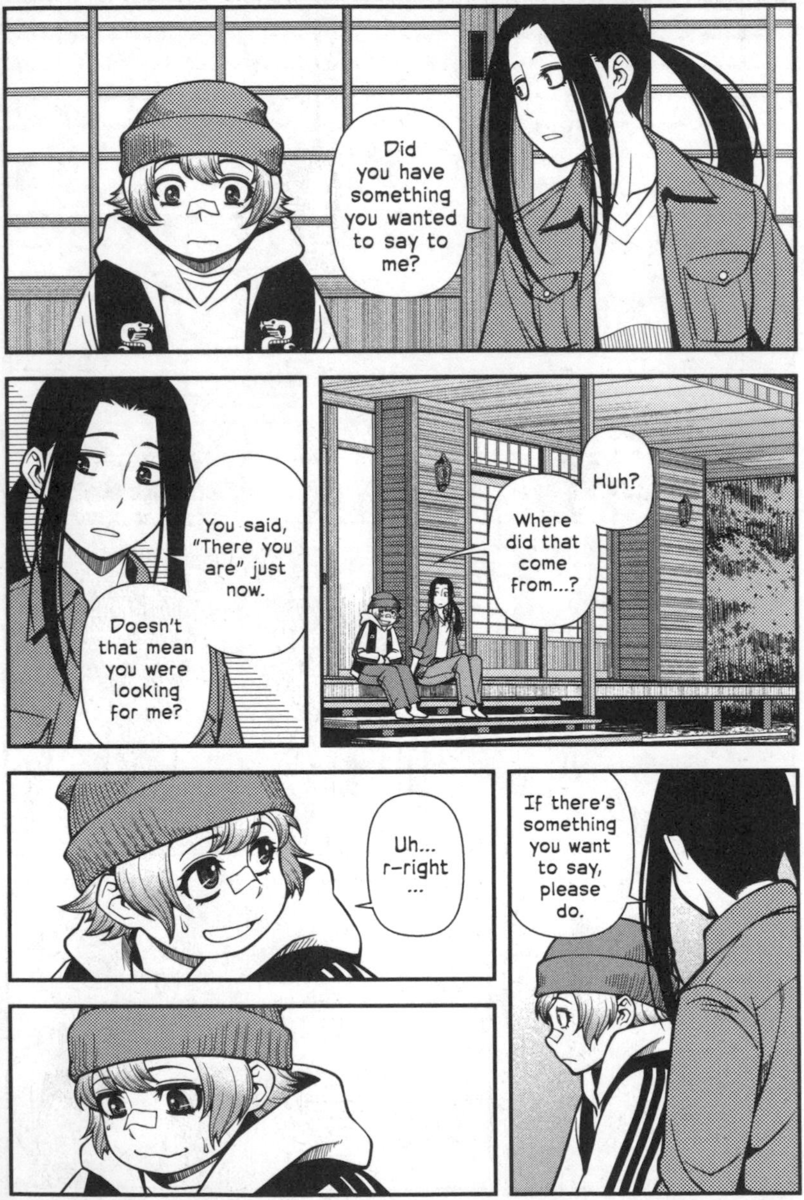
Did you have something you wanted to say to me?
Huh?
Where did that come from...?
You said, "There you are" just now.
Doesn't that mean you were looking for me?
If there's something you want to say, please do.
Uh... r-right ...

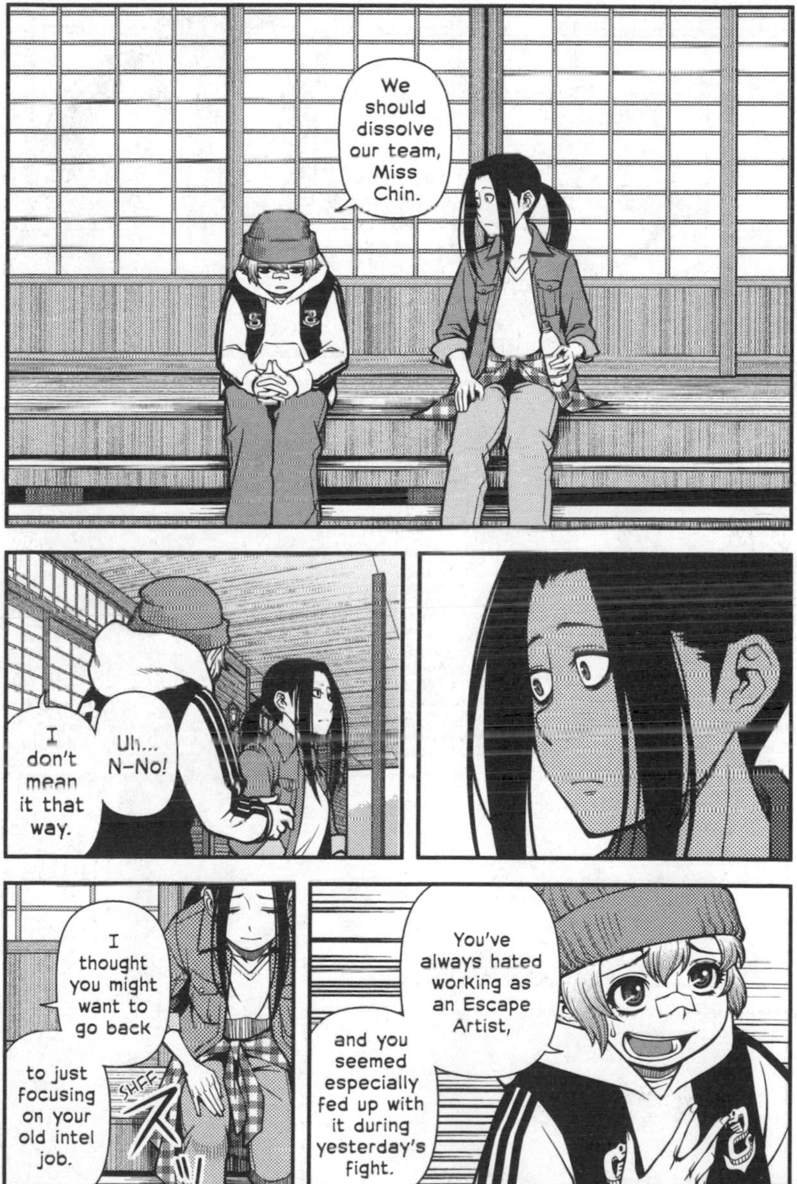
We should dissolve our team, Miss Chin.
Uh... N-No!
I don't mean it that way.
You've always hated working as an Escape Artist,
and you seemed especially fed up with it during yesterday's fight.
I thought you might want to go back
to just focusing on your old intel job.
SHFF

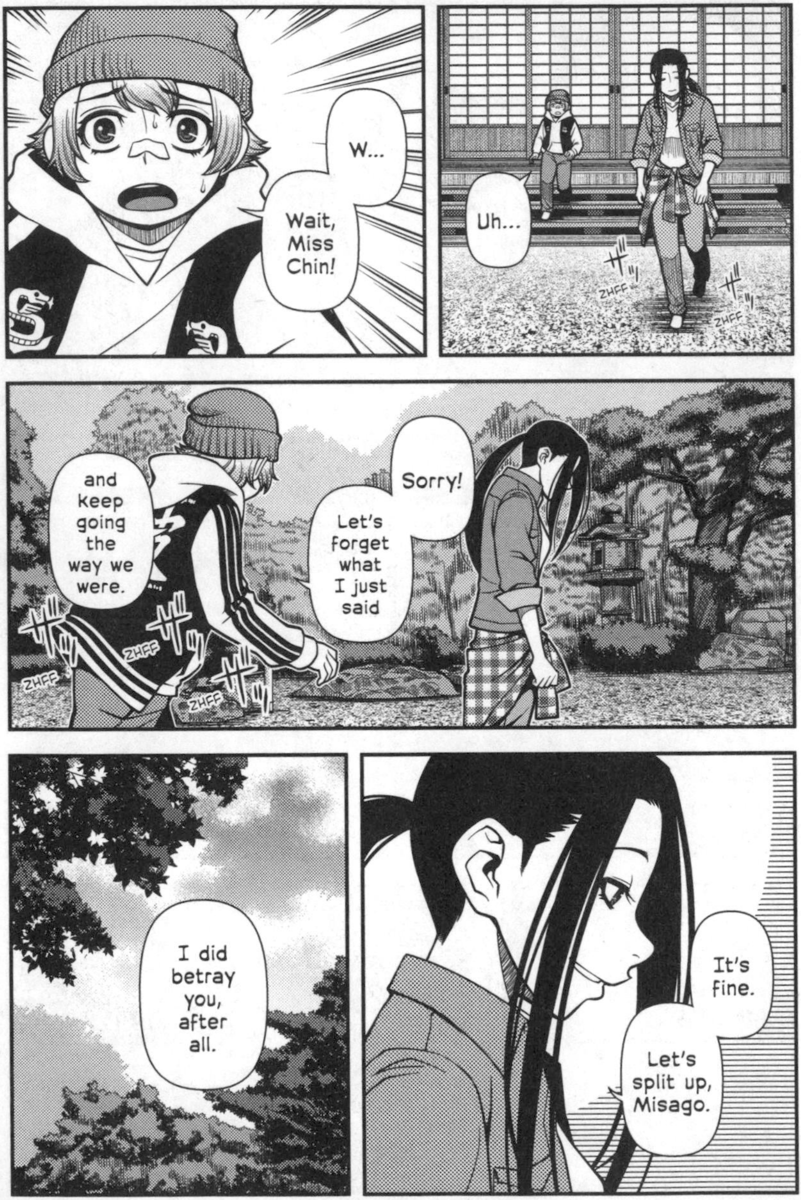
Uh...
ZHFF
ZHFF
W...
Wait, Miss Chin!
Sorry!
Let's forget what I just said
and keep going the way we were.
ZHFF
ZHFF
ZHFF
It's fine.
Let's split up, Misago.
I did betray you, after all.

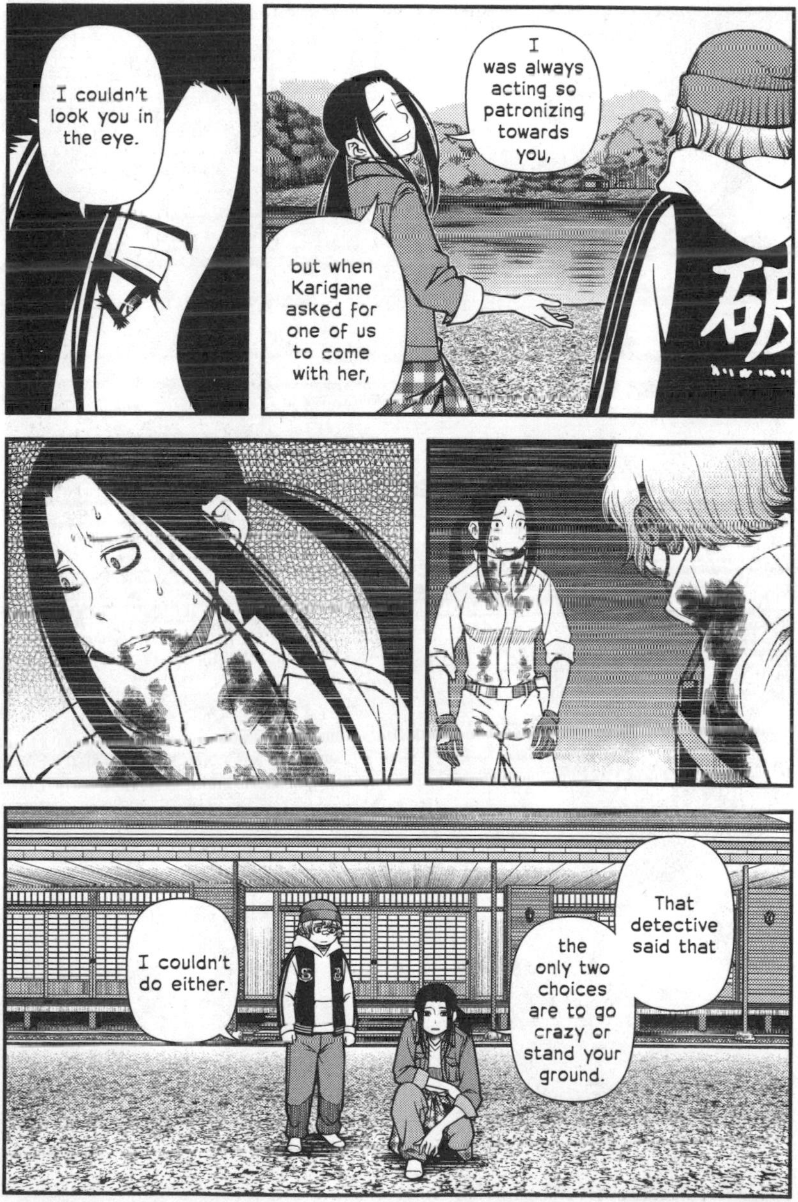
I was always acting so patronizing towards you,
but when Karigane asked for one of us to come with her,
I couldn't look you in the eye.
That detective said that
the only two choices are to go crazy or stand your ground.
I couldn't do either.

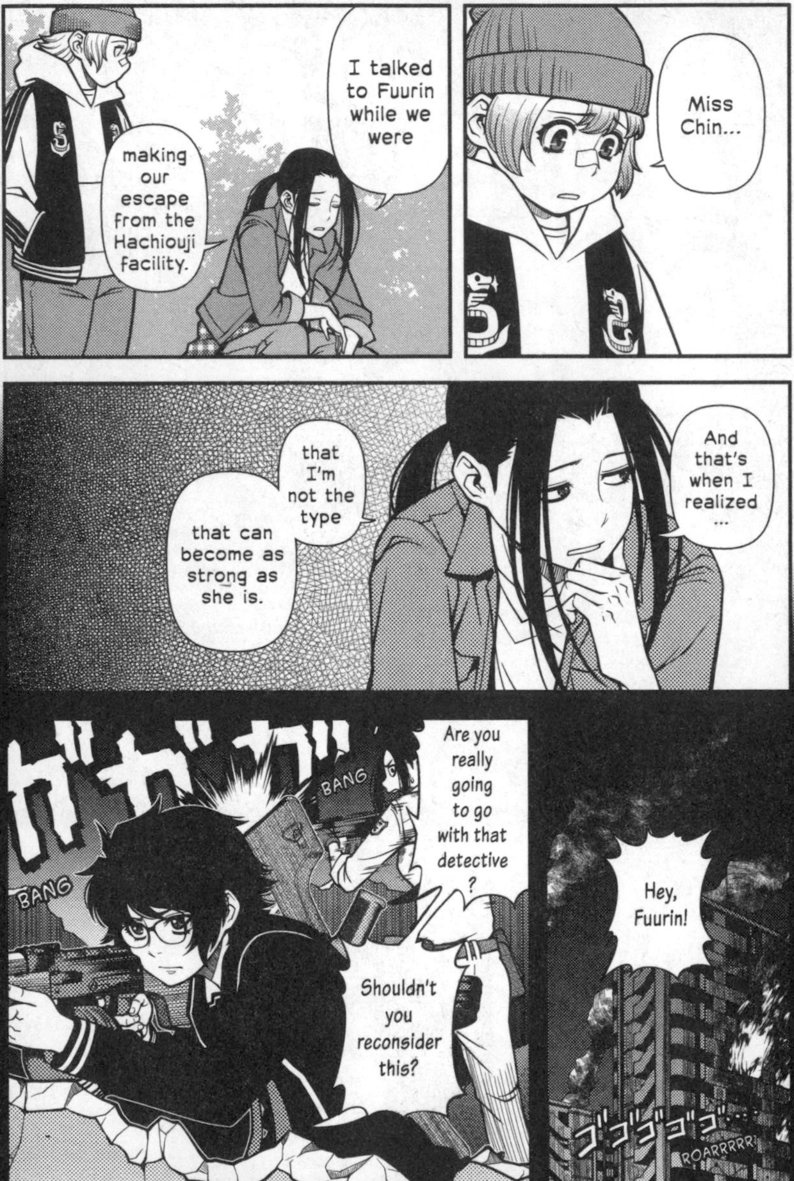
Miss Chin...
I talked to Fuurin while we were
making our escape from the Hachiouji facility.
And that's when I realized ...
that I'm not the type
that can become as strong as she is.
Hey, Fuurin!
ゴゴゴゴゴ…
ROARRRRR
Are you really going to go with that detective ?
BANG
Shouldn't you reconsider this?
BANG

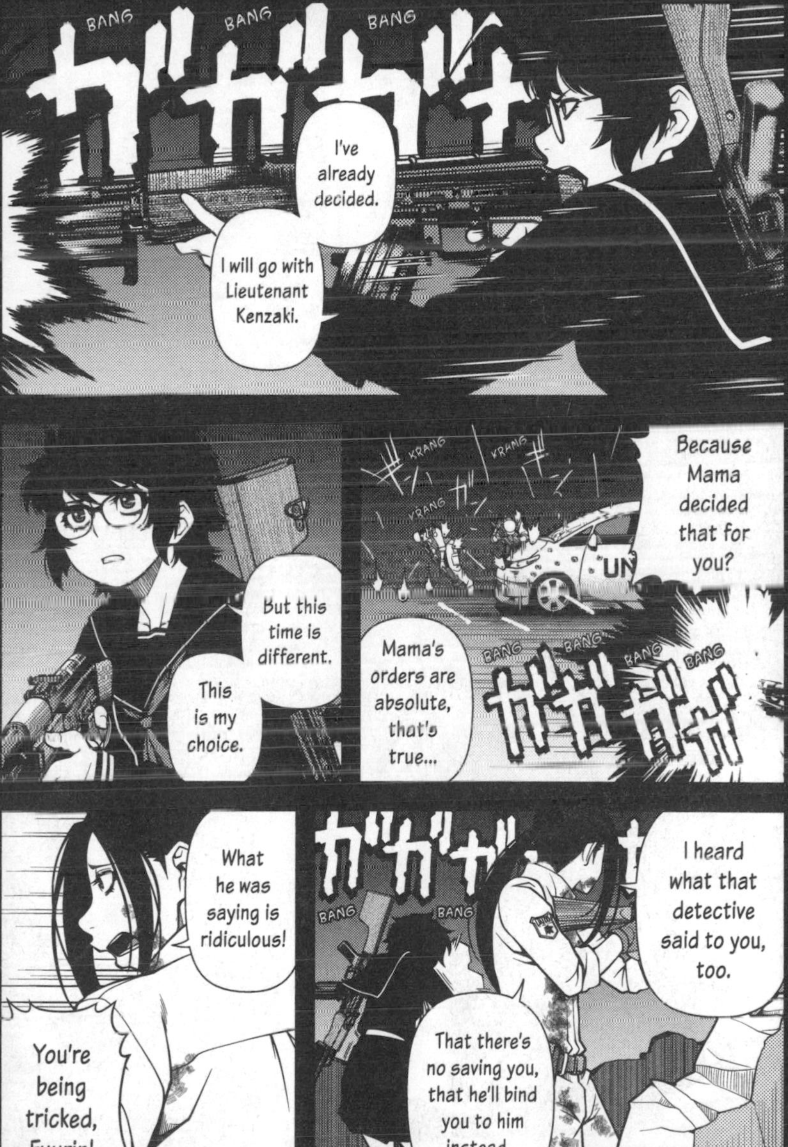
BANG BANG BANG
I've already decided.
I will go with Lieutenant Kenzaki.
KRANG KRANG KRANG
Because Mama decided that for you?
Mama's orders are absolute, that's true...
BANG BANG BANG BANG
But this time is different.
This is my choice.
I heard what that detective said to you, too.
BANG BANG
That there's no saving you, that he'll bind you to him instead...
What he was saying is ridiculous!
You're being tricked, Fuurin!

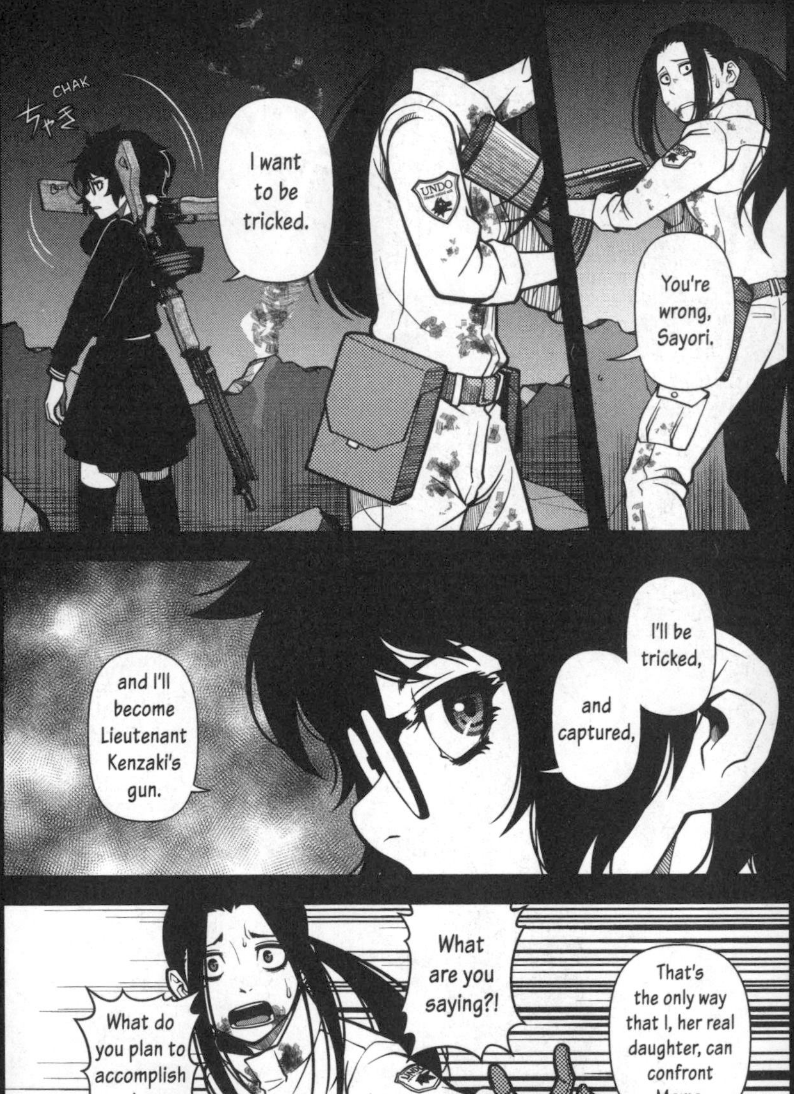
You're wrong, Sayori.
CHAK
ちゃき
I want to be tricked.
I'll be tricked,
and captured,
and I'll become Lieutenant Kenzaki's gun.
That's the only way that I, her real daughter, can confront Mama.
What are you saying?!
What do you plan to accomplish by confronting Mama?!

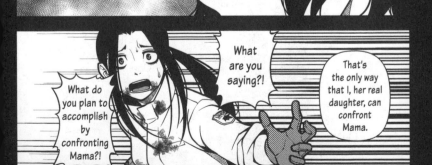

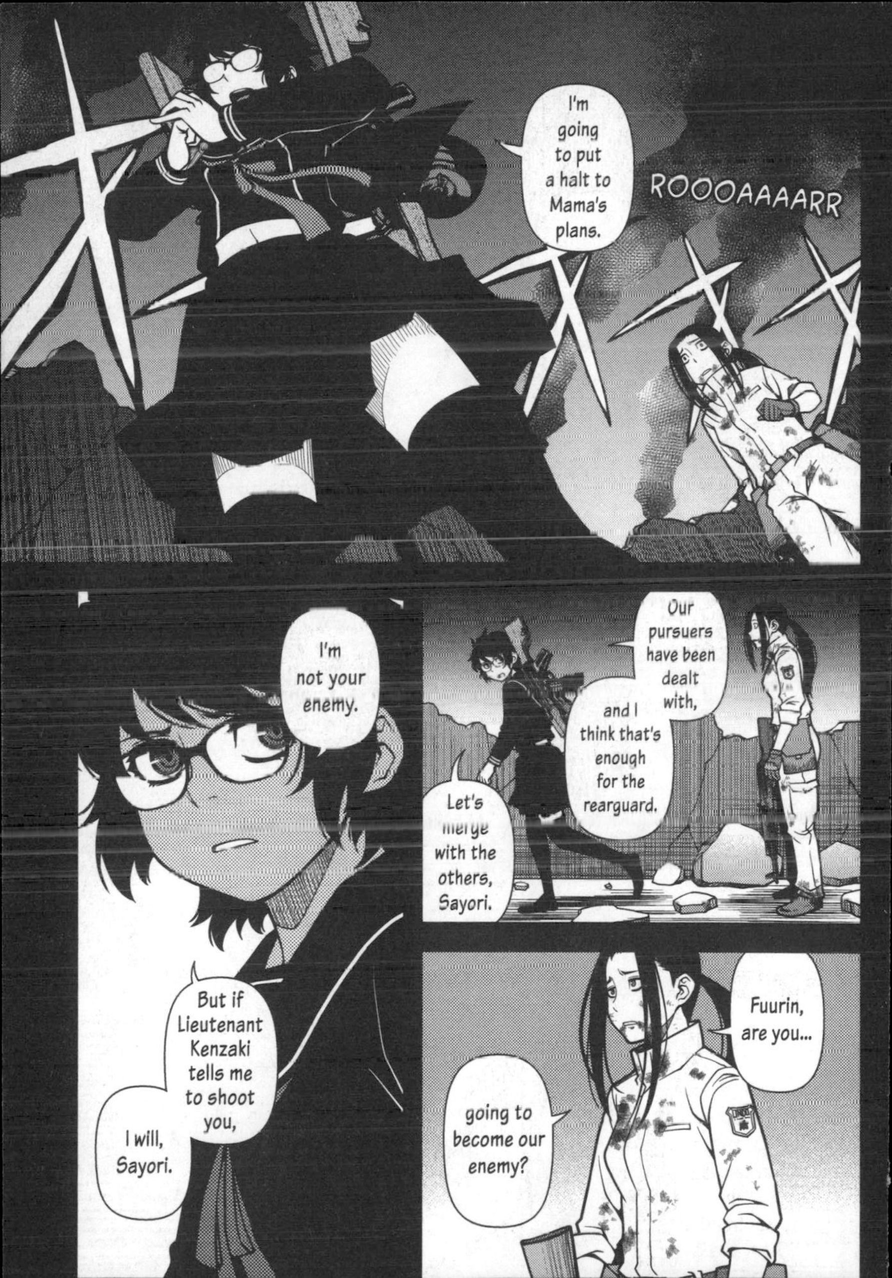
I'm going to put a halt to Mama's plans.
ROOOAAAARR
Our pursuers have been dealt with,
and I think that's enough for the rearguard.
Let's merge with the others, Sayori.
Fuurin, are you...
going to become our enemy?
I'm not your enemy.
But if Lieutenant Kenzaki tells me to shoot you,
I will, Sayori.

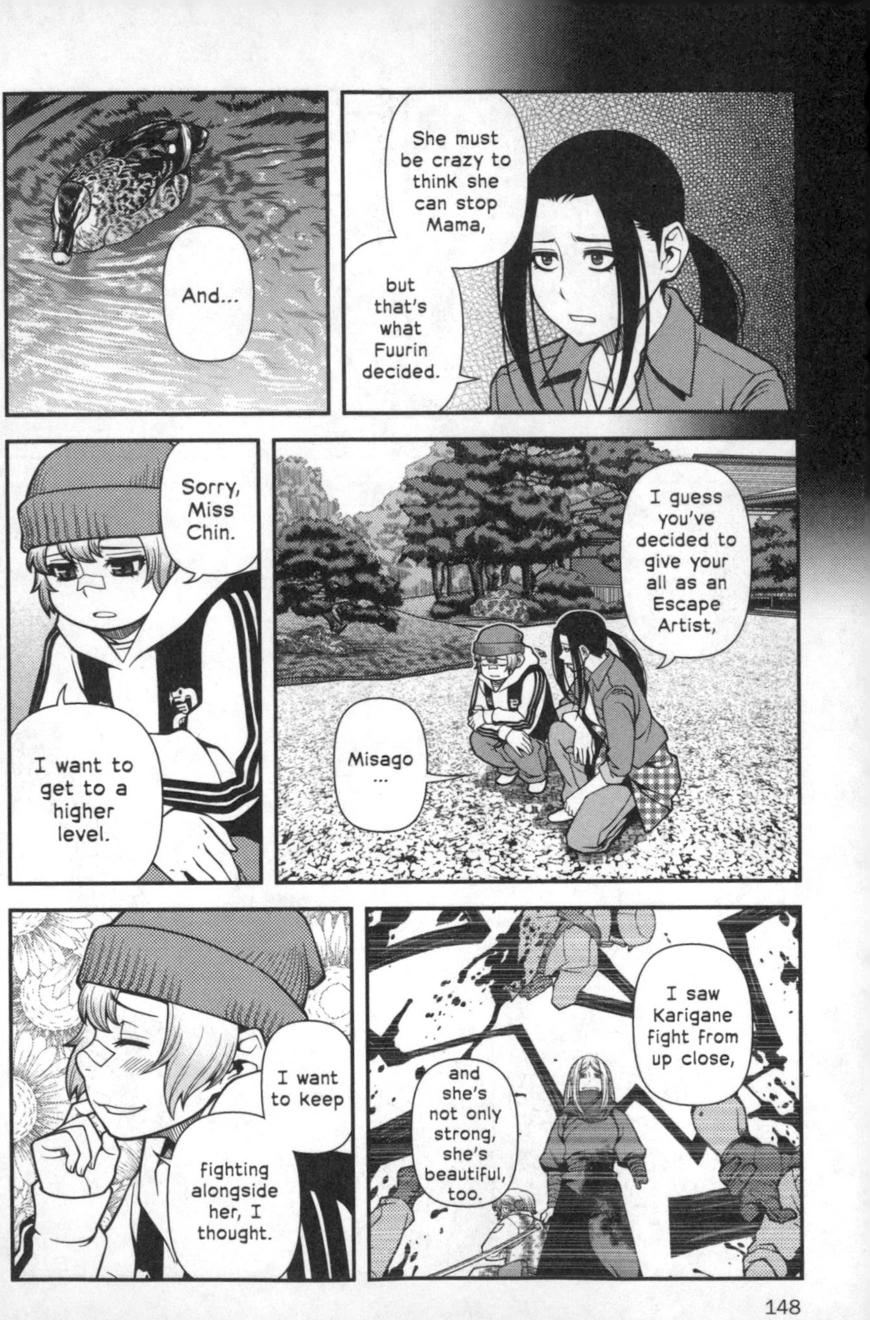
She must be crazy to think she can stop Mama,
but that's what Fuurin decided.
And...
I guess you've decided to give your all as an Escape Artist,
Misago ...
Sorry, Miss Chin.
I want to get to a higher level.
I saw Karigane fight from up close,
and she's not only strong, she's beautiful, too.
I want to keep
fighting alongside her, I thought.

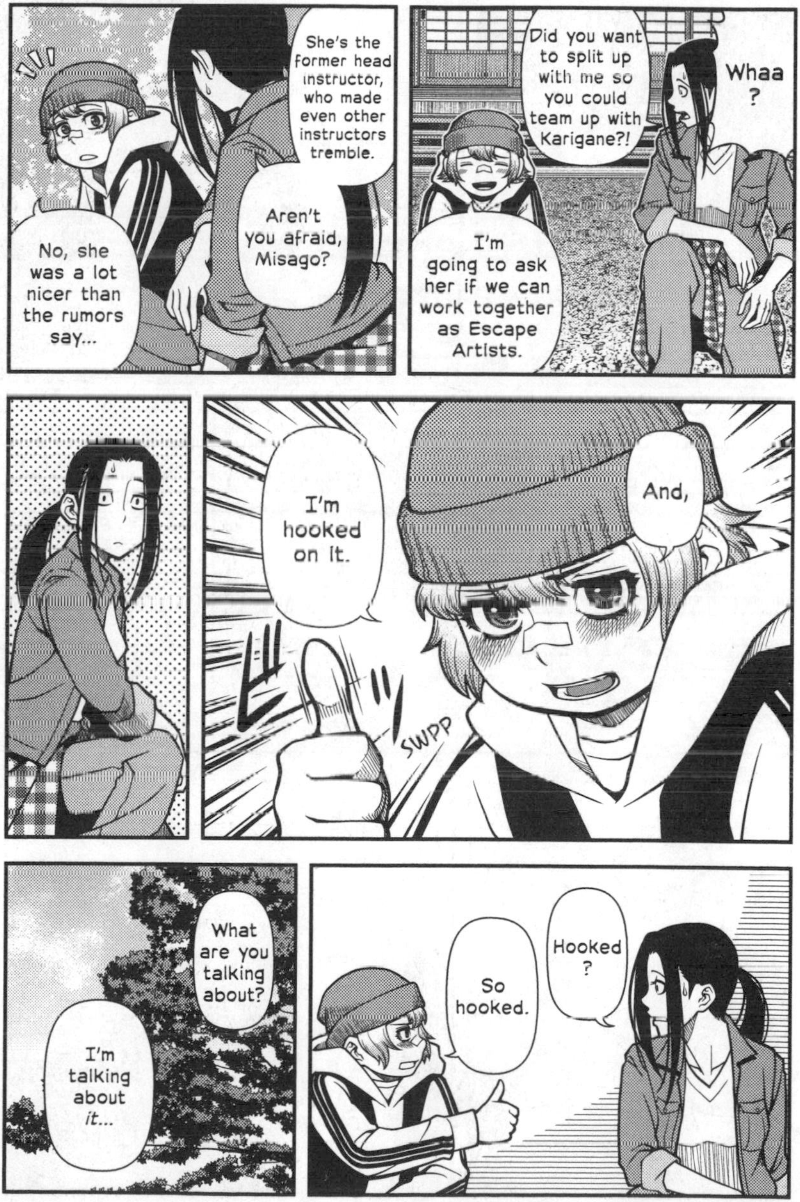
Did you want to split up with me so you could team up with Karigane?!
Whaa ?
I'm going to ask her if we can work together as Escape Artists.
She's the former head instructor, who made even other instructors tremble.
Aren't you afraid, Misago?
No, she was a lot nicer than the rumors say...
And,
I'm hooked on it.
SWPP
Hooked ?
So hooked.
What are you talking about?
I'm talking about *it*...

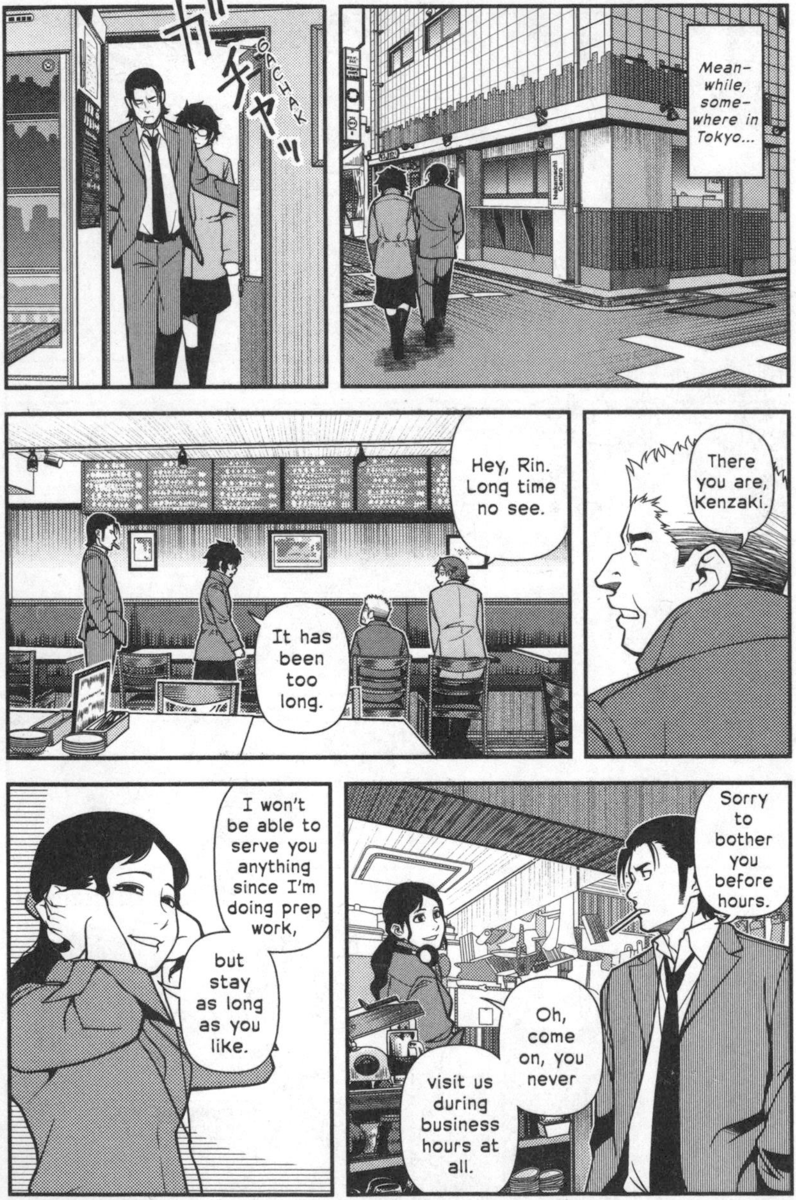
Mean-while, some-where in Tokyo...
ガチャッ
GACHAK
There you are, Kenzaki.
Hey, Rin. Long time no see.
It has been too long.
Sorry to bother you before hours.
Oh, come on, you never
visit us during business hours at all.
I won't be able to serve you anything since I'm doing prep work,
but stay as long as you like.

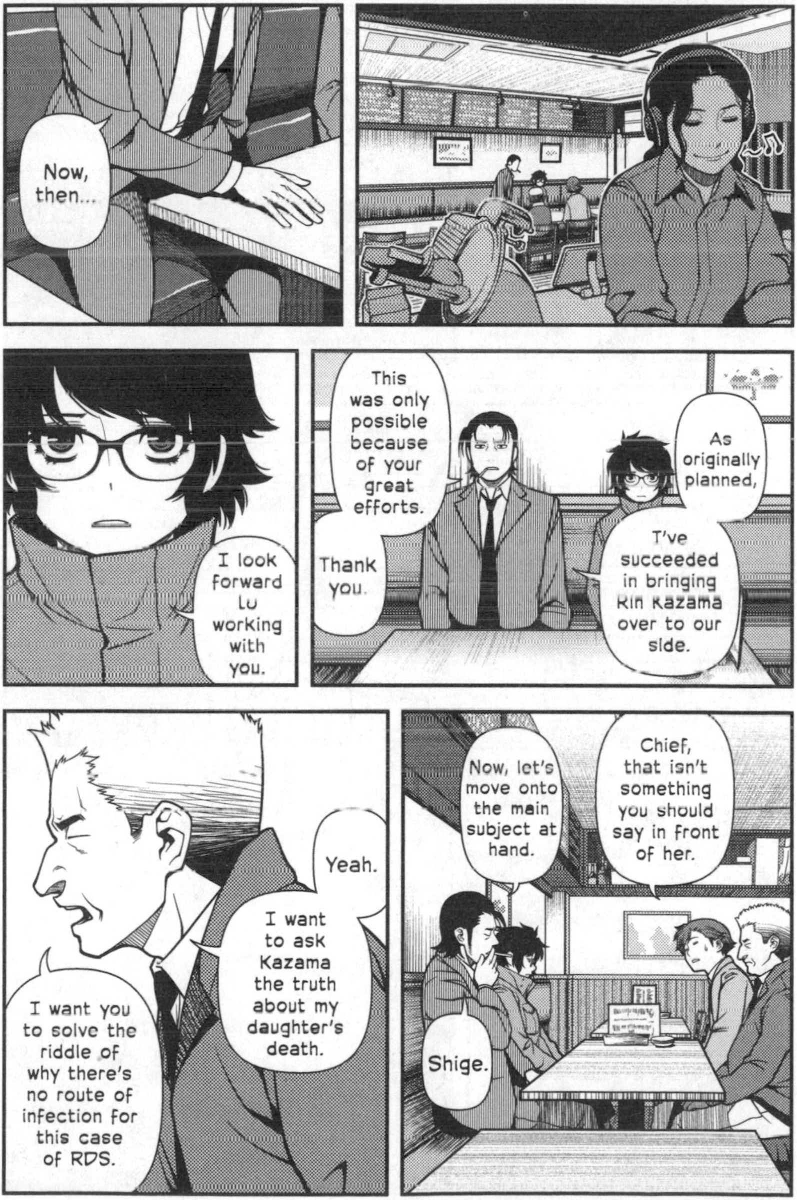
Now, then...
As originally planned,
I've succeeded in bringing Rin Kazama over to our side.
This was only possible because of your great efforts.
Thank you.
I look forward to working with you.
Chief, that isn't something you should say in front of her.
Now, let's move onto the main subject at hand.
Shige.
Yeah.
I want to ask Kazama the truth about my daughter's death.
I want you to solve the riddle of why there's no route of infection for this case of RDS.

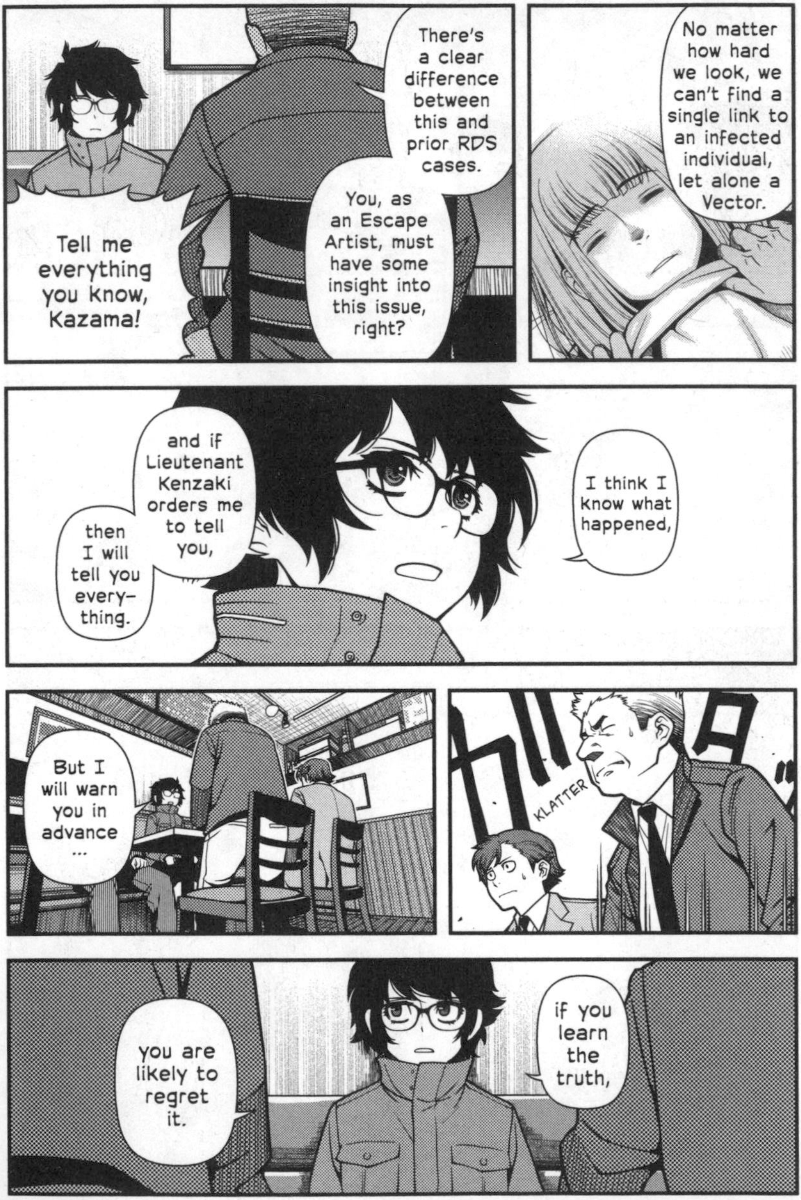
No matter how hard we look, we can't find a single link to an infected individual, let alone a Vector.
There's a clear difference between this and prior RDS cases.
You, as an Escape Artist, must have some insight into this issue, right?
Tell me everything you know, Kazama!
I think I know what happened,
and if Lieutenant Kenzaki orders me to tell you,
then I will tell you every-thing.
KLATTER
But I will warn you in advance ...
if you learn the truth,
you are likely to regret it.

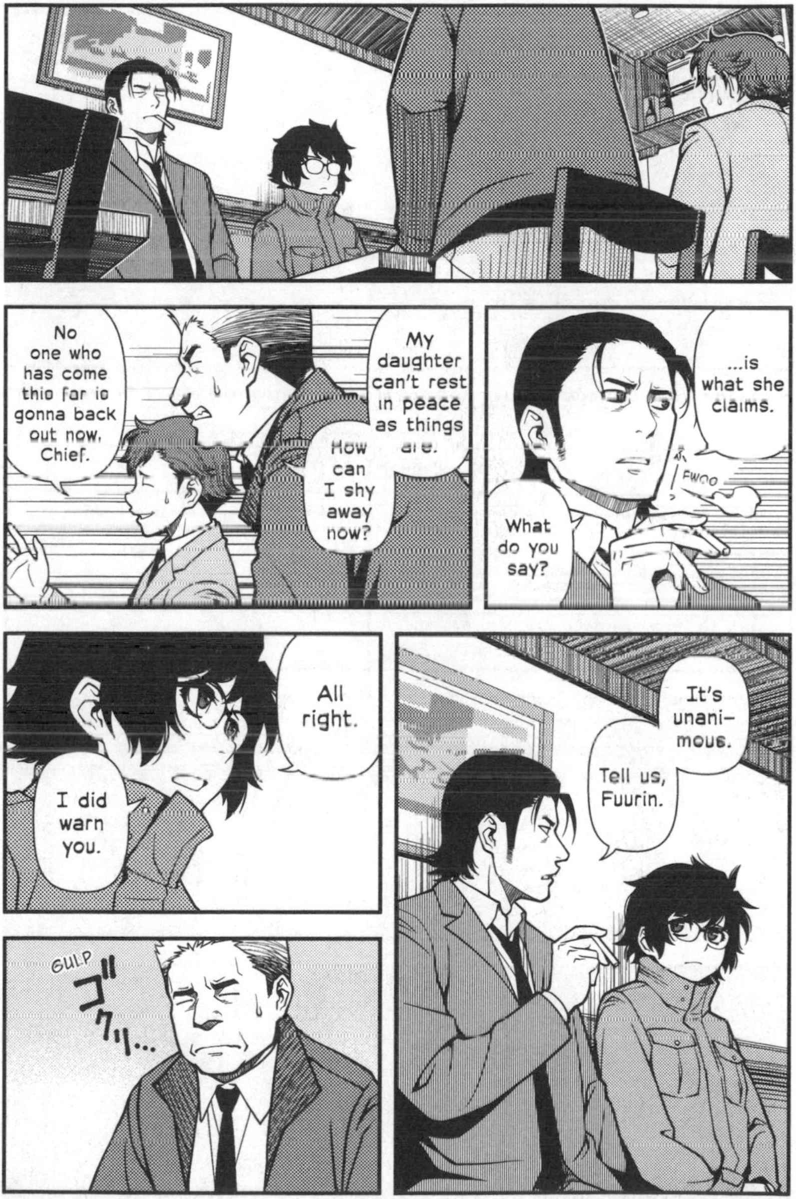
...is what she claims.
FWOO
What do you say?
My daughter can't rest in peace as things are.
How can I shy away now?
No one who has come this far is gonna back out now, Chief.
It's unani-mous.
Tell us, Fuurin.
All right.
I did warn you.
GULP
ゴクリ...

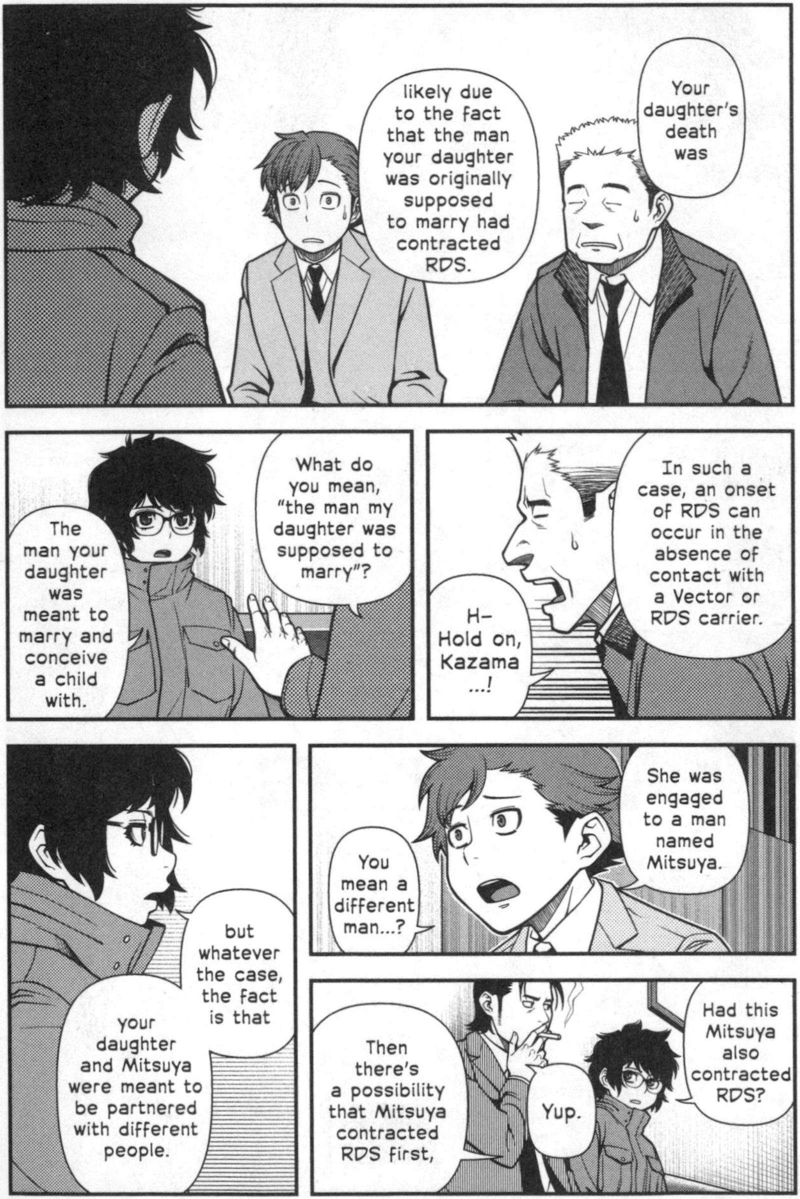
Your daughter's death was
likely due to the fact that the man your daughter was originally supposed to marry had contracted RDS.
In such a case, an onset of RDS can occur in the absence of contact with a Vector or RDS carrier.
H–Hold on, Kazama ...!
What do you mean, "the man my daughter was supposed to marry"?
The man your daughter was meant to marry and conceive a child with.
She was engaged to a man named Mitsuya.
You mean a different man...?
Had this Mitsuya also contracted RDS?
Yup.
Then there's a possibility that Mitsuya contracted RDS first,
but whatever the case, the fact is that
your daughter and Mitsuya were meant to be partnered with different people.

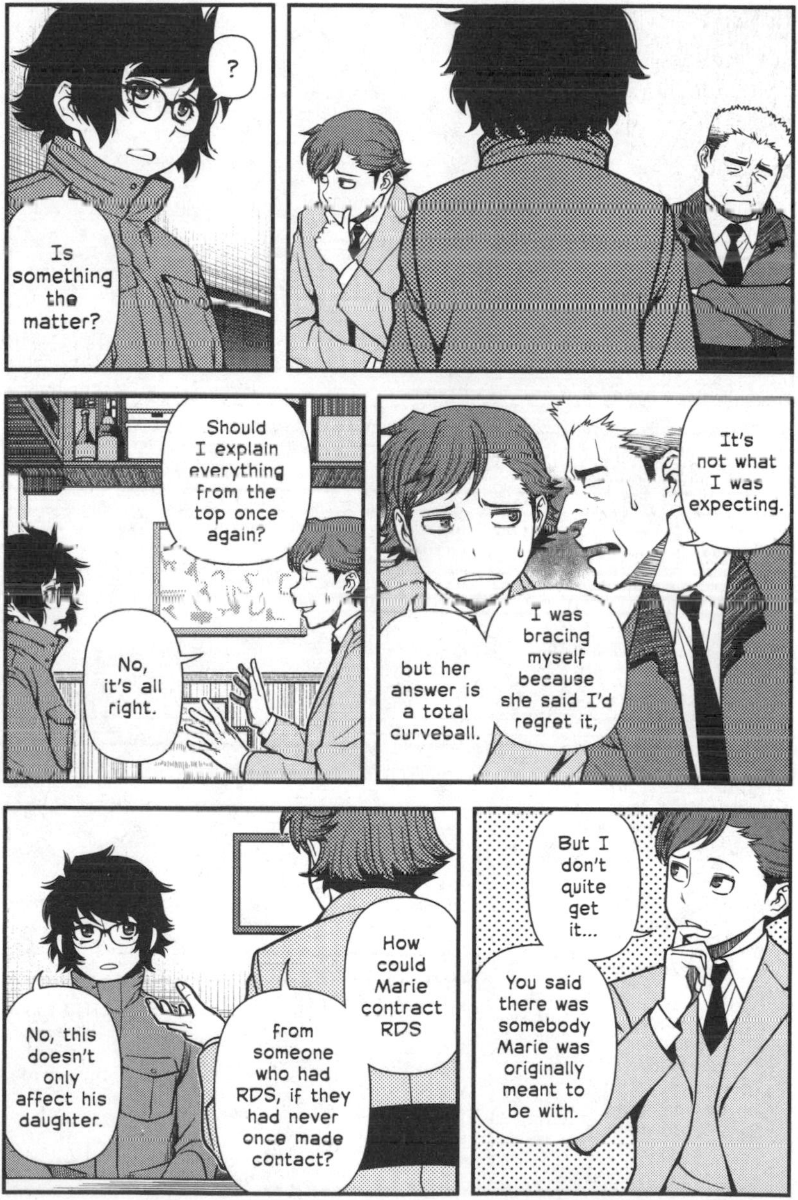
?
Is something the matter?
It's not what I was expecting.
I was bracing myself because she said I'd regret it,
but her answer is a total curveball.
Should I explain everything from the top once again?
No, it's all right.
But I don't quite get it...
You said there was somebody Marie was originally meant to be with.
How could Marie contract RDS
from someone who had RDS, if they had never once made contact?
No, this doesn't only affect his daughter.

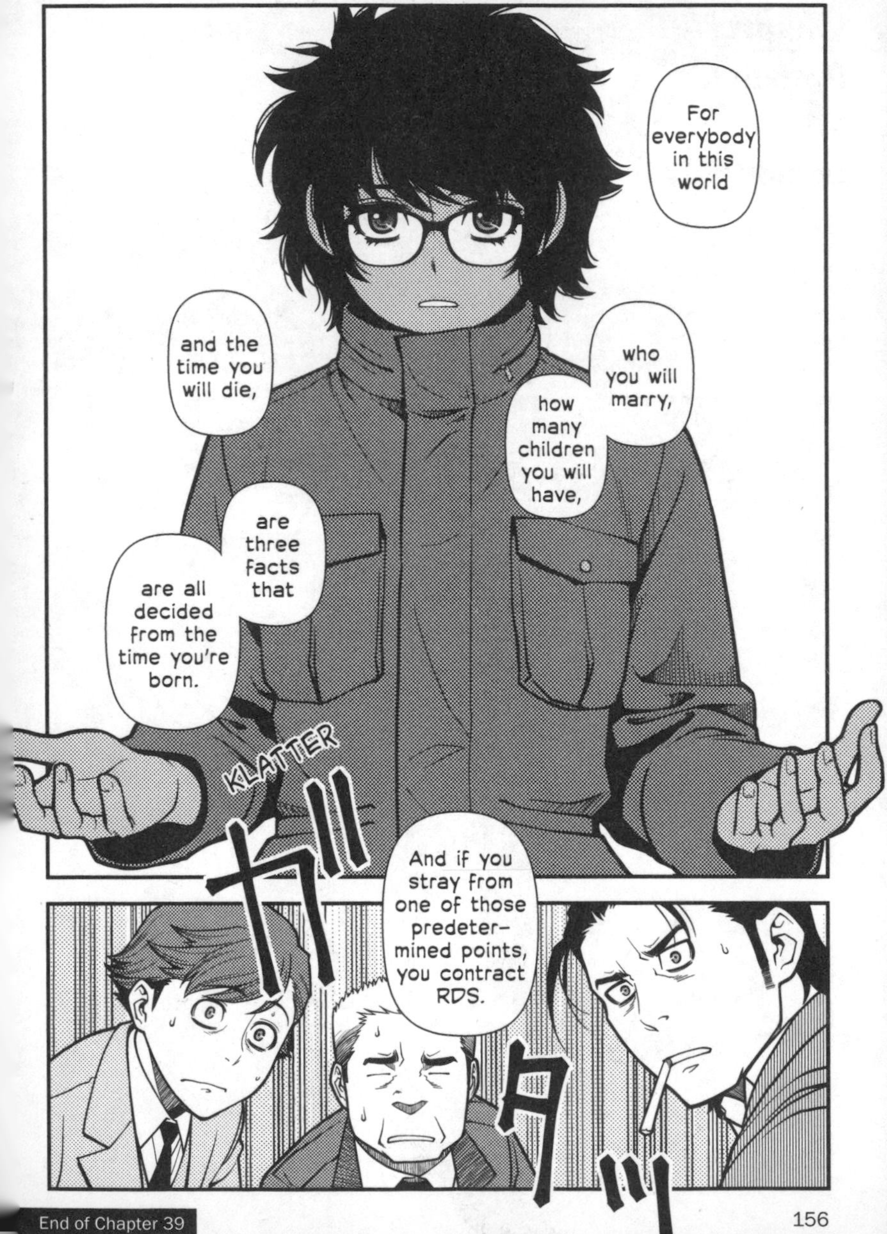
For everybody in this world
who you will marry,
how many children you will have,
and the time you will die,
are three facts that
are all decided from the time you're born.
KLATTER
And if you stray from one of those predeter-mined points, you contract RDS.

Chapter 40
System of Immortality

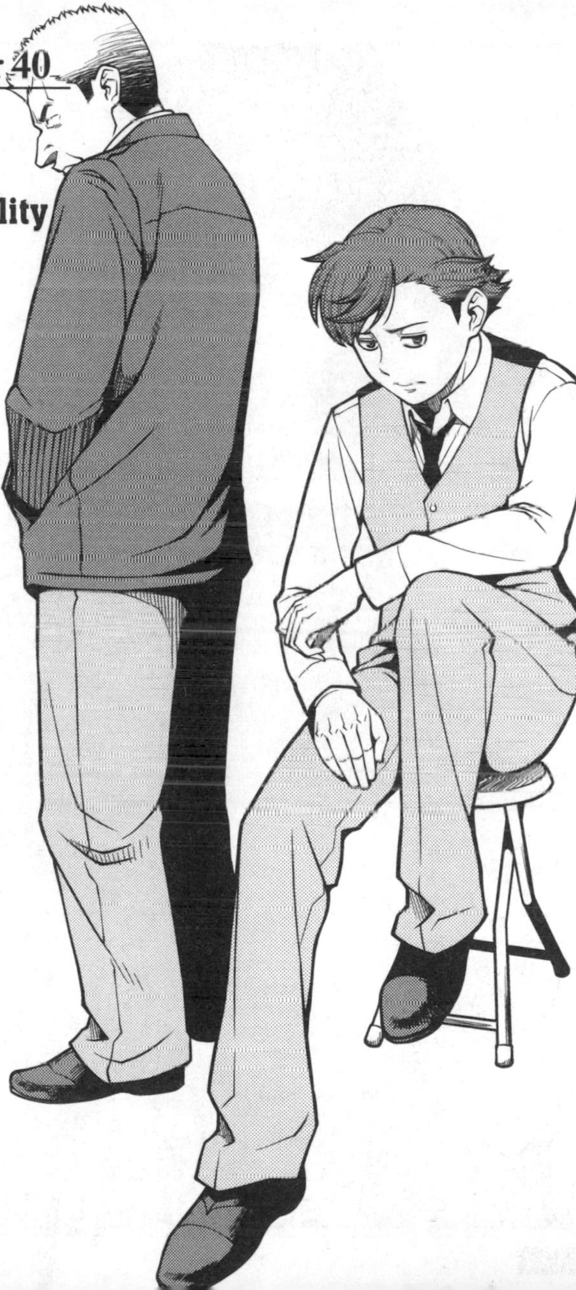

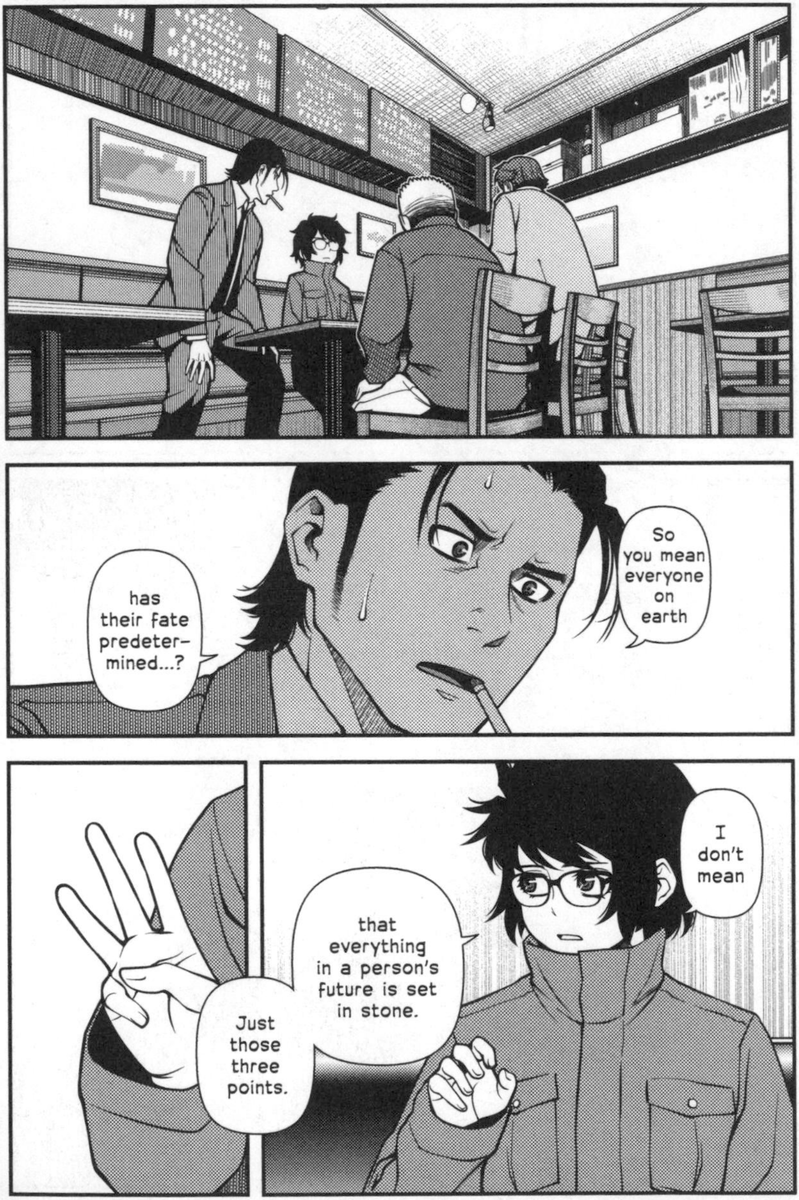
So you mean everyone on earth
has their fate predetermined...?
I don't mean
that everything in a person's future is set in stone.
Just those three points.

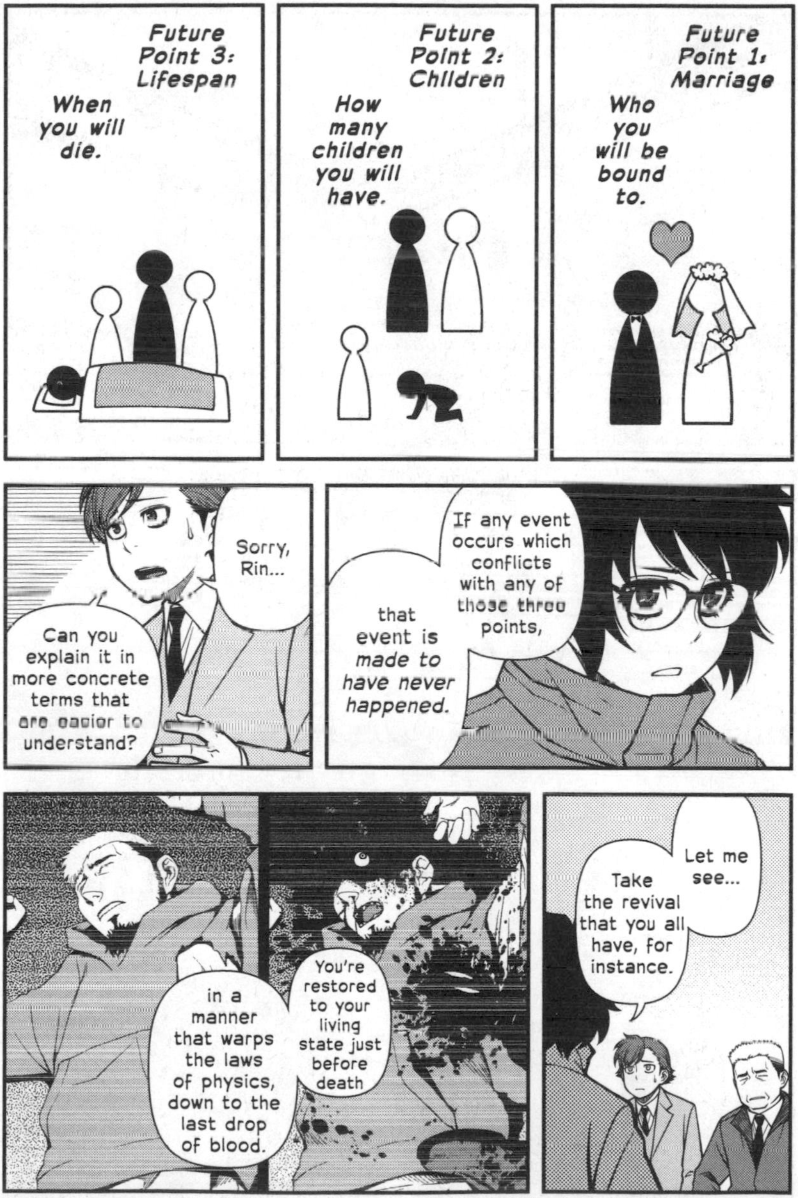
Future Point 1: Marriage
Who you will be bound to.
Future Point 2: Children
How many children you will have.
Future Point 3: Lifespan
When you will die.
If any event occurs which conflicts with any of those three points,
that event is made to have never happened.
Sorry, Rin...
Can you explain it in more concrete terms that are easier to understand?
Let me see...
Take the revival that you all have, for instance.
You're restored to your living state just before death
in a manner that warps the laws of physics, down to the last drop of blood.

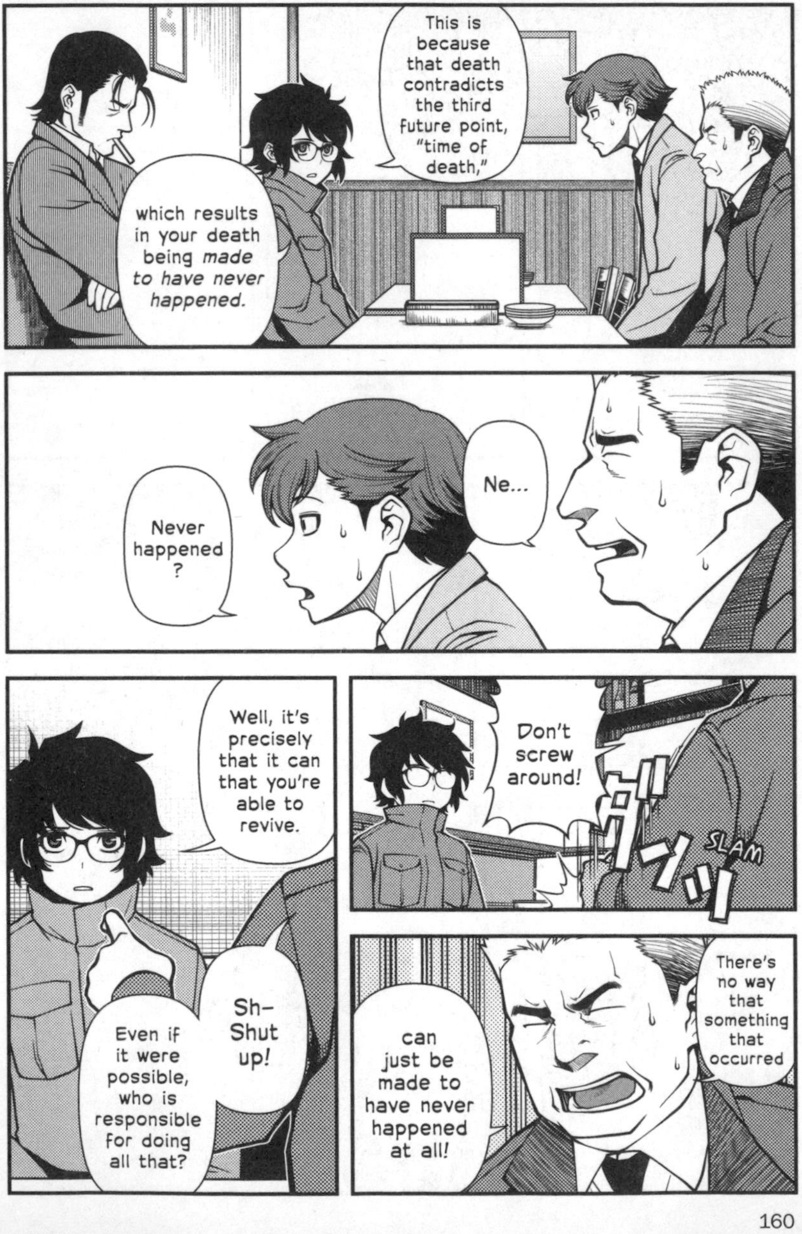
This is because that death contradicts the third future point, "time of death,"
which results in your death being *made to have never happened.*
Ne...
Never happened?
Don't screw around!
ダンッ
SLAM
There's no way that something that occurred
can just be made to have never happened at all!
Well, it's precisely that it can that you're able to revive.
Sh- Shut up!
Even if it were possible, who is responsible for doing all that?

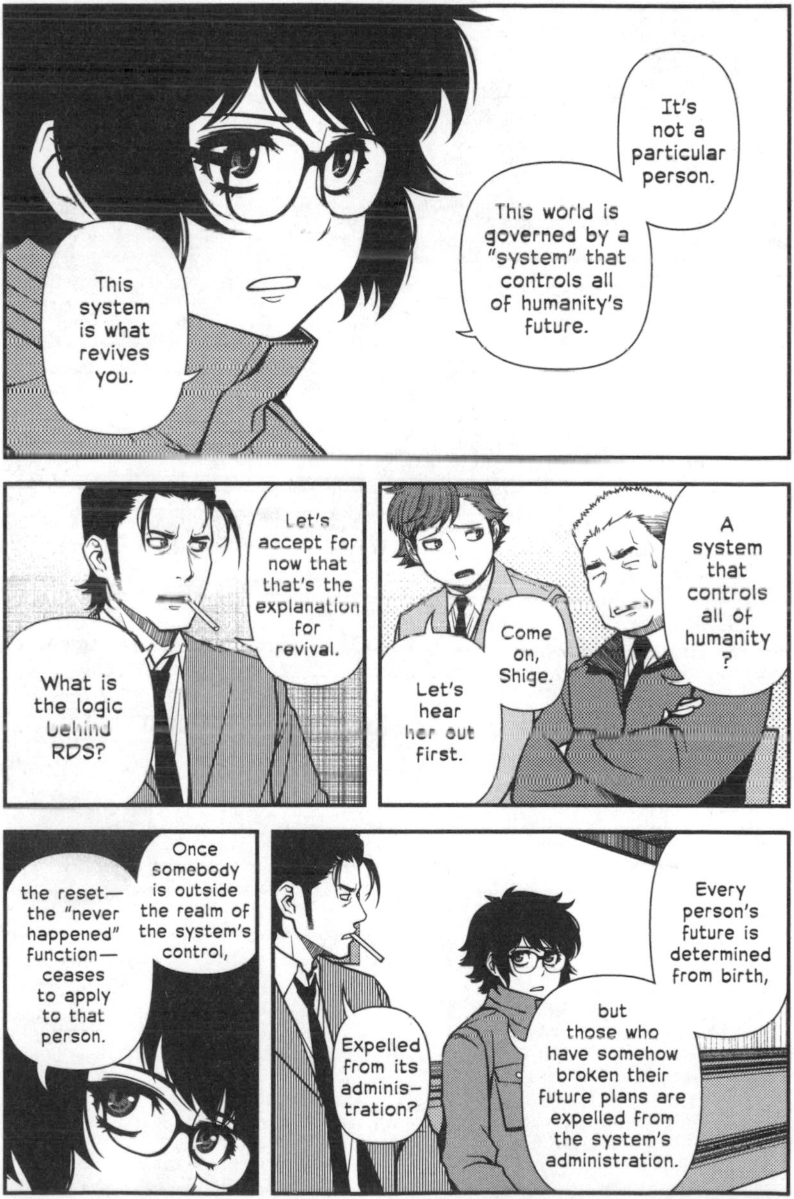
It's not a particular person.
This world is governed by a "system" that controls all of humanity's future.
This system is what revives you.
A system that controls all of humanity?
Come on, Shige.
Let's hear her out first.
Let's accept for now that that's the explanation for revival.
What is the logic behind RDS?
Every person's future is determined from birth,
but those who have somehow broken their future plans are expelled from the system's administration.
Expelled from its adminis- tration?
Once somebody is outside the realm of the system's control,
the reset— the "never happened" function— ceases to apply to that person.

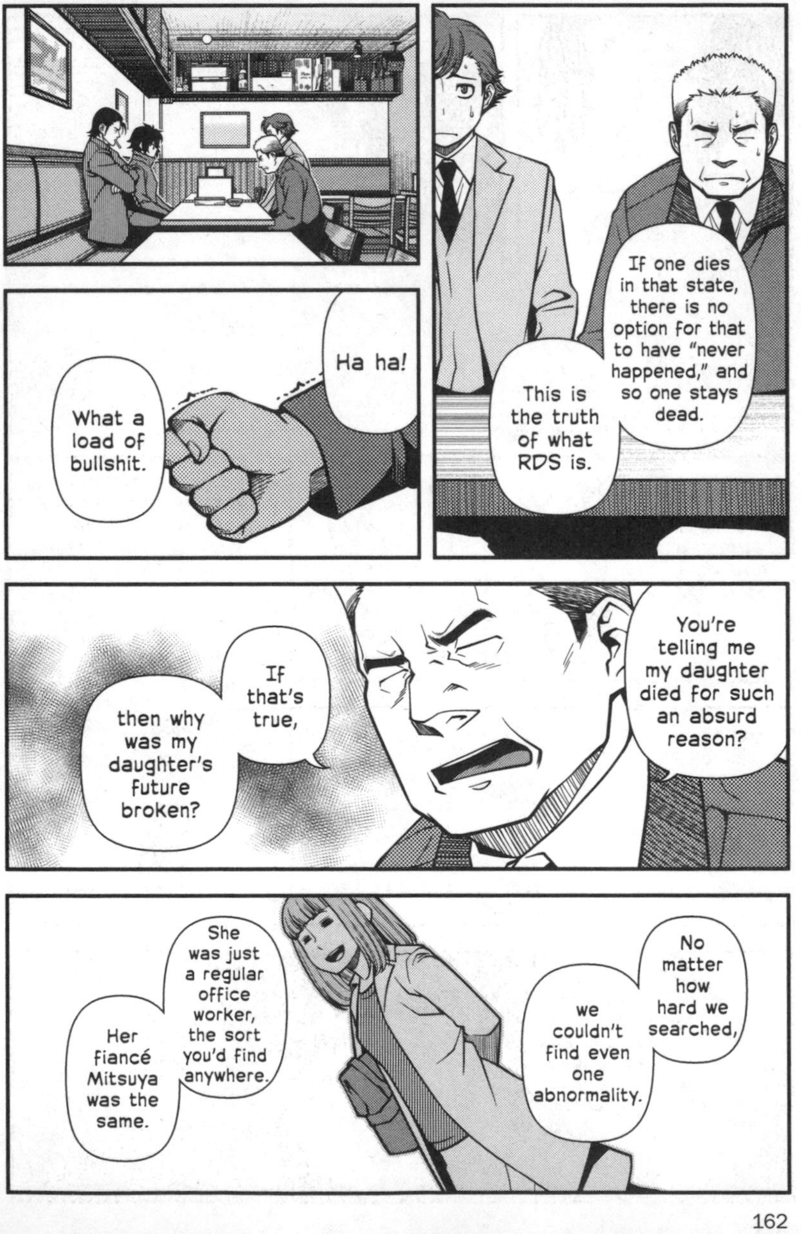
If one dies in that state, there is no option for that to have "never happened," and so one stays dead.
This is the truth of what RDS is.
Ha ha!
What a load of bullshit.
You're telling me my daughter died for such an absurd reason?
If that's true,
then why was my daughter's future broken?
No matter how hard we searched,
we couldn't find even one abnormality.
She was just a regular office worker, the sort you'd find anywhere.
Her fiancé Mitsuya was the same.

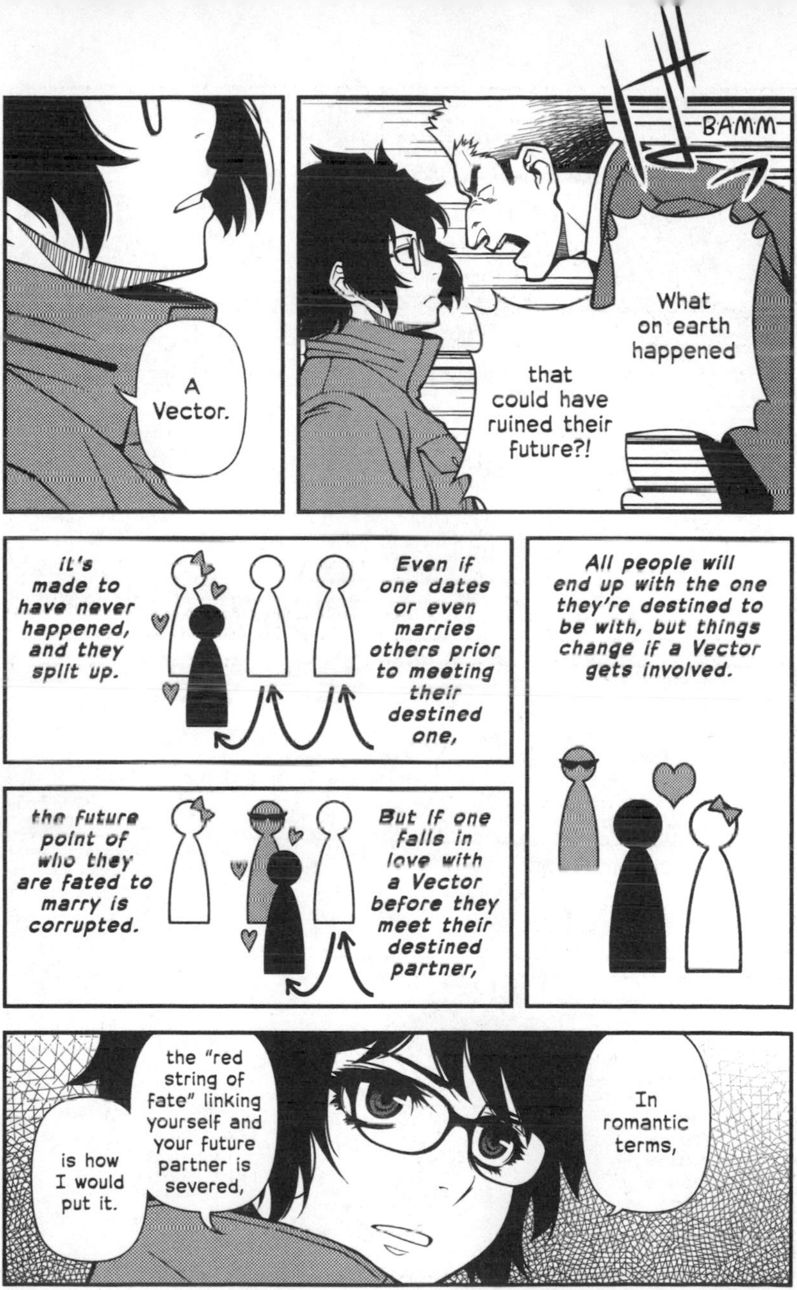
BAMM
What on earth happened
that could have ruined their future?!
A Vector.
All people will end up with the one they're destined to be with, but things change if a Vector gets involved.
Even if one dates or even marries others prior to meeting their destined one,
it's made to have never happened, and they split up.
But if one falls in love with a Vector before they meet their destined partner,
the future point of who they are fated to marry is corrupted.
In romantic terms,
the "red string of fate" linking yourself and your future partner is severed,
is how I would put it.

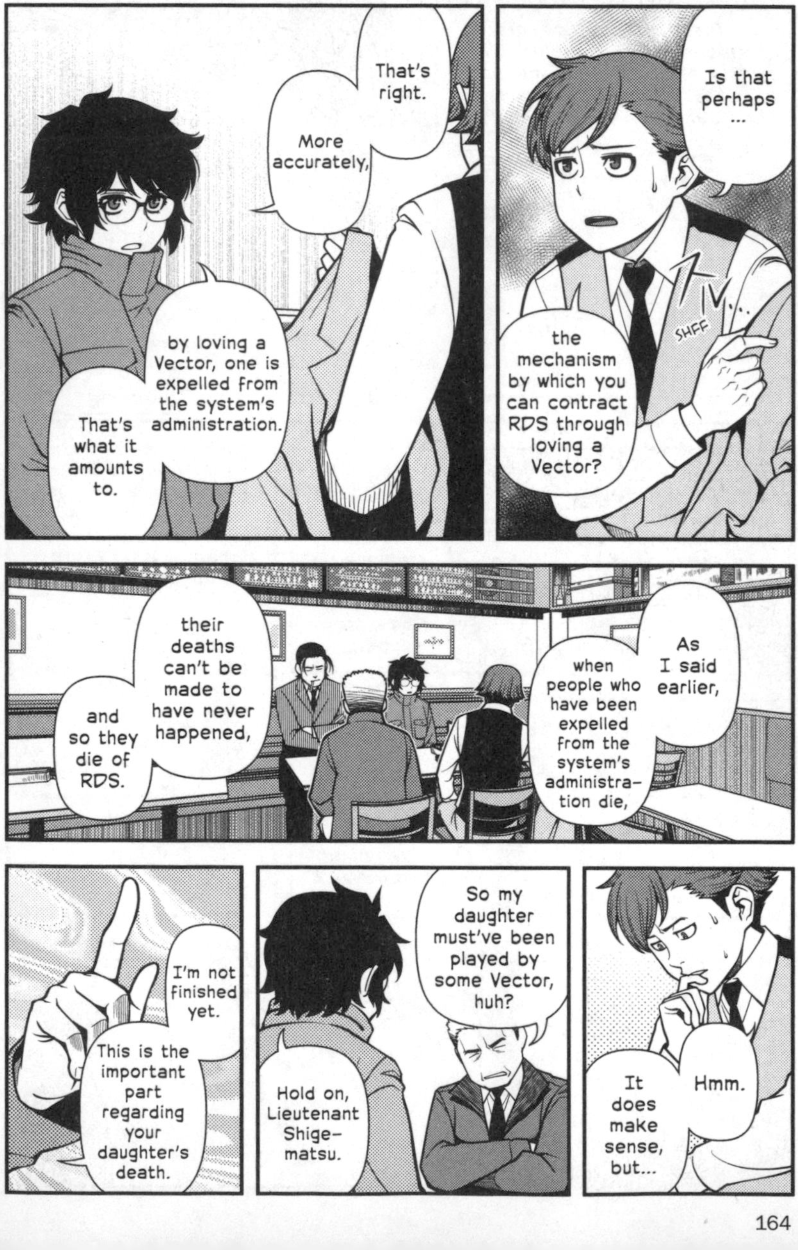
Is that perhaps ...
SHFF
the mechanism by which you can contract RDS through loving a Vector?
That's right.
More accurately,
by loving a Vector, one is expelled from the system's administration.
That's what it amounts to.
As I said earlier,
when people who have been expelled from the system's administration die,
their deaths can't be made to have never happened,
and so they die of RDS.
Hmm.
It does make sense, but...
So my daughter must've been played by some Vector, huh?
Hold on, Lieutenant Shige-matsu.
I'm not finished yet.
This is the important part regarding your daughter's death.

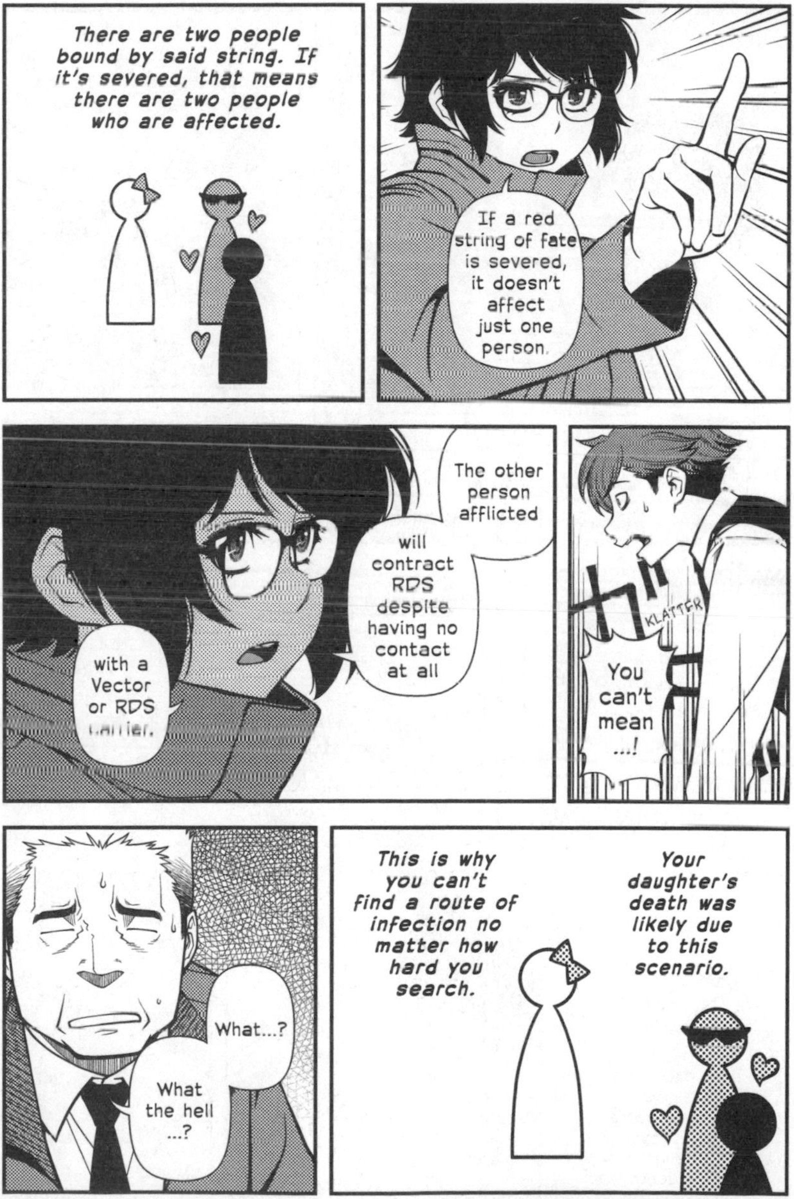
If a red string of fate is severed, it doesn't affect just one person.
There are two people bound by said string. If it's severed, that means there are two people who are affected.
KLATTER
You can't mean ...!
The other person afflicted
will contract RDS despite having no contact at all
with a Vector or RDS carrier.
Your daughter's death was likely due to this scenario.
This is why you can't find a route of infection no matter how hard you search.
What...?
What the hell ...?

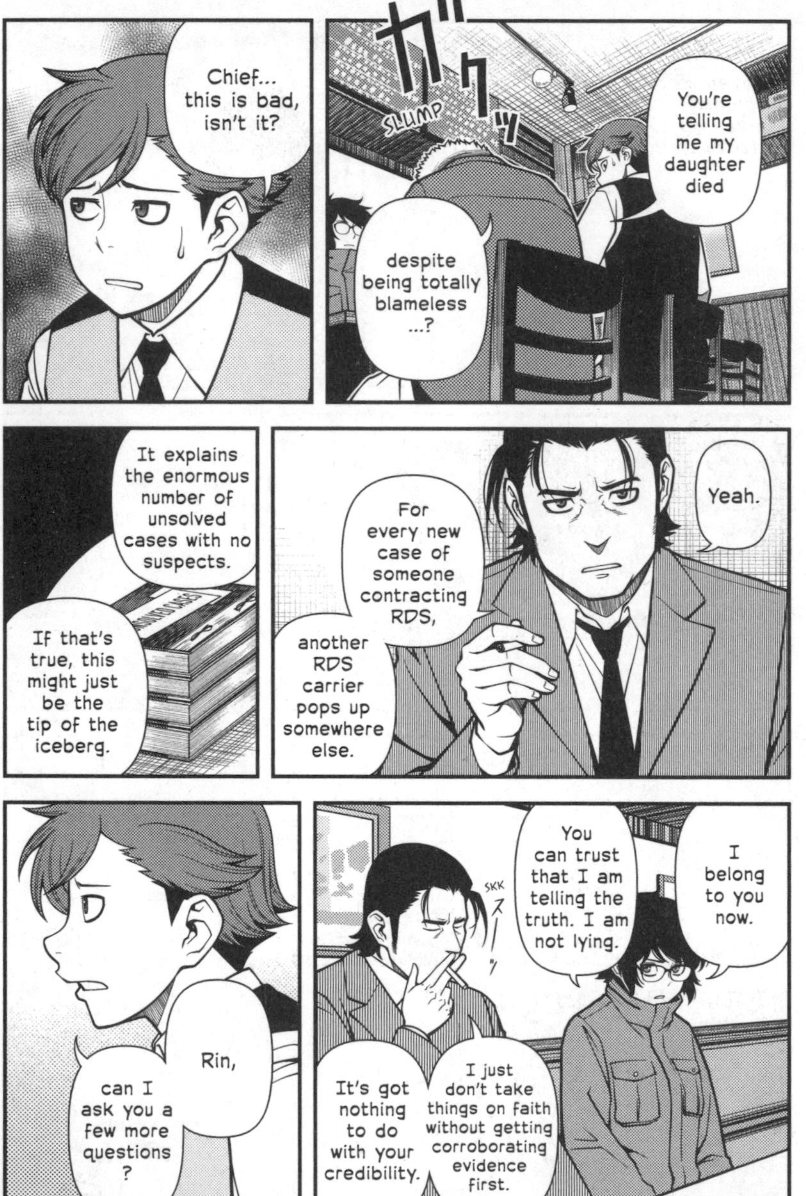
SLUMP
You're telling me my daughter died
despite being totally blameless ...?
Chief... this is bad, isn't it?
Yeah.
For every new case of someone contracting RDS,
another RDS carrier pops up somewhere else.
It explains the enormous number of unsolved cases with no suspects.
If that's true, this might just be the tip of the iceberg.
I belong to you now.
You can trust that I am telling the truth. I am not lying.
SKK
I just don't take things on faith without getting corroborating evidence first.
It's got nothing to do with your credibility.
Rin,
can I ask you a few more questions ?

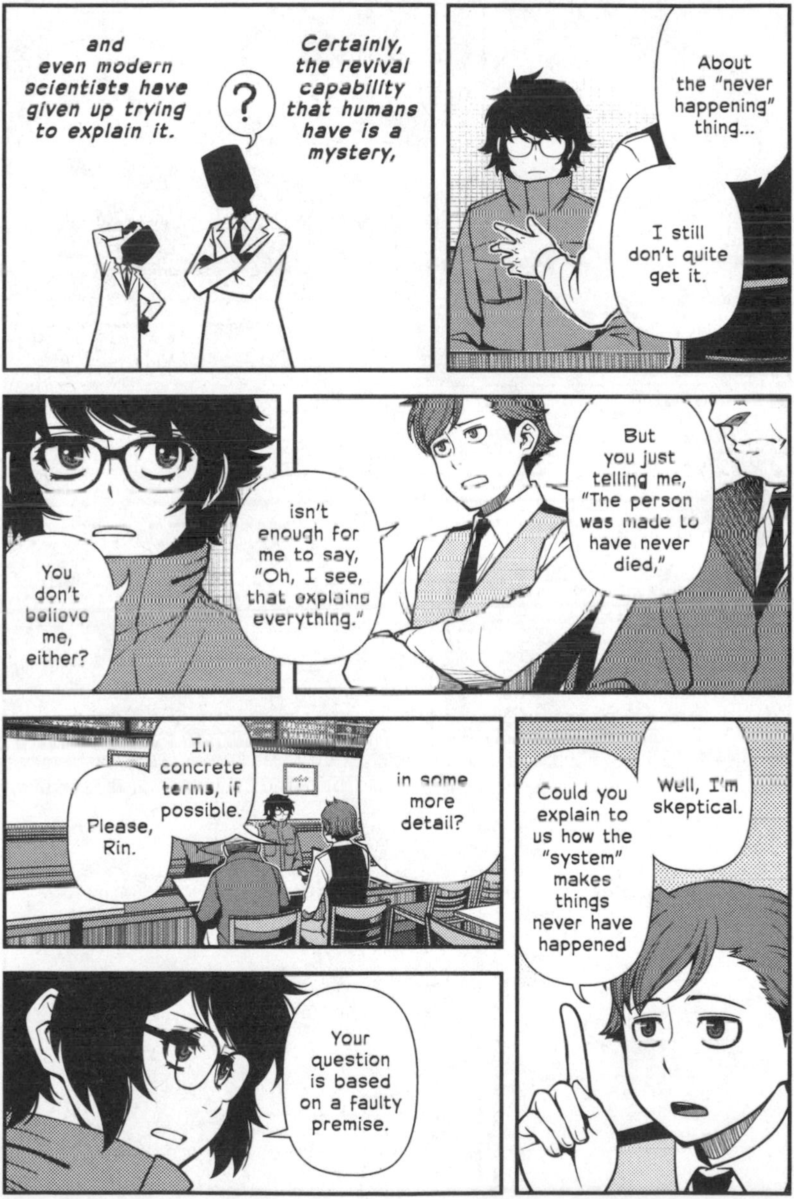

About the "never happening" thing...
I still don't quite get it.
Certainly, the revival capability that humans have is a mystery,
?
and even modern scientists have given up trying to explain it.
But you just telling me, "The person was made to have never died,"
isn't enough for me to say, "Oh, I see, that explains everything."
You don't believe me, either?
Well, I'm skeptical.
Could you explain to us how the "system" makes things never have happened
in some more detail?
In concrete terms, if possible.
Please, Rin.
Your question is based on a faulty premise.

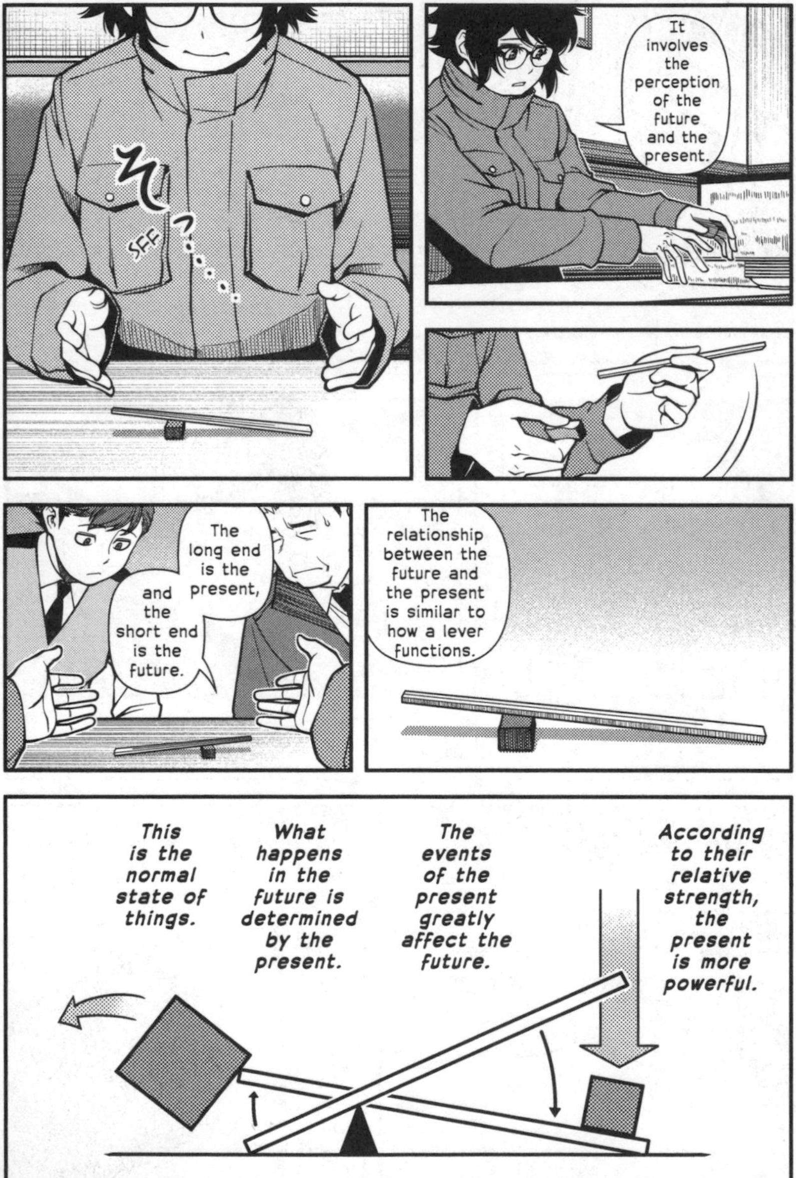
It involves the perception of the future and the present.
SFF
The relationship between the future and the present is similar to how a lever functions.
The long end is the present,
and the short end is the future.
According to their relative strength, the present is more powerful.
The events of the present greatly affect the future.
What happens in the future is determined by the present.
This is the normal state of things.

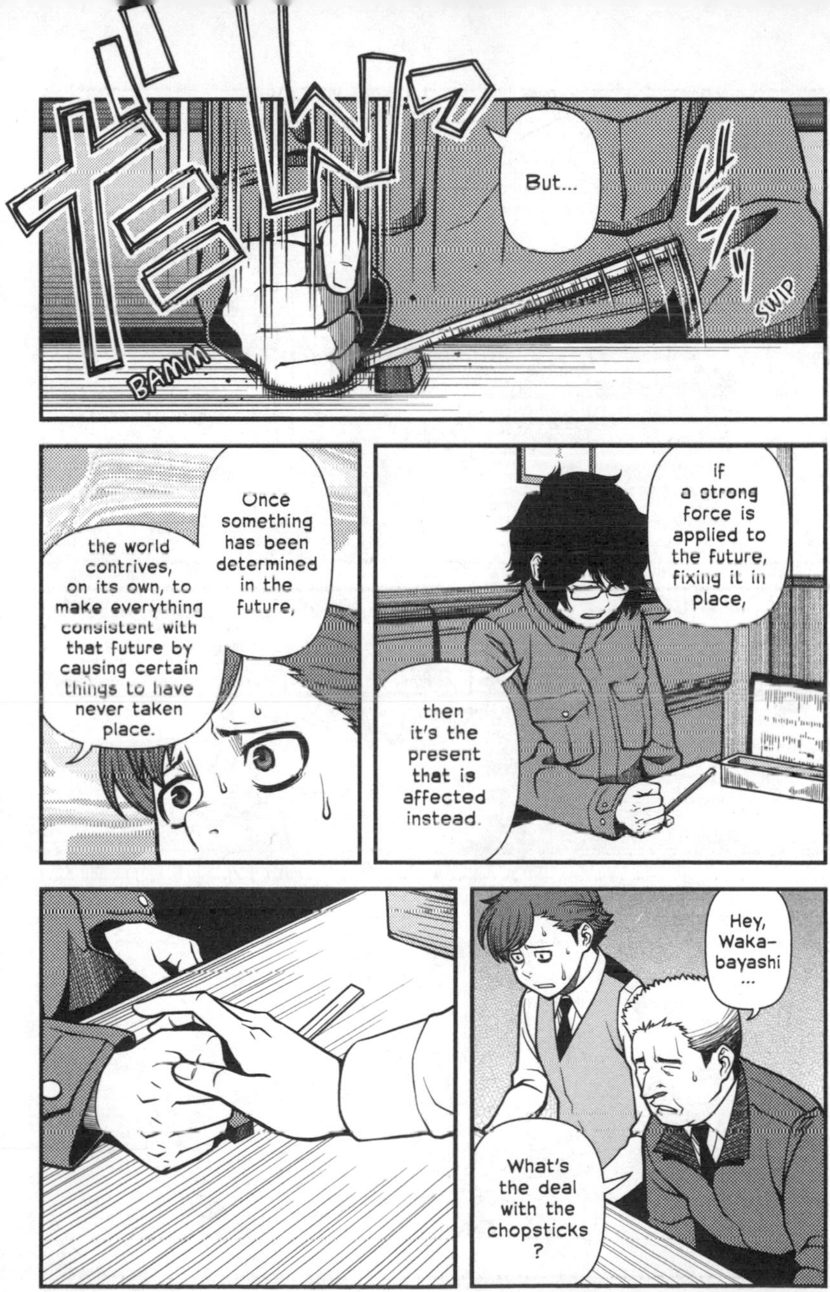
But...
SWIP
BAMM
if a strong force is applied to the future, fixing it in place,
then it's the present that is affected instead.
Once something has been determined in the future,
the world contrives, on its own, to make everything consistent with that future by causing certain things to have never taken place.
Hey, Waka-bayashi ...
What's the deal with the chopsticks ?

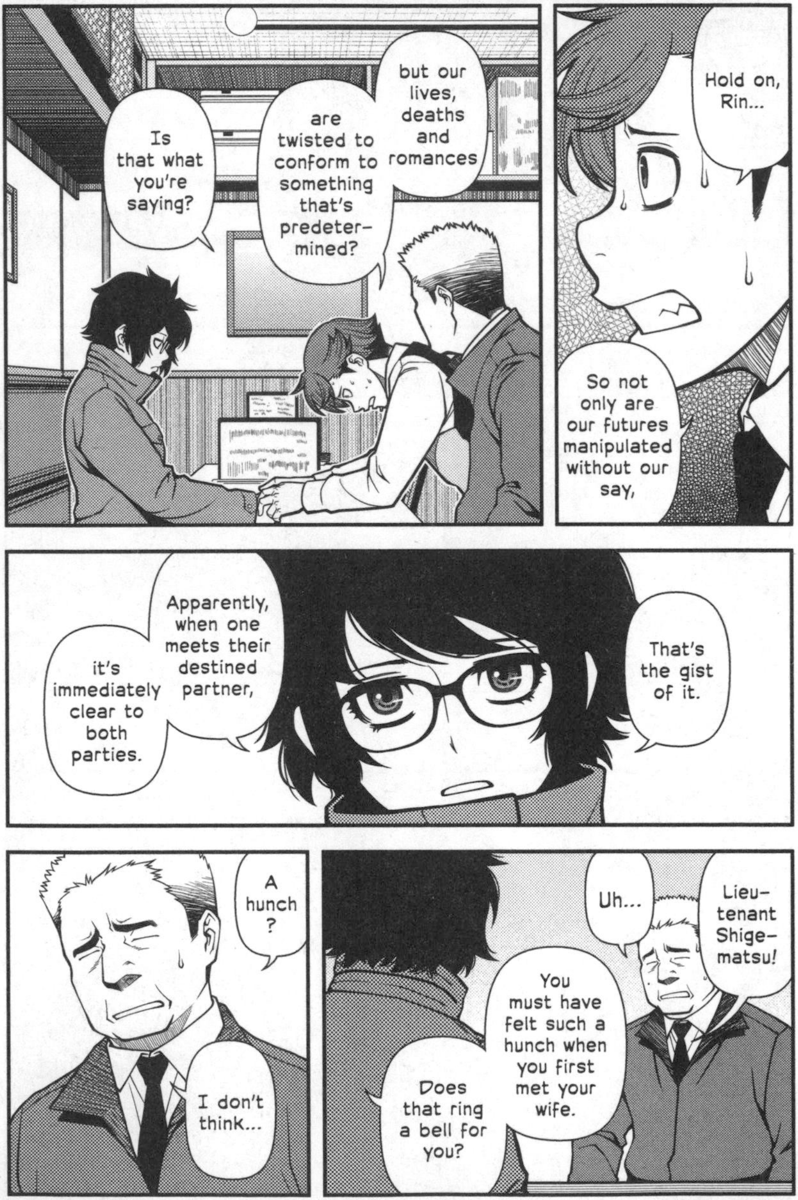
Hold on, Rin...
So not only are our futures manipulated without our say,
but our lives, deaths and romances
are twisted to conform to something that's predeter-mined?
Is that what you're saying?
That's the gist of it.
Apparently, when one meets their destined partner,
it's immediately clear to both parties.
Lieu-tenant Shige-matsu!
Uh...
You must have felt such a hunch when you first met your wife.
Does that ring a bell for you?
A hunch?
I don't think...

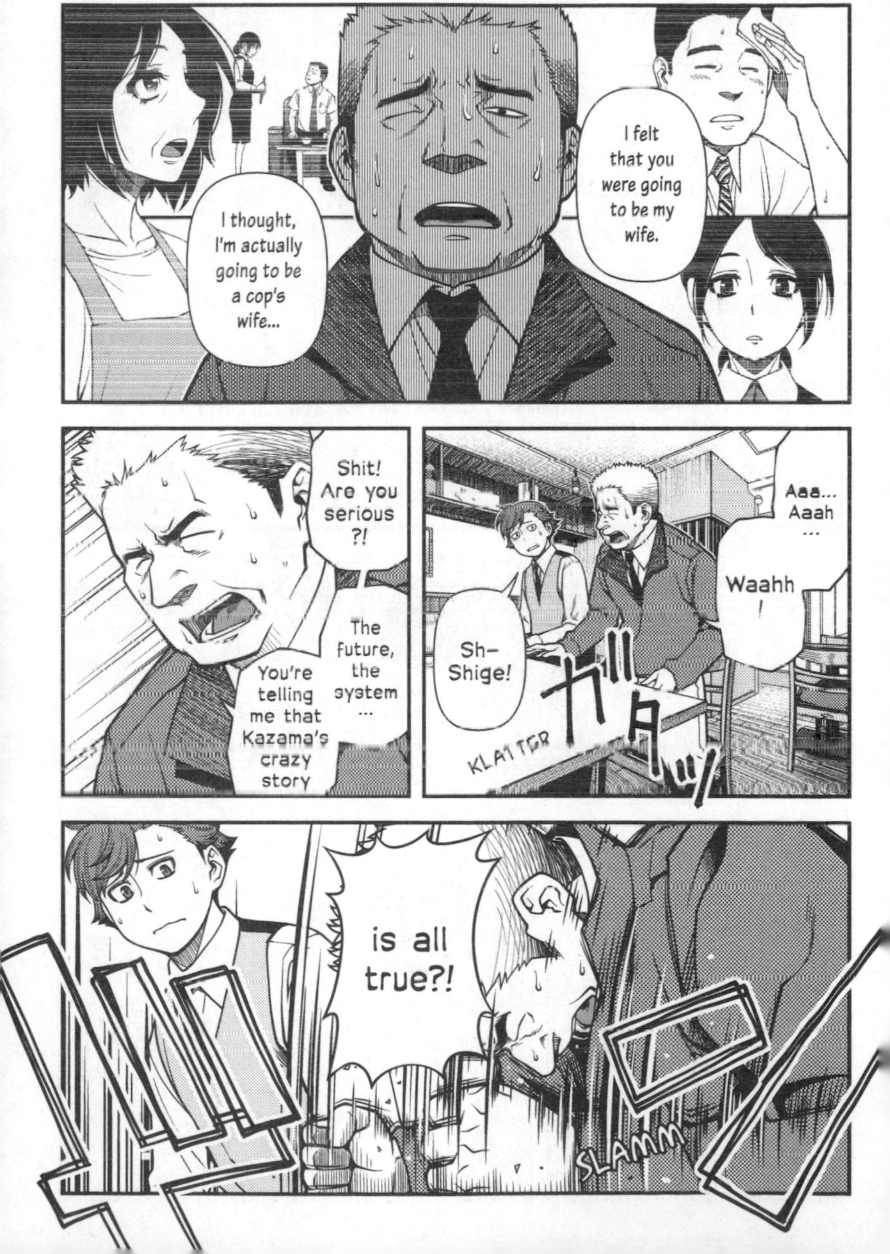
I felt that you were going to be my wife.
I thought, I'm actually going to be a cop's wife...
Aaa... Aaah ...
Waahh !
Sh- Shige!
KLATTER
Shit! Are you serious ?!
The future, the system ...
You're telling me that Kazama's crazy story
is all true?!
SLAMM

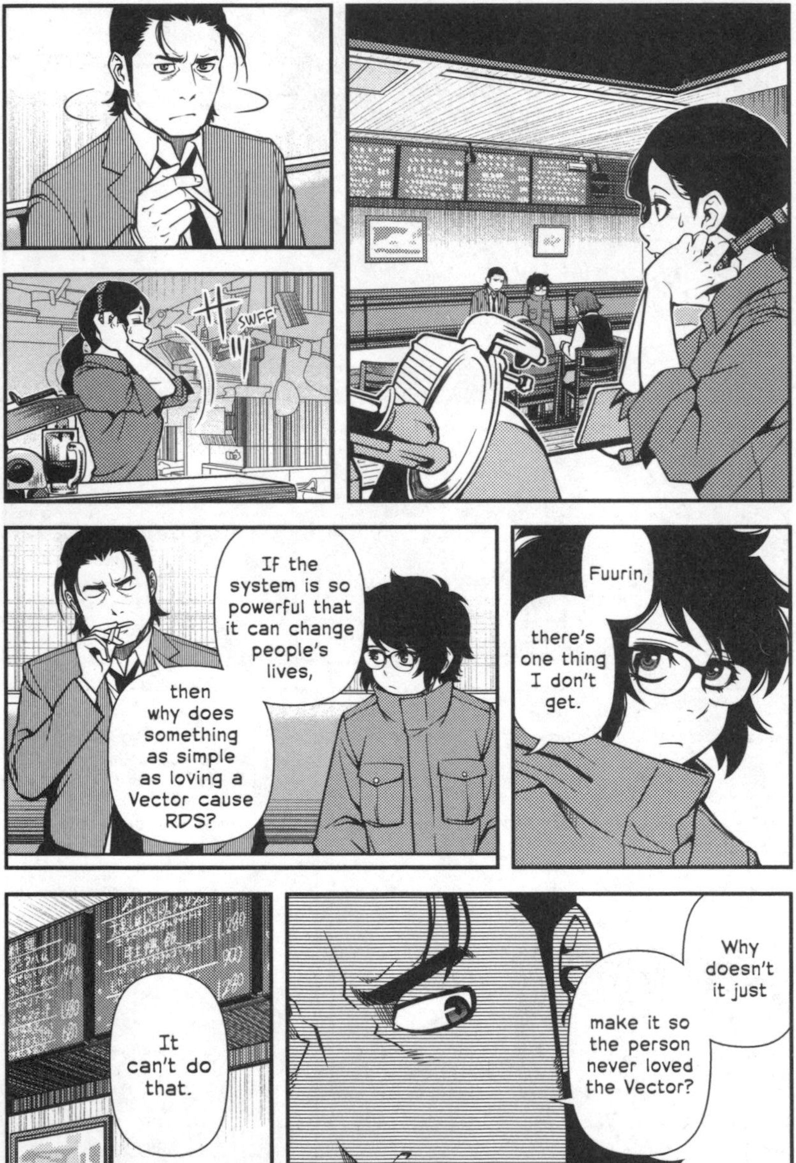
SWFF
Fuurin,
there's one thing I don't get.
If the system is so powerful that it can change people's lives,
then why does something as simple as loving a Vector cause RDS?
Why doesn't it just
make it so the person never loved the Vector?
It can't do that.

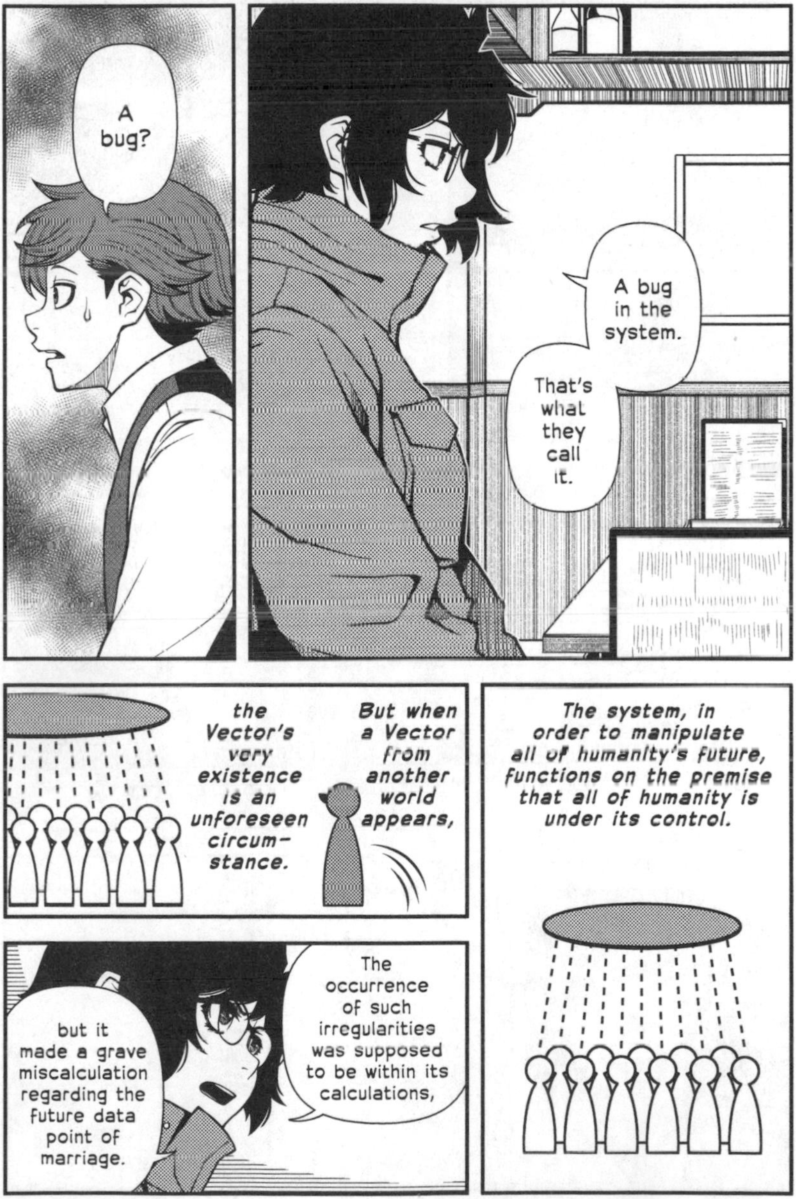
A bug in the system.
That's what they call it.
A bug?
The system, in order to manipulate all of humanity's future, functions on the premise that all of humanity is under its control.
But when a Vector from another world appears,
the Vector's very existence is an unforeseen circum-stance.
The occurrence of such irregularities was supposed to be within its calculations,
but it made a grave miscalculation regarding the future data point of marriage.

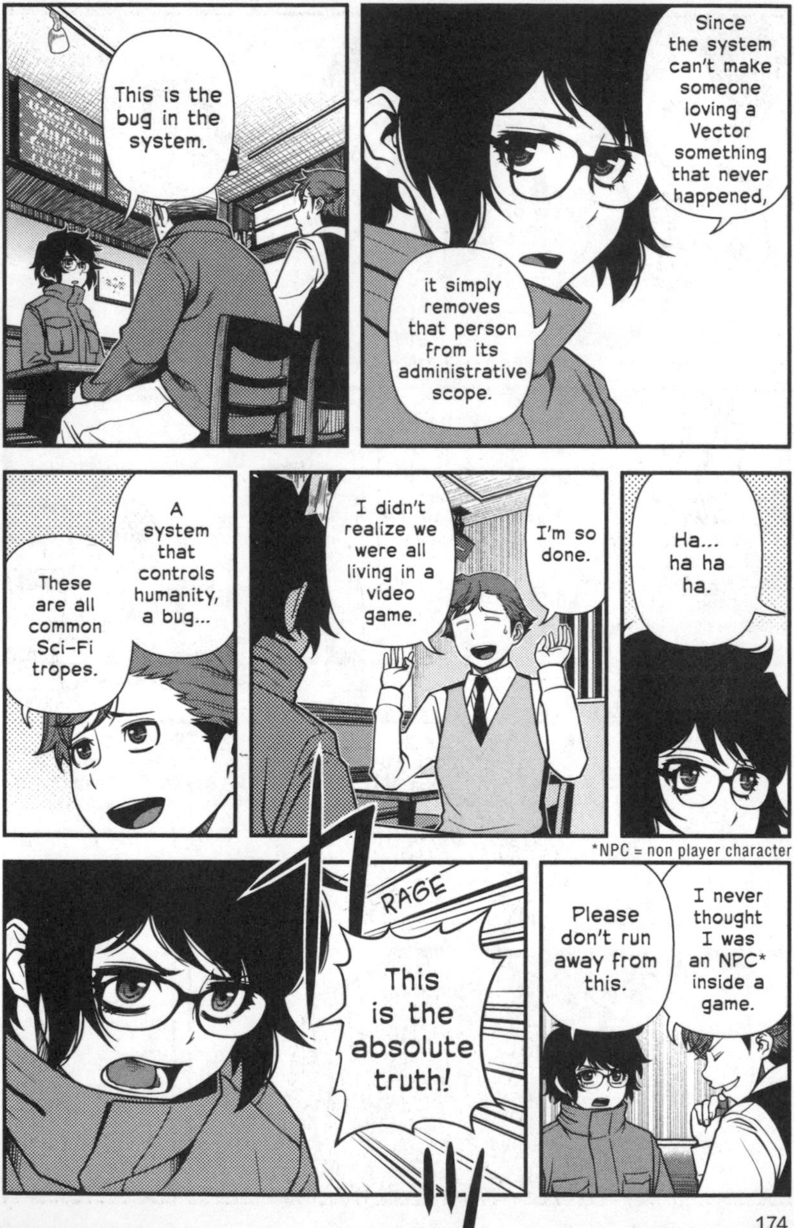
Since the system can't make someone loving a Vector something that never happened,
it simply removes that person from its administrative scope.
This is the bug in the system.
Ha... ha ha ha.
I'm so done.
I didn't realize we were all living in a video game.
A system that controls humanity, a bug...
These are all common Sci-Fi tropes.
I never thought I was an NPC* inside a game.
Please don't run away from this.
RAGE
This is the absolute truth!

*NPC = non player character

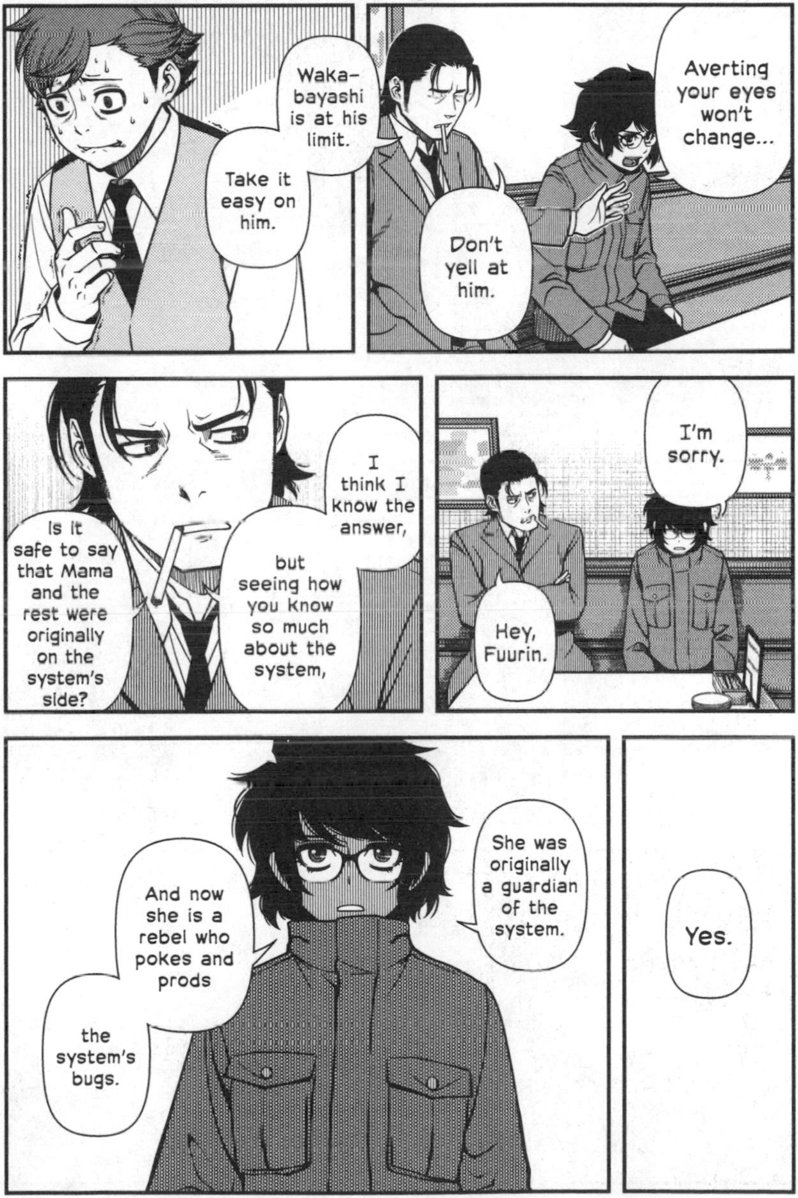
Averting your eyes won't change...
Don't yell at him.
Waka-bayashi is at his limit.
Take it easy on him.
I'm sorry.
Hey, Fuurin.
I think I know the answer,
but seeing how you know so much about the system,
Is it safe to say that Mama and the rest were originally on the system's side?
Yes.
She was originally a guardian of the system.
And now she is a rebel who pokes and prods
the system's bugs.

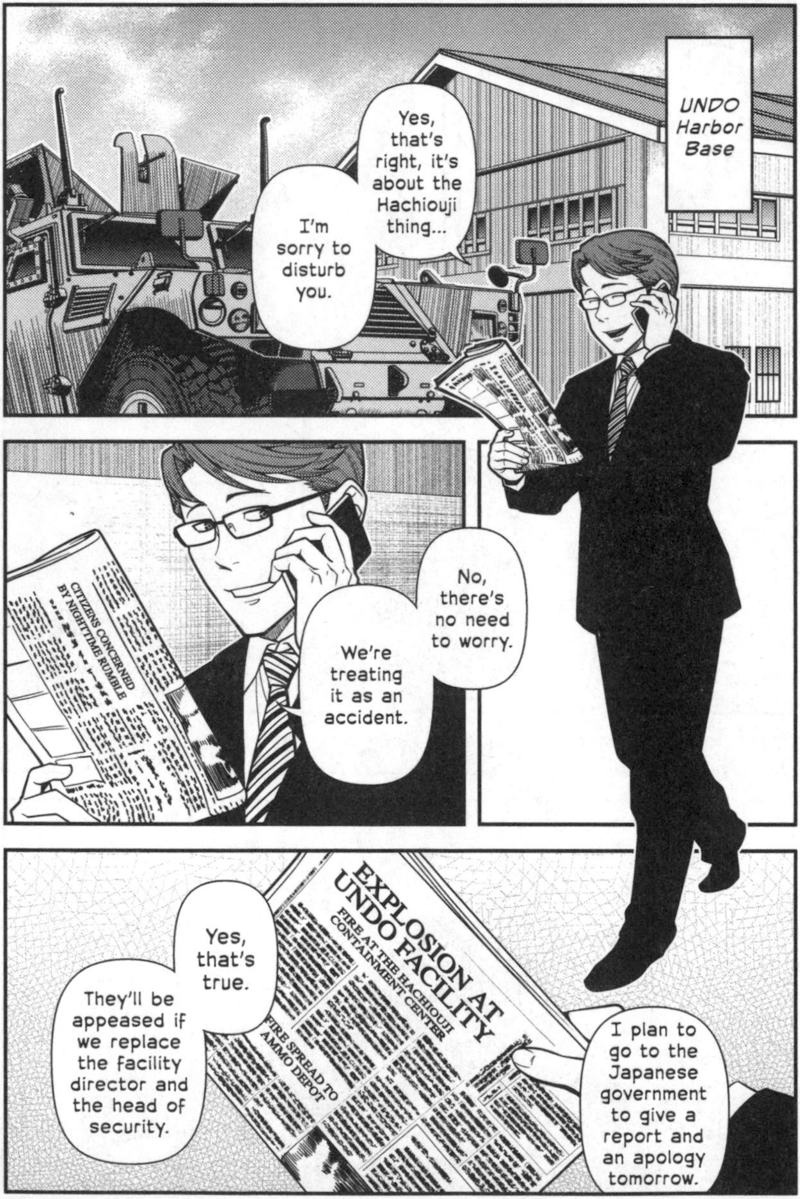
UNDO Harbor Base
Yes, that's right, it's about the Hachiouji thing...
I'm sorry to disturb you.
No, there's no need to worry.
We're treating it as an accident.
CITIZENS CONCERNED BY NIGHTTIME RUMBLE
EXPLOSION AT UNDO FACILITY
FIRE AT THE HACHIOUJI CONTAINMENT CENTER
FIRE SPREAD TO AMMO DEPOT
I plan to go to the Japanese government to give a report and an apology tomorrow.
Yes, that's true.
They'll be appeased if we replace the facility director and the head of security.

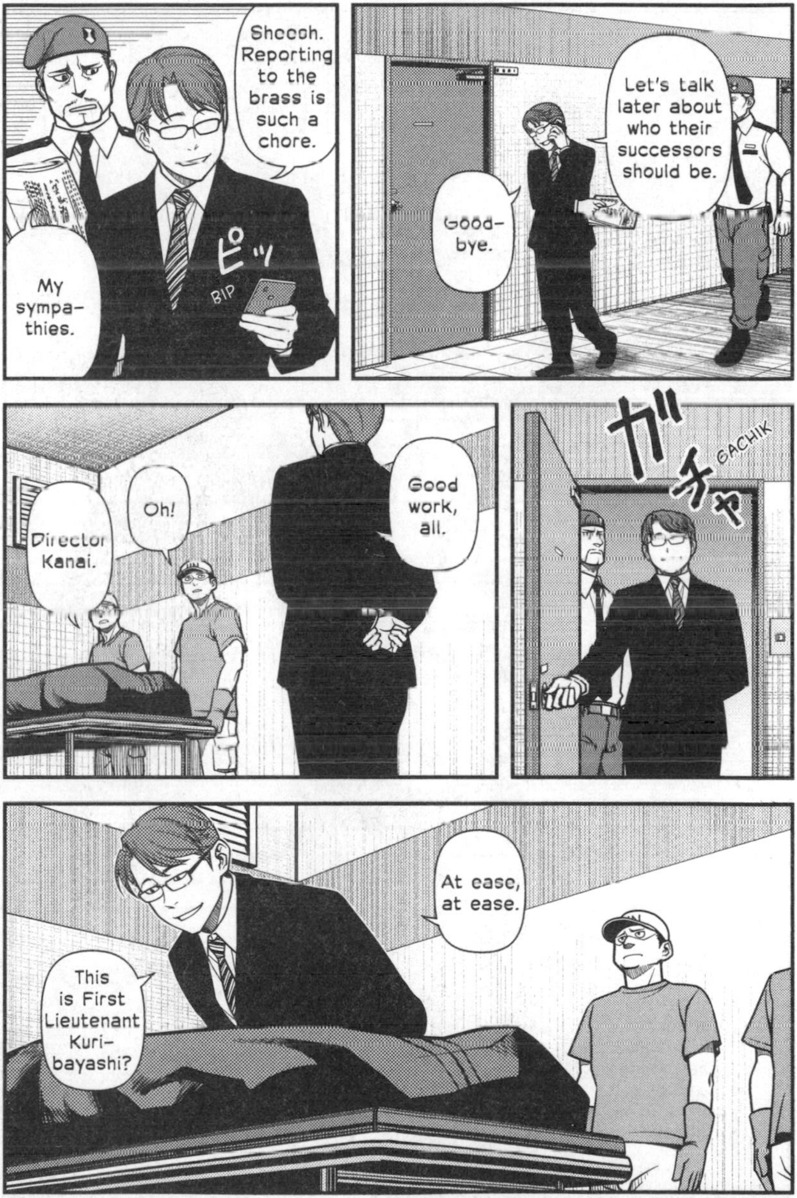
Let's talk later about who their successors should be.
Good-bye.
Sheesh. Reporting to the brass is such a chore.
ピッ
BIP
My sympathies.
ガチャ
GACHIK
Good work, all.
Oh!
Director Kanai.
At ease, at ease.
This is First Lieutenant Kuri-bayashi?

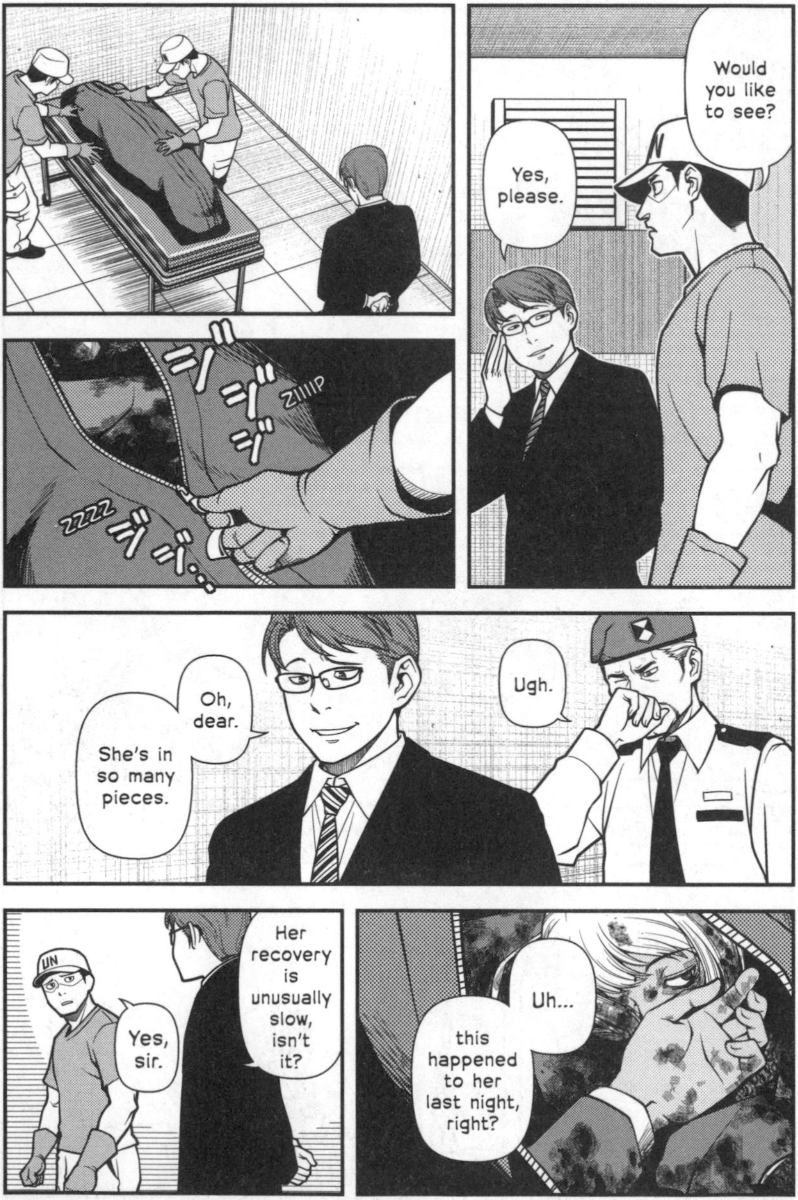

Would you like to see?
Yes, please.
ZIIIP
ZZZZ
Ugh.
Oh, dear.
She's in so many pieces.
Uh...
this happened to her last night, right?
Her recovery is unusually slow, isn't it?
Yes, sir.

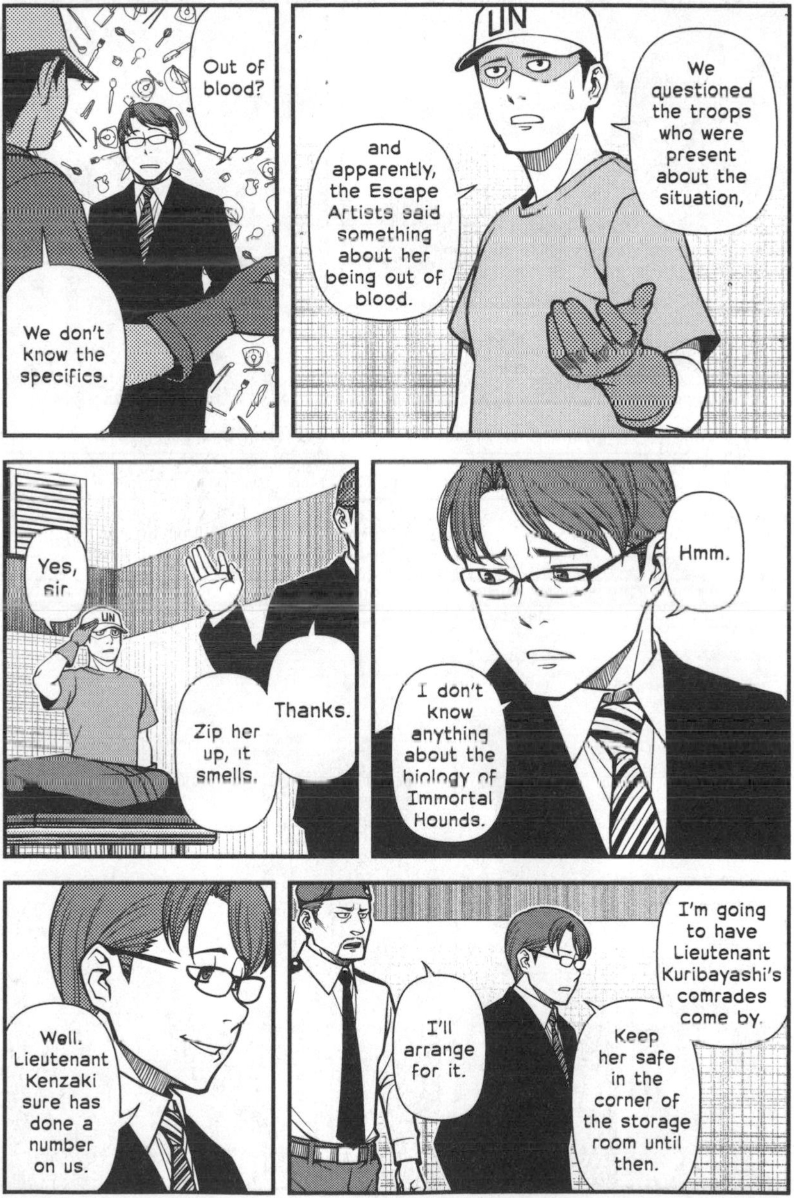
We questioned the troops who were present about the situation,
and apparently, the Escape Artists said something about her being out of blood.
Out of blood?
We don't know the specifics.
Hmm.
I don't know anything about the biology of Immortal Hounds.
Thanks.
Zip her up, it smells.
Yes, sir.
I'm going to have Lieutenant Kuribayashi's comrades come by.
Keep her safe in the corner of the storage room until then.
I'll arrange for it.
Well. Lieutenant Kenzaki sure has done a number on us.

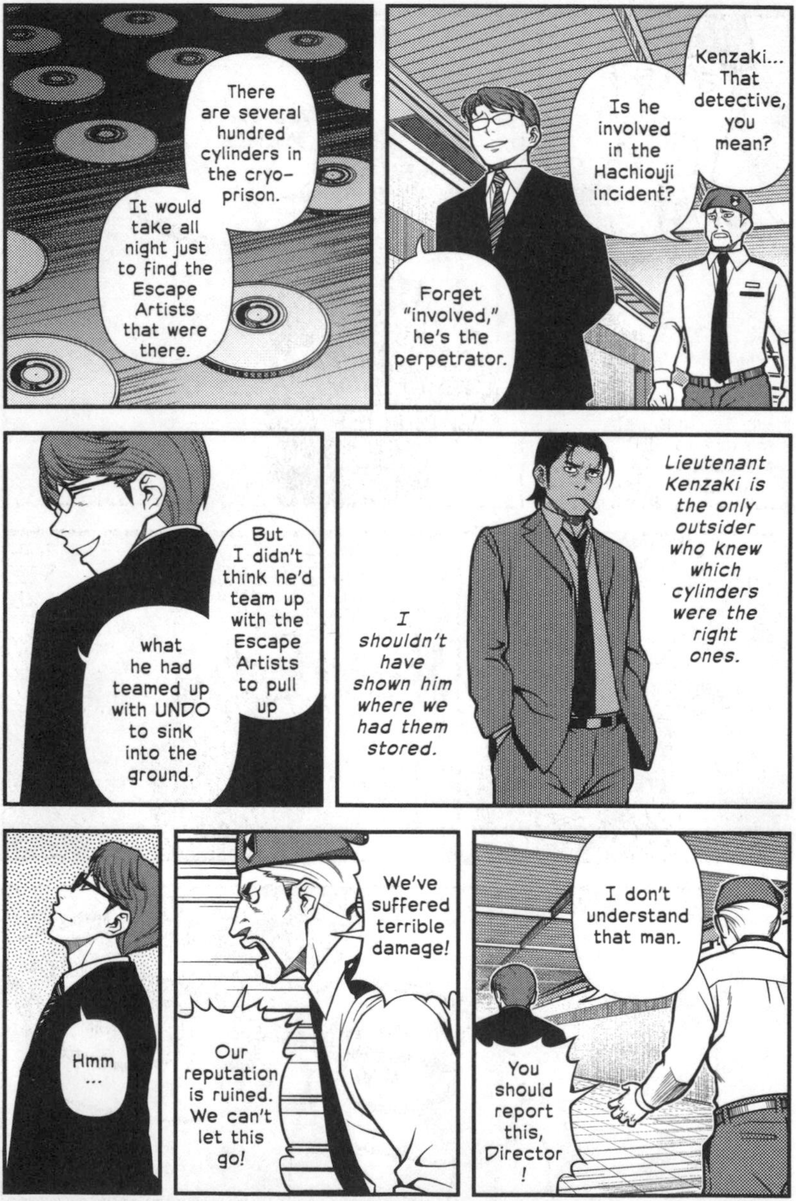
Kenzaki... That detective, you mean?
Is he involved in the Hachiouji incident?
Forget "involved," he's the perpetrator.
There are several hundred cylinders in the cryo-prison.
It would take all night just to find the Escape Artists that were there.
Lieutenant Kenzaki is the only outsider who knew which cylinders were the right ones.
I shouldn't have shown him where we had them stored.
But I didn't think he'd team up with the Escape Artists to pull up
what he had teamed up with UNDO to sink into the ground.
I don't understand that man.
You should report this, Director!
We've suffered terrible damage!
Our reputation is ruined. We can't let this go!
Hmm ...

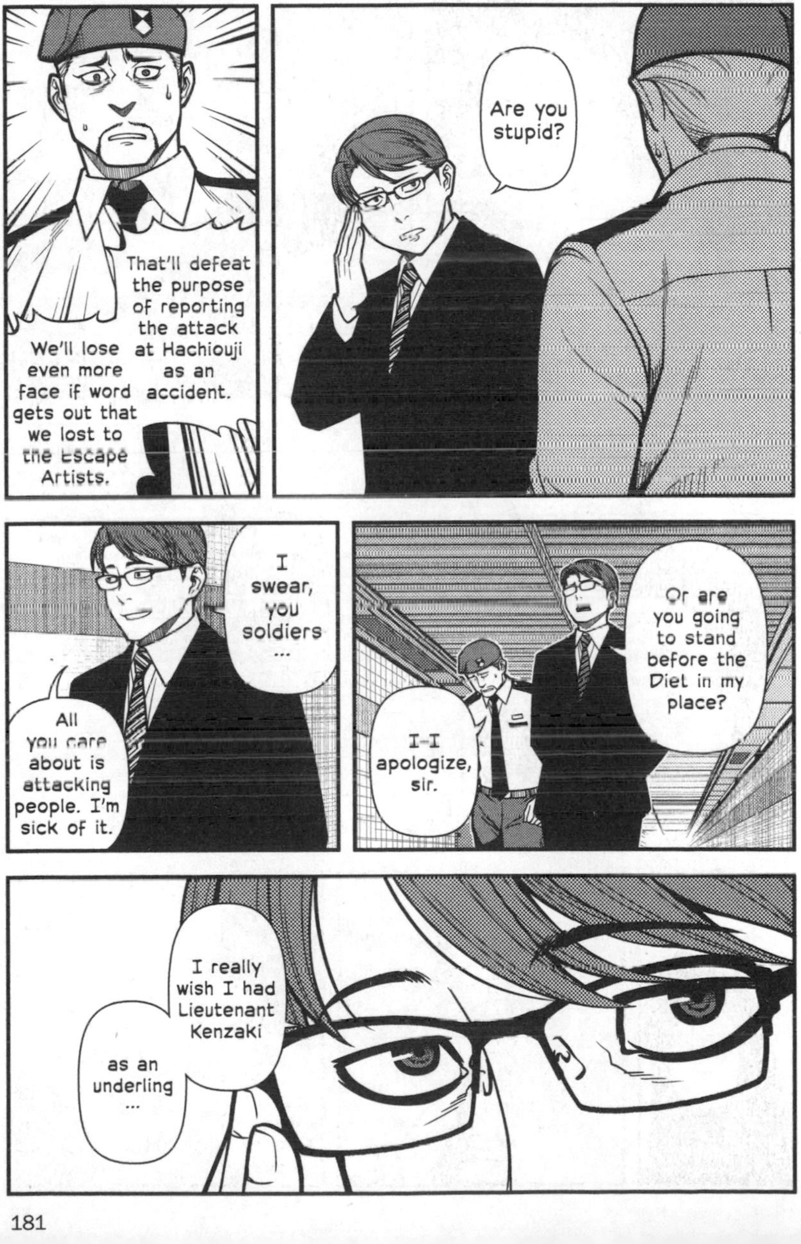
Are you stupid?
That'll defeat the purpose of reporting the attack at Hachiouji as an accident.
We'll lose even more face if word gets out that we lost to the Escape Artists.
Or are you going to stand before the Diet in my place?
I-I apologize, sir.
I swear, you soldiers ...
All you care about is attacking people. I'm sick of it.
I really wish I had Lieutenant Kenzaki
as an underling ...

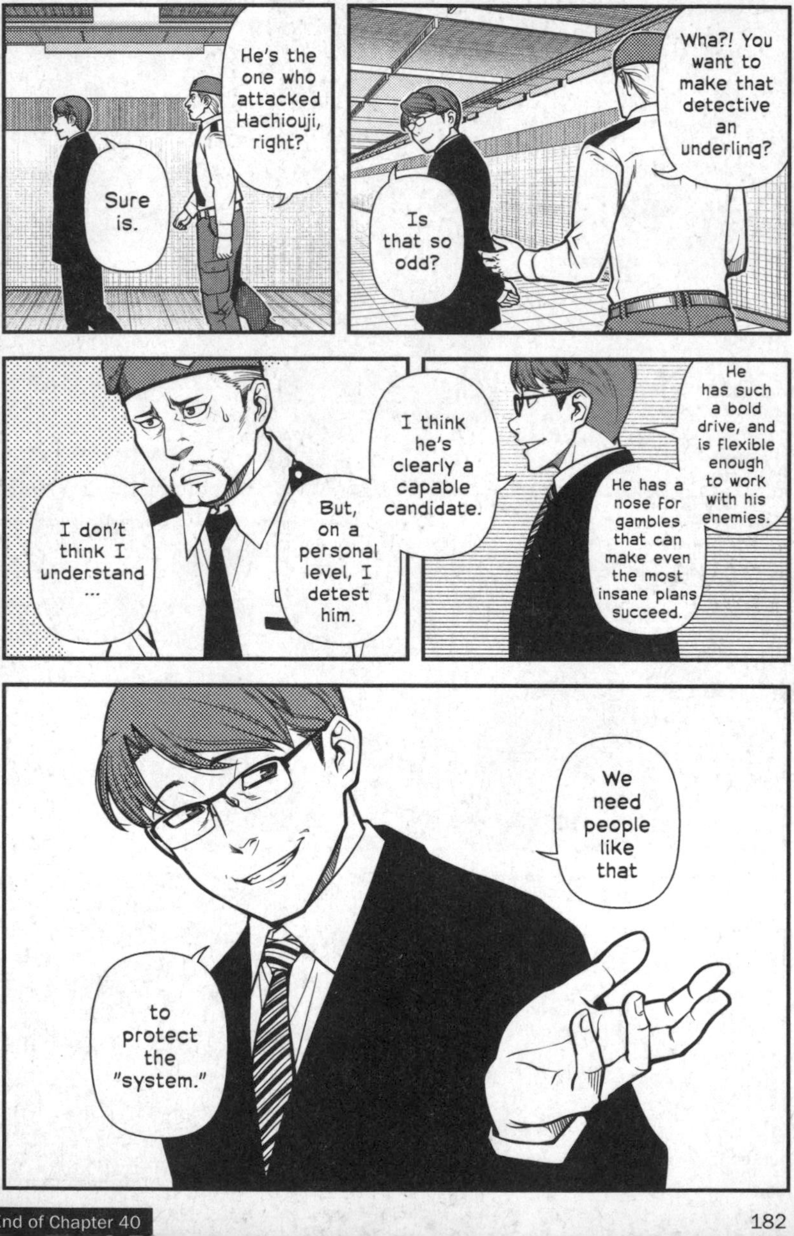
He's the one who attacked Hachiouji, right?
Sure is.
Wha?! You want to make that detective an underling?
Is that so odd?
He has such a bold drive, and is flexible enough to work with his enemies.
He has a nose for gambles that can make even the most insane plans succeed.
I think he's clearly a capable candidate.
But, on a personal level, I detest him.
I don't think I understand ...
We need people like that
to protect the "system."

Immortal Hounds 6

A Vertical Comics Edition

Translation: Yota Okutani
Production: Grace Lu
          Anthony Quintessenza

© Ryo Yasohachi 2017
First published in Japan in 2017 by KADOKAWA CORPORATION, Tokyo.
English translation rights arranged with KADOKAWA CORPORATION, Tokyo
through TUTTLE-MORI AGENCY, INC., Tokyo.

Translation provided by Vertical Comics, 2018
Published by Vertical Comics, an imprint of Vertical, Inc., New York

Originally published in Japanese as *Shinazu no Ryouken 6* by Kadokawa Corporation, 2017
Shinazu no Ryouken first serialized in *Harta*, Kadokawa Corporation, 2013-

This is a work of fiction.

ISBN: 978-1-945054-57-0

Manufactured in Canada

First Edition

Vertical, Inc.
451 Park Avenue South
7th Floor
New York, NY 10016
www.vertical-comics.com

Vertical books are distributed through Penguin-Random House Publisher Services.